THE PADDY CAMPS

The Irish of Lowell
1821–61

Brian C. Mitchell

University of Illinois Press

Urbana and Chicago

Publication of this work was supported in part by a grant
from the Lowell Historic Preservation Commission.

This book is printed on acid-free paper.

Library of Congress Cataloging-in-Publication Data

Mitchell, Brian Christopher, 1953–
    The paddy camps: the Irish of Lowell, 1821–61 / Brian C.
Mitchell.
        p.   cm.
    Bibliography: p.
    Includes index.
    ISBN 0-252-01371-9 (alk. paper)
    1. Irish Americans—Massachusetts—Lowell—History—19th century.
2. Lowell (Mass.)—Ethnic relations.   3. Lowell (Mass.)—History.
I. Title.
F74.L9M64   1988   87-16724
                     CIP

To Mary Jane

CONTENTS

ILLUSTRATIONS

ACKNOWLEDGMENTS

A number of scholars have examined this manuscript in various stages of development. They include Mary Blewett, Thomas N. Brown, Jay P. Dolan, Thomas Dublin, John B. Duff, Bruce Laurie, Lawrence McCaffrey, Timothy J. Meagher, William V. Shannon, James P. Walsh, and Kevin Whelan. My thanks to them and to Arthur L. Eno, Jr., M. Brendan Fleming, and Elmer P. Rynne, Sr., for their important insight into Lowell's fascinating history and the role of the Irish in it. Mary E. Young and Milton Berman of the University of Rochester offered much initial encouragement. I tested portions of the manuscript at the Female Sphere Conference, New Harmony, Indiana; the Fourth Annual Meeting of the Society for Historians of the Early American Republic, Memphis, Tennessee; the Perspectives on American Catholicism Conference, University of Notre Dame; and the Seventy-seventh Annual Meeting of the Organization of American Historians, Los Angeles, California. I benefited greatly from the thoughtful and provocative comments at each session. The *Historical Journal of Massachusetts* allowed me to reprint portions of an earlier article on immigrants and public education.

I also wish to thank Most Rev. Thomas V. Daily, administrator, Archdiocese of Boston; James M. O'Toole and John J. Treanor, former archivist and assistant archivist, respectively; and Rev. Thomas J. Walsh for their assistance. Sr. Jane Catherine, S.N.D.; Sr. Marie Roberta, S.N.D.; and the late Sr. Dorothea of the Sacred Heart, S.N.D., opened the Provincial Archives of the Sisters of Notre Dame to me. In St. Patrick's parish, Rev. Richard C. Conway, pastor; Rev. Vincent Maffei; Rev. Raymond Mahoney, S.S.C.C.; and James J. Heafy made available appropriate parish records. On a local level, William Busby, city clerk; Lieutenant Thomas Conlon, Lowell Police Department; and the staffs of the city clerk, tax assessor, license commission, city engineer, and election commission opened their records or made certain that I had seen all records which survived. I also wish to thank Kay Curran, Middlesex County Superior Court, Northern District, Lowell; David Quinn, Middlesex County Superior Court, Southern District, Cambridge; and the staff of the Lowell District Court.

Joseph V. Kopycinski, director, Alumni Lydon Library; Martha Mayo, head of special collections, University of Lowell; Mildred Wahlgren and the late Marion Morse, both of the Lowell Historical Society; and Robert W. McLeod, formerly of the Pollard Memorial Library, opened private and public collections, nineteenth-century newspapers, and the holdings of the Lowell Historical Society. I also benefited from the research of Ann Grady on housing patterns in the Acre and of Fred Kennedy on the life of Daniel McElroy. John E. Dyer, assistant vice-president, Lowell Institution for Savings, and Ralph Jenkins, Jr., vice-president and controller, Colonial Gas Company, allowed me to view their early company records.

I also wish to thank the Board of Directors, Colonial Gas Company; Robert Lovett, now retired from the Baker Business Library; the late Helen Landreth, director, Irish Special Collections, Boston College; and Jeanne Lindquist, Anna Maria College, as well as the staffs of the National Park Service and St. Patrick's Cemetery, Lowell. I deeply appreciated the graciousness of the staffs of the National Library of Ireland; University College, Galway; Alumni Lydon Library, North Campus, University of Lowell; American Antiquarian Society; Baker Business Library, Harvard University; Bapst Library, Boston College; Boston Public Library; Library of Congress; Massachusetts Historical Society, Massachusetts State Archives; Mondor-Eagen Library, Anna Maria College; Mullen Library, Catholic University; Mugar Library, Boston University; O'Leary Library, South Campus, University of Lowell; Pollard Memorial Library, Lowell; Rush Rhees Library, University of Rochester; Xaverian Brothers Provincial Archives, Kensington, Maryland; Widener Library, Harvard University; and the various libraries of the Worcester Consortium of Colleges. For permission to reproduce maps, photographs, and paintings, I would like to thank the Lowell Historical Society, Lowell Museum, University of Lowell Special Collections, Museum of American Textile History, Archives, Archdiocese of Boston, and Arthur L. Eno, Jr.

Funding for this manuscript has come from an Albert J. Beveridge Grant for Research in American History, American Historical Association; from the Lowell Historic Preservation Commission, United States Department of Interior; from an NEH Summer Fellowship; from a Grant-in-Aid from the American Council of Learned Societies; and from a Faculty

Research and Development Grant, Anna Maria College. I would also like to acknowledge the support of Sr. Bernadette Madore, S.S.A., Ph.D., president, Anna Maria College. Marie-Rose Rodrique and Craig Roscoe reproduced figures and tables. In Worcester, Leine Manning provided daily technical assistance. My thanks to Richard Wentworth and to Patricia Hollahan of the University of Illinois Press. Patricia Moore, Kitty Green, and Candice Feldman typed this manuscript; each displayed a great sense of humor and patience throughout the various drafts. I deeply appreciate the kindness of my colleagues in the Division of State Programs at the National Endowment for the Humanities, who allowed me time to complete the manuscript before joining them in Washington.

My father, the late Christopher J. Mitchell, and my mother, Doris K. (McEvoy) Mitchell, were extremely supportive of my research. My sons, Jeffrey and Patrick, could always persuade me to put down my pen. This work is dedicated to my wife, Maryjane, with whom I have shared this experience and so many others.

CHAPTER 1

Introduction

Historians interested in labor, women's, urban, and economic history, among others, have looked to conditions in Lowell, Massachusetts, in their efforts to understand American industrialism. The early work of Caroline Ware and Hannah Josephson described working conditions, housing, labor protest, and the substitution of Irish for Yankee labor in Lowell's famous textile mills, using newspaper reports, local records, and contemporary accounts.[1] More recent historians, especially Leo Marx, John Kasson, Thomas Bender, and Jonathan Prude, examined the impact of the "machine in the garden" by assessing industrialization and its impact upon the New England countryside and by identifying the conflict between technology and republican values.[2] A few economic historians, including George Gibb, Robert Layer, and Alexander Field, focused upon general industrial growth and textile industry innovations, while Marxists such as Samuel Bowles and Herbert Gintis explored the impact of capitalism upon public schools.[3]

All chose Lowell because of what it represented to American industrialism. Lowell was the largest of the antebellum mill towns and the model for the "Waltham" type which predominated in northern New England. In its early development, Lowell was the acknowledged leader in textile innovation. Its agents made decisions affecting the organization of production which were copied widely throughout New England. By 1850 Lowell's mill owners, the Boston Associates, operated mills in Chicopee, Taunton, and Lawrence, Massachusetts; Manchester, Dover, Somersworth, and Nashua, New Hampshire; Saco and Biddeford, Maine; and, shortly after, in Holyoke, Massachusetts.[4] This interlocking network of mill owners watched industrywide trends as well as local conditions. As part of such a network, Lowell shared in the most important change to occur within the textile industry in the mid-nineteenth century—the shift in the pattern of employment as the Irish replaced Yankee farm women in New England's textile mills.[5]

The Boston Associates' decision to employ Irish labor marked a significant departure from the "republican" community of Yankee factory women. Thomas Dublin recently examined this change in his seminal *Women at Work: The Transformation of Work and Community in Lowell, Massachusetts, 1826–1860.* Dublin used local records, private family letters, and the records of the Hamilton Manufacturing Company, particularly payroll accounts, to describe the movement of Yankee farm women into Lowell's textile mills. He found that these women carried with them rural values stressing friendship and kinship and, while at Lowell, built a close-knit community of factory operatives. This sense of community grew in response to the labor situation, the power of the peer group within the boardinghouses in which these women resided, and the homogeneity of the work force. It underscored the fascinating paradox that, as these women challenged paternal capitalists, they did so as a direct result of the increasing opportunities available to them within paternal capitalism. Dublin argued that the labor unrest of the 1830s was a defensive effort to maintain wages but, with the revival following the Panic of 1837, the mill women renewed their labor agitation by expanding their efforts to demand an increased role for women within factory life. At the same time, the Boston Associates' efforts to maintain profits through wage cuts and increased production undermined the existing system. The Boston Associates turned to eager Irish immigrants as a new system of family wage labor appeared.[6]

Dublin's work is important because, in describing the transformation of Lowell's economy, he added a new dimension with his discussion of a developing sense of community among mill women. He used the Hamilton Company's records to determine when and how the transformation occurred and to show why the community spirit among Yankee factory women diminished as the Boston Associates turned to Irish labor. Dublin, however, did not draw heavily upon the full range of Irish experiences in Lowell, preferring instead to define the role of the Irish in terms of their impact upon the pattern of employment, the subject of his attention.[7] Still, Dublin's contribution is essential to understanding the role of women, even if they are largely Yankee women, in the textile mills of antebellum America. His application of Hamilton Company records, combined with private letters, has set a standard by which future research will be measured. If some questions were beyond the scope of his research, Dublin did place Lowell's Irish firmly in the textile mills with a perceptive analysis of where they obtained work and, to a lesser degree, what awaited them there. He demonstrated that the Irish were central to the transformation of labor and, by doing so, opened a discussion of an ethnic community which has long been neglected but which has important implications for industrial America.

Still, the sheer number of Irish entering the mills and the speed with which they entered them make their entry crucial to an explanation of Lowell's metamorphosis from a Yankee factory village into an immigrant industrial city. Hence, there is great value in a more detailed investigation of the role of the Irish not only as a complement to Dublin's impressive treatment of the labor system but also as an addition to the growing body of research on immigrants in American industrial communities. When the Boston Associates created Lowell, they did not foresee a permanent Irish working class. The Boston Associates saw the Irish as a transient collection of unskilled workers, whose stay in the new factory village would be determined only by the length of time needed to complete the Associates' construction projects and whose impact on the community would be minimal. Instead, they found that these immigrants had their own set of values, family, neighborhood, and institutional associations. The Irish created a distinctive subculture within Lowell and, in the process, became a major force in shaping its development. By the 1840s, it was hardly surprising that the mill agents should turn to local Irish labor, especially given the size of the labor pool and Irish eagerness to enter the mills. While we know *why* Lowell's labor system changed, it is also important to explain *how* that change occurred. To complete the story, the Irish must become more important players in the drama.

This approach is useful because it also allows us to broaden our perception of community. With the Irish activity in Lowell, we witness the dynamic growth of an Irish community while placing it squarely within the context of Lowell's development. Such volatile issues as public schools, city services, and poor relief arose as the structure of community changed among the Irish and in Lowell generally. We see the various dimensions of human experience and the full range of that experience—warts and all. In such an analysis, the concept of community emerges as a constantly changing interactive process based upon a number of "givens" such as the role of the Irish in Lowell's economy but determined ultimately by the simple truth that the Irish lived in nineteenth-century Lowell.

Lowell had the largest Irish community in New England, excluding

Boston, in the mid-nineteenth century and, while the Irish community in Lowell remains largely unexplored, the wider story of the Irish in America has attracted considerable research. William Forbes Adams, Carl Wittke, and Marcus Hansen took the first tentative steps in the 1930s with their work on the transatlantic crossing and on general Irish contributions to America.[8] The real impetus to additional research, however, came with the publication of Oscar Handlin's *Boston's Immigrants: A Study in Acculturation* in 1941. Handlin closely examined one community and found that the Irish had dramatically changed the closed, homogeneous city which had existed before 1820. He also depicted the growing conflict between Boston's Yankees and the Irish between 1820 and 1860, arguing that the Irish formed a separate subculture before the Civil War. By then, the Irish had achieved a foothold as they wrested political control of Boston from the Yankees, although the Yankees retained social, cultural, and economic dominance. Handlin also described immigrants such as Boston's Irish as disoriented European peasants, "uprooted" from their traditional culture, who were caught up in an alien environment.[9]

Handlin's work was hailed widely as a pathbreaking effort and his research set the limits within which many historians thought about the American Irish. Handlin's approach appeared, with some variation, in the writings of Robert Ernst on New York and Dennis Clark on Philadelphia who, much like Lynn Lees recently, emphasized the internal dynamics of Irish communities while stressing the problem of acculturation.[10] Other historians focused upon particular issues or relationships, with Thomas N. Brown's *Irish-American Nationalism, 1870–1890* the best in this group.[11] A few, notably William V. Shannon, Lawrence McCaffrey, and, to some extent, Andrew Greeley, examined the impact of the American Irish over the broad range of American culture. Greeley identified what he suggested were Irish-American characteristics measured typically in relationship to other immigrant groups.[12] Finally, noted Catholic historians, particularly John Tracy Ellis and Thomas T. McAvoy, have discussed relationships between the Irish and American Catholicism.[13]

By the mid-1960s, revisionists began to examine Handlin's basic thrust carefully and some like Stephan Thernstrom turned once again to community studies. In 1964 Thernstrom published his impressive *Poverty and Progress: Social Mobility in a Nineteenth Century City*, in which he turned an analysis of social mobility into a fascinating tale of Newburyport's Irish and their efforts to secure a niche for themselves within the social and economic structure of nineteenth-century Newburyport.[14]

Thernstrom's wide-ranging use of records echoed the work of the late Herbert Gutman who, about the same time, called for a shift in both research focus and technique to rewrite history "from the bottom up." Gutman's call produced a profusion of research and the "new social," "new urban," and "working-class" history grew rapidly.[15]

As research techniques became more specialized, the scope of many studies narrowed, although most retained their ethnic character and "ethnic" history flourished. Much of the recent "urban-ethnic" history flowed originally from the 1968 Yale Conference on Urban History and, more recently, from Harvard's "Studies in Urban History" series, where immigrant neighborhoods and associations, social mobility, and "status and power" questions received treatment.[16] A second group of "ethnic-labor" studies dealt with economic opportunity and labor protest, while a third set enlarged upon Thernstrom's discussion of social mobility.[17] A fourth group stressed immigrant religious life. Among this set, Jay Dolan's work stood out for his ability to depict the immigrant "in the pew."[18] Additional themes included cultural transmission, education, and politics, among others.[19]

Most recent ethnic studies have dealt with late nineteenth-century America, where the records are better, the immigrant experience was longer, particularly for the Irish, and the trends are more apparent. In this light, Handlin's original research is impressive because he looked at Boston's Irish when they first arrived in large numbers at mid-century. He also perceptively questioned a wide range of immigrant experiences. In particular, Handlin saw acculturation as defined by cultural transmission, the internal dynamics of an immigrant community, and the outside environment. The specialization which has occurred since the late 1960s has limited studies in acculturation which paralleled Handlin. Those who come close, such as Thernstrom on Newburyport, generally have the most to say about immigrants and the American experience.[20]

This study examines the Irish in Lowell, Massachusetts, before the Civil War by focusing upon cultural transmission, internal community dynamics, and the outside environment with careful attention to arguments in support of writing a readable history.[21] As a case study, Lowell's Irish can tell us much about the immigrant's role in American industrialism, providing a number of "if's" are satisfied. Lowell's Irish are important to the Irish- American experience if Lowell is important to American industrial history. (In view of recent work, a struggle over Lowell's "representativeness" within American industrialism seems unnecessary.) Lowell's

Irish are important if, in the process of writing history "from the bottom up," these immigrants do not appear as a formless mass but rather as a group of individuals building a neighborhood with internal dynamics of its own. Finally, Lowell's Irish are important if a study of their contribution to Lowell's history adds to previous scholarship. We know, for example, how Lowell's Irish transformed work and community in mid-nineteenth-century Lowell but we also need to know why and at what cost.

I have attempted to satisfy these stipulations by producing a work which places the Irish firmly in Lowell while accounting for their traditions and while stressing the internal development of the Irish community. My research is intended to complement Dublin's work on Yankee mill women but also to go beyond his discussion of the Irish role by broadening his discussion of the transformation of labor. Lowell's Irish formed a separate community which existed simultaneously with the planned Yankee mill village and which grew faster than that village. They developed customs and traditions which suited their new environment and, when the transformation of labor occurred at mid-century, the Irish were already entrenched in Lowell. They were never helpless pawns in the Boston Associates' scheme to maintain profits and quell Yankee mill women's labor agitation but, at the same time, they were hardly free agents skillfully negotiating to their own advantage. The story of Lowell's Irish is a dramatic tale of assimilation and alienation, tolerance and nativism, opportunity and rejection, and, perhaps most important, compromise.

The first Irish in Lowell were mainly either naturalized Americans or Irish who had lived in America for some time. The early settlers arrived not from Ireland but primarily from the Boston docks and were familiar with American work habits. They worked in Irish labor gangs headed by an Irish foreman to whom they owed allegiance and with whom they often shared a common ancestry. Lowell's early Irish settlement was a rough collection of "paddy camps," where employment was seasonal and where the Irish lived separately from those employed in the planned Yankee mill village. The lives of Lowell's early Irish settlers reflected a pattern common throughout the history of Lowell's Irish community—the Irish worked separately, lived apart, and retained those customs which could be adapted to America or which facilitated acculturation. While the Irish laborer understood American work traditions, he retired to a rough-hewn cabin "as seen in Ballyshannon," often built within sight of the factory boardinghouses.[22]

It was almost a decade before the Irish "paddy camps" were established permanently, but inevitably an Irish neighborhood took shape. That neighborhood, eventually called "the Acre," retained the flavor of the paddy camps, divided by factional disputes. It also took on a certain social structure. At the top was a small middle class, largely shopkeepers and construction foremen, as well as a few lawyers and teachers. This middle class was American in outlook but Irish in spirit and, initially, shaped the Irish outlook toward Lowell. Institutions developed to serve them, and soon the "Lowell Irish Benevolent Society" became the most powerful lay organization in the neighborhood. Beneath the Irish middle class was the mass of unskilled Irish laborers. The cyclical nature of Lowell's building boom encouraged transiency among laborers, preventing stronger working-class loyalties and fostering dependence upon the resident Irish middle class who were more stable, had established the beginnings of an institutional network, and both understood and helped to shape the definition of being Irish in Lowell.

Although feelings between Irish and Yankee laborers ran high, relations between Lowell's Yankee and Irish leaders were cordial, and the two groups shared certain characteristics and patterns. The Irish middle class applauded the image of Lowell as an industrial paradise; they voted Whig; and they socialized with Lowell's Yankees at Benevolent Society gatherings. In response to the need for education among the children of Irish laborers, the Irish middle class and the Yankee leadership worked out a remarkable education compromise which effectively enlisted Catholic support for Lowell's public schools. Both groups also contributed to Daniel O'Connell's Repeal campaign and to Famine relief.

In the early 1840s, economic and social conditions changed in Lowell. The Panic of 1837 had stopped construction of Lowell's mills and its canal system, although these complexes were already largely complete.[23] Other mill towns sprang up throughout New England, which created some new employment opportunities even during the Panic, while those Irish poor who remained in Lowell benefited from private relief. When business revived, however, the Boston Associates faced new difficulties as the demands for high dividends remained constant and labor unrest intensified. At the same time, Famine Irish, direct from Ireland and ignorant of American work habits and of Lowell's social and economic structure, streamed into Lowell. These newcomers offered the Boston Associates a partial solution to the problem of finding an alternative to the employment of Yankee farm women.[24]

With the new Irish in the mills, the "low class" Irish whose numbers were sufficient to wreck the social fabric of the Lowell system, cordial re-

lations between Irish and Yankees disappeared. To control the unruly
Famine immigrants and to prepare their children for factory employment,
Lowell's officials joined Massachusetts's authorities in devising a house of
reformation and a poor farm. Perhaps most significant, they changed the
education compromise, transforming Lowell's public schools from a setting for innovative experimentation designed to bring to Irish children
the full benefits of the American republic into institutions which instilled
work discipline into immigrant students who would become factory workers. This change in the official attitude produced a marked shift in the way
the Irish viewed their position in Lowell. The Irish middle class in particular reacted defensively, turning inward and redefining their presence
in Lowell in sharply ethnic terms.

During this period of change, the middle-class Benevolent Society remained conspicuously silent, and a new source of authority arose within
the Irish community. In 1848 Frs. John and Timothy O'Brien arrived to
end the schismatic disputes which had embroiled Lowell's Catholics for
fifteen years. These priests represented the bishop at the parish level and
combined personal charisma with a sense of duty to increase the Church's
influence, as well as their own, over the Irish. As nativism increased and
diocesan officials took a position which advised Catholic immigrants to lie
low in defense of their religious beliefs, the O'Briens' influence grew.[25]
They supported the traditions of American republicanism, encouraged
Irish mill employment, and upheld immigrant customs, all the while forging a new identity among Lowell's Irish which was "Irish American,"
working class, and heavily Catholic.

The rise in the power of the O'Brien brothers coincided with the increase in the number of Irish mill workers. Absentee mill owners and their
agents by now viewed Lowell's Irish as a permanent work force through
which they might maintain dividends by depressing wages. When Lowell's
mills opened to Irish, their admission sparked a furious debate which
raged throughout Lowell's newspapers and in the Irish Catholic Boston
Pilot, particularly after one corporation, the Prescott Company, permanently replaced Yankee operatives with Irish. The debate focused upon
the quality of Irish labor, their moral and physical character, and their social pretensions among "educated" Yankee women. Beneath this debate,
however, lay an intense rage at absentee Boston capitalists who had hitherto enjoyed widespread support among Lowell's Yankees and who were
now abandoning them. Its Yankees claimed that Lowell had deteriorated

into an immigrant industrial city. The Irish, represented in the Boston *Pilot*, agreed and commended the change.[26]

The debate over the Irish presence has significant implications because it broadens Dublin's definition of community by raising important questions about Lowell's overall growth, of which the community of Yankee mill women was also a part. Cordial relations ended when the Famine Irish entered Lowell's mills because they had become symbols of deteriorating status within American industrialism. While Handlin, for example, saw growing animosity between Boston's Yankees and Irish in the mid-nineteenth century, the experience at Lowell indicates that this deterioration, initiated by "outside" Boston capitalists, caused a sudden collapse of Lowell's intricate social structure.[27] The experience of Lowell's Irish is also important because it enlarges upon a conflict which Dublin confined to mobility within the mill.

The story of Lowell's Irish is a complex tale of economic, social, political, and religious pressures precipitating changes within the Irish community and, more generally, within Lowell. Boston's capitalists were the shapers and movers behind the economic transformation of Lowell, but the Irish seized opportunity when it arose. Lowell's Yankees spoke out not only against the loss of their near-monopoly on mill employment but also at the destruction of a quality of life within American industrialism. As Lowell changed from a Yankee mill village into an immigrant industrial city, the Know-Nothings emerged. When the furor passed, Lowell's Irish had obtained their toehold in the mills but the Yankees shunned Irish Benevolent Society dinners. The Irish developed strong religious institutions, a growing political presence, and a sense of common traditions within their community, but these traditions were initially generated more by Yankee hostility than from within the Irish community. Lowell had become an immigrant industrial city but at the cost of its reputation as an industrial showcase.

CHAPTER 2

The Early Immigrants
1821–30

In November, 1821, a group of Boston investors, the Boston Associates, visited East Chelmsford, Massachusetts, where the Merrimack River dropped thirty-two feet. They "perambulated the grounds and scanned the capabilities of the place."[1] The group included Paul Moody, a master mechanic who had designed a successful experimental complex for Francis Cabot Lowell at Waltham; Patrick Tracy Jackson, Lowell's brother-in-law; Nathan Appleton, a business associate; Kirk Boott, whom the Associates had hired to direct their new endeavor; his brother, John W. Boott; and Warren Dutton, who would serve as first president of the Merrimack Manufacturing Company. They agreed that East Chelmsford was an ideal location for a new and much larger complex of factories than those which they operated at Waltham. The Associates quietly bought up the surrounding farmland and purchased the water rights to the Merrimack River.[2]

The East Chelmsford site presented serious problems. A decaying canal, the Pawtucket, had been built in a rough semicircle around the drop in the Merrimack River in the 1790s. The Associates planned to transform this into a power canal, while retaining its transportation function. The revitalized canal would then supply water to a new complex of mills. Unfortunately the terrain, particularly the southwest section close to where the Pawtucket took water from the Merrimack River, was hilly, and the canal's path made it impossible to tap all potential mill sites without constructing secondary waterways that would divert water from the Pawtucket to the mills. In addition, the Pawtucket was an earthen canal and its water flowed unimpeded into low-lying marshes and fields. The Associates' expensive redesign required not only the reconstruction of the Pawtucket but also the addition of numerous branch canals.[3]

The Associates' vision of a large manufacturing city at East Chelmsford also presumed a long-term mill-building program. Beginning with the

construction of the Merrimack Manufacturing Company, new mills, carefully designed for maximum efficiency, arose as canals were dug. In addition to the mills, countinghouses, dye houses, bleacheries, and stables, as
well as housing for the mill workers and for resident mill agents, were
required. As mills opened, the Associates laid out new streets, and by the
time workers entered the mills, a commercial district and small residential
neighborhoods appeared. In their developments, the Associates wished to
harmonize their mill village with the surrounding New England countryside, planting trees and cultivating flowers at mill windows and grassy
plots in mill yards. In 1826, the flourishing mill village was separated from
Chelmsford and named Lowell.

In its early days, Lowell seemed to glisten and sparkle, most especially
because the Associates followed Francis Cabot Lowell's wish that the new
enterprise avoid the psychological horrors of England's Lancashire. In
their planned mill village, the Associates paid close attention to a variety
of amenities. They sent recruiters to central and northern New England,
promising Yankee farm women not only cash wages but also the excite-
ment of a cosmopolitan city in a rural setting.[4] They eased homesickness
by placing these women with friends or, where possible, with relatives
from their farm homes.[5] They encouraged Yankee farm women to picnic in
the pristine countryside which was always visible from their factory window. To promote cultural opportunities, the Associates provided invigo-
rating lecture series which attracted the likes of Emerson, Hawthorne,
and Thoreau.

In these and other ways, the Associates safeguarded Lowell's cherished
reputation and promoted the refreshing contrast between American and
English industrialism.[6] Lowell's sponsors depicted it as the "pretty sister"
of American industrialism, although scores of other towns experienced
similar conditions and some, like Manchester, New Hampshire, were
even more successful in constructing a pleasant environment. Lowell welcomed a steady stream of domestic and foreign visitors and soon became a
mandatory stop for European travelers. The Associates received Andrew
Jackson warmly, for example, despite their distaste for his politics. "We
will feed him gold dust, if he will eat it," reportedly crowed one of the
Associates, Amos Lawrence, a year after Kirk Boott, their chief agent for
Lowell, had warned ominously that "grass will grow in your streets, owls
will build their nests in the mills and foxes burrow in your highways" if
Jackson was elected.[7]

Jackson, like so many of Lowell's visitors, went away impressed. From

Lowell in the 1820s. Courtesy of the Lowell Historical Society.

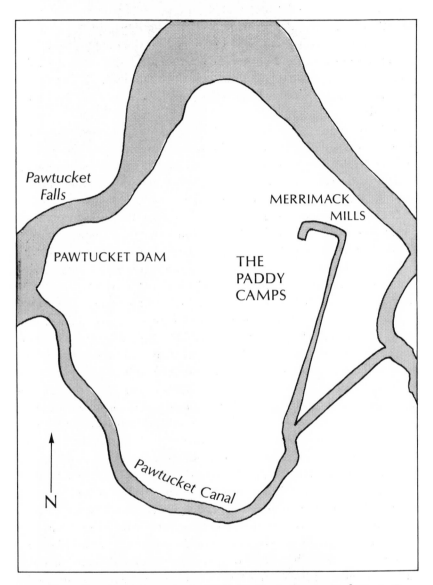

Lowell's mill and canal system in 1823. By Craig Roscoe and Marie Rose
Rodrique.

Europe came Harriett Martineau, Frederika Bremer, Anthony Trollope, Michel Chevalier, and Charles Dickens.[8] In 1842, Dickens described Lowell as large, populous, thriving, and youthful: "One would swear that every 'Bakery,' 'Grocery,' and 'Bookbindery,' and other kind of store, took its shutters down for the first time, and started in business yesterday. The golden pestles and mortars fixed as signs upon the sun-blind frames outside the Druggists' appear to have been just turned out of the United States Mint."[9]

Dickens's impressions are fascinating because he recorded them at a time when several thousand Irish lived in miserable hovels close to the mill district. Curiously, he never mentioned them. Like other dignitaries, Dickens, who was escorted by agent Samuel Lawrence, saw only the mill district, "the object of my visit." Once there, Dickens toured attractively laid out mills and boardinghouses and watched the Yankee factory women engaged in productive employ. His visit illustrated the success of Lowell's officials in protecting and promoting their image of Lowell. Even Richard Cobden, an English businessman passing through Lowell in 1835, noted in the only surviving reference to Lowell's Irish of this type that "*even the Irish* always wash" before leaving the Lowell Machine Shop.[10]

It is clear that the planned industrial community at Lowell did not include a permanent place for Irish laborers. The enormous task of building the mill village required extensive use of unskilled labor, which attracted many of the younger sons of New England farmers, but there was still no large pool of unskilled workers. Kirk Boott understood that other sources of employment drained New England's manpower, but he wished to complete development quickly and efficiently. To accomplish this, he hired all available unskilled laborers during peak construction periods, including itinerant Yankees and Irish. Word that laborers were needed spread quickly along such routes as the Middlesex Canal, which connected Lowell with Boston Harbor at Charlestown, and as construction picked up in the spring of 1822, Irish from the Boston area applied to Boott for work.[11]

There had been Irish in the vicinity of Lowell for over twenty-five years. The records of the Middlesex Canal Company from the 1790s, for example, contained the names of Irish employees, although, undoubtedly, most returned to Boston when work was completed.[12] As early as the summer of 1822, Fr. Patrick Byrne, an Irish missionary priest, visited the Catholics living in East Chelmsford. On 20 August 1822, he baptized Ellen Harrigan near the mill village and held services for a small group of

Irish employed at the Chelmsford Glass Works in nearby Middlesex Village. During his visit, Byrne bapitzed a total of eight children and lectured to Catholics in Gaelic on the importance of preserving their faith. These small, isolated groups of Irish grew as Lowell attracted new residents.[13]

The migration had really begun when Hugh Cummiskey, an Irish foreman who worked on the Charlestown docks, the terminus of the Middlesex Canal, petitioned Kirk Boott for employment, just as construction began. Cummiskey met Boott at Frye's Tavern, a local inn not far from the Pawtucket Canal, on 5 April 1822. Cummiskey represented thirty laborers who had walked with him from Charlestown to Lowell, a distance of about twenty-seven miles. Perhaps in consideration of their journey, Boott generously gave the Irish laborers "money to refresh themselves." He and Cummiskey concluded an agreement and, on the following morning, Cummiskey and his men began enlarging and deepening the Pawtucket Canal.[14]

The thirty laborers formed a work gang who were personally loyal to Cummiskey, making him a dominant figure in local Irish affairs. A native of County Tyrone, Cummiskey had come to America in 1790 and, shortly after, obtained his citizenship. He became a construction foreman and general supervisor on the Charlestown docks. Initially, Lowell represented little more to him than a lucrative employment opportunity; in fact, he settled permanently in Lowell only in 1828. Still, Cummiskey had a number of traits which ideally suited him for his position in Lowell.[15] First, he found work for his men. As jobs were scarce, Cummiskey was willing to work at anything. In 1831, for example, Lowell's officials paid him for "digging fenceposts in the Protestant cemetery."[16] Second, he cultivated warm and lasting friendships with Lowell's Yankee leaders, particularly Ezra Worthen, Paul Moody, Luther Lawrence, and Kirk Boott, and after their deaths he referred to them as "dear, departed friends."[17] Third, he was actively involved in the early development of a Catholic church and participated prominently in the early years of the Benevolent Society. Further, Cummiskey patrolled the paddy camps as a town constable, served as the local agent for Boston's Irish Catholic newspaper, the Boston *Pilot*, and contributed regularly to O'Connell's Repeal campaign.[18] Despite such involvement, he judiciously refrained from embroiling himself in volatile disputes which wracked the Irish community on several levels throughout much of its early history. Finally, Cummiskey also remained a resident of the old Irish neighborhood even after his resources permitted him to move elsewhere, as many other middle-class Irish had done. In short, he produced results for those under him and was respected throughout the paddy camps.

Cummiskey and his men were typical of the Irish who settled in Lowell in the 1820s. Most had been in America for a number of years, many coming from tiny Irish settlements which dotted the New England coastline. The largest of these was in Boston, where Irish laborers were attracted by employment along its waterfront. They lived nearby in a small Irish district centered around Broad Street and for the most part worshipped at the Church of the Holy Cross.[19] Other Irish had settled in the New England countryside, where they worked at whatever jobs were available. Because of the relative size of the undertaking, Lowell held the promise of significant employment and laborers from nearby Irish settlements such as Boston applied to Lowell's agents for employment.

Still, the localized nature of Lowell's building boom was not sufficient to generate emigration directly from Ireland but, as word of the scale of construction spread, some Canadian Irish also migrated there.[20] In this sense, the early Irish settlers were a fairly cosmopolitan group, as well as seasoned veterans of the region's unskilled labor market. The informal network through which employment opportunities for unskilled labor were broadcast worked sufficiently well for Lowell to hold four thou Irish by 1844.[21]

Although the U.S. federal census recorded only 44,000 Irish-born residents in the United States in 1790, their number increased steadily after 1815.[22] Between 1815 and 1845, over one million Irish left for North America. Many emigrants chose Canada because passage on Canadian timber and flax seed ships was much less expensive than the cost of a direct passage to a port in the United States and because English legislation allowed Canadian ships "to carry more passengers per registered ton and superficial deck space than the American Congress tolerated."[23]

Once Irish emigrants landed in Canada, they reached Lowell in several ways. Many walked through northern New England from Quebec or New Brunswick; in fact, Irish emigrants settled in scores of small villages along the Maine coast when they decided not to push farther south.[24] George Potter discovered, for example, that "before leaving County Sligo, men were heard to declare they planned to walk from Quebec to New York. The town of Concord, New Hampshire, buried an Irishman who died while walking from the Canadian border."[25] Potter also noted that the route through Eastport, Maine, was a popular, well-traveled path: "From St.

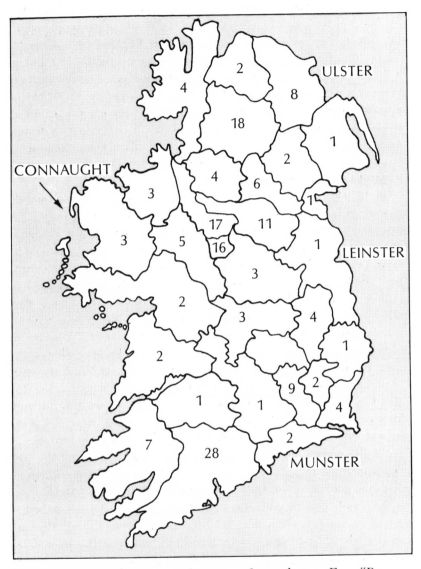

Lowell's Repeal Association: Irish origins of contributors. From "Progress of Repeal in the United States: Lowell," Boston *Pilot*, 29 May 1841, p. 171.

John's in New Brunswick, starting in the mid-1820s, a steamboat crossed the Bay of Fundy to Eastport in Maine, which was the transshipment point for Boston and and the New England states, and for New York, Philadelphia, and Baltimore by coastal vessel. Later steamboat supplemented sail, and the ancestors of thousands of New England Irish arrived in Boston from Eastport on the well-known steamboat *Admiral*."[26] But not all Irish entered the United States so openly. Because Massachusetts required sea captains to post bond that their Irish passengers would not become paupers, many vessels carrying Irish emigrants sailed into unwatched harbors where the Irish disembarked and walked to their destinations. As early as 1823, authorities arrested a Belfast, Maine, sea captain who smuggled Irish illegally into Massachusetts. Despite such action, officials failed to discourage the trade.[27]

The 1850 federal census confirms the importance of the Canadian route for some of Lowell's Irish, for whom emigration had been a painstakingly slow process. By 1850, most of Lowell's Irish had been in North America for at least five years and many had been here for over ten years. Many families contained children who had been born in Canada. By recording the birthplaces of all the individuals who lived in the heart of the Irish neighborhood in 1850, an area bounded by Dutton, Merrimack, Pawtucket, and Willie streets, the census documents the preeminence of Canada's Atlantic Provinces as a debarkation point. In the 650 Irish households examined, sixty-four births occurred outside Massachusetts or Great Britain, including Ireland. Of these sixty-four births, forty-seven (73 percent) were in Quebec, New Brunswick, Nova Scotia, Prince Edward Island, Maine, New Hampshire, and Vermont, with the Atlantic Provinces representing the largest percentage of births. New York, Connecticut, and Rhode Island contributed the other seventeen births.[28]

It is also possible to make some tentative suggestions about the Irish origins of these emigrants. Several accounts described the process by which emigration to North America gained respectability. McDonough and Kerr and, more recently, Lees and Anderson have shown that the first emigration impulse, originating in Ulster and spreading through the eastern coastal region toward Cork, rooted emigration in the Irish mind. Later, the collapse precipitated by the Great Famine spurred Irish in the central and western regions to leave as well, although decades after the initial impulse.[29] Whatever the cause, emigration was an especially handy solution to the difficulties encountered by the Irish in the first half of the nineteenth century. Many gravitated temporarily to Lancashire, earning

The Irish in steerage. From the *London Illustrated Weekly*, 9 July 1840. Courtesy of the Lowell Museum.

enough money to meet their rent or other obligations upon return to Ireland. For others, permanent emigration was a more attractive alternative. A number of these Irish eventually found their way to Lowell.[30]

In Lowell, there are three sources which allow us to draw tentative conclusions about birthplaces: city death records, "Declarations of Intentions" among naturalized Irishmen, and the records of Lowell's Repeal Association as reported in the Boston *Pilot*. The city death records were the least useful because, like the federal census, birth origin was listed almost invariably as "Ireland." These records list 1,396 births in the Dutton-Willie-Pawtucket-Merrimack Street area from 1832 to 1862, but only 127 entries (9 percent) specified origin within Ireland. These 127 births, which were scattered over thirty years, indicated that Lowell's Irish emigrated from throughout Ireland, although the earliest records showed a tendency for Irish to have emigrated from the north.[31] A more consistent pattern emerged, however, in the "Declaration of Intentions" among naturalized Irishmen and in the records of contributors to Lowell's Repeal Association published in 1841–42. Of the 132 declarations in which Irishmen specified birth by county, the pattern confirmed the theory that pre-Famine emigration originated in Ulster and adjacent counties, in eastern coastal regions, and in Cork, with Tyrone (22), Cavan (13), Leitrim (12), Fermanagh (11), and Cork (13) sending the largest number of emigrants to Lowell. In the contributors' records, 173 Irishmen, all of whom lived in Lowell before the Famine emigrants arrived, reported their county of origin. As in the declarations, northern counties, such as Leitrim and Tyrone, contributed 9.8 and 10.4 percent respectively, while Cork sent 16.1 percent of the group in Lowell. By contrast, the western counties of Mayo (3), Sligo (3), Galway (2), and Clare (2), when combined, represented only 5.7 percent of the total group.[32]

Oscar Handlin employed many of the same sources for Boston in the same period. Handlin used the Boston Repeal Association contributors' records published in the Boston *Pilot* between 1841 and 1843 as well and his conclusions support the findings for Lowell. Handlin noted that only about two thousand Irish passed through Boston annually before 1830 and that, except for 1837, the number of Irish arriving annually in Boston before 1840 never rose above four thousand. Among those Irish who settled in Boston, Handlin found in the Boston Repeal Association records and in the lists of Irish seeking information about Ireland in the Boston *Pilot* that the largest numbers came from Ulster and from Tyrone, although Cork also sent a sizable contingent. Handlin argued quite properly that the pattern shifted with the Famine toward the south and west, which coincided also with the pattern among the "Declarations of Intentions" at Lowell.[33] The similarities of these findings indicated that the economy of a city had little direct effect upon its attractiveness to specific groups of Irishmen. Industrial and commercial cities both shared Canadian-based emigration of unskilled Irish into New England.

The "Declarations of Intentions" also provided information on the median age of Irishmen arriving at the American port of entry. Among those Irishmen who arrived before 1850, the median age was twenty-five. Of the 171 Irishmen examined, only fifteen were teenagers. The majority of Irishmen (55.5 percent) arrived in America in their twenties, although several came who were in their fifties. Although a few Irishmen declared their intentions to become American citizens almost immediately upon arrival, most waited several years before expressing their intent.[34] Overall, the number of Irish increased steadily in Lowell before the Civil War. In 1830, the Irish accounted for about 7 percent of Lowell's population.[35] It is important to remember that their experiences in Lowell were not exclusively work related but rather were directly affected by the image which Lowell's officials projected of their factory village and by the cultural values which these officials espoused. Lowell was a noble enterprise, set into the New England countryside by enlightened, progressive entrepreneurs who symbolized the potential of the new American republic. Like everyone else, the Irish could not help but be impressed and influenced by this image of Lowell. As the pace of construction continued unabated throughout the 1820s, many of them remained in Lowell.

At first, the nature of employment largely governed the position of the Irish in Lowell. In the early years, most of Lowell's Irish were men whose presence there was dictated by the "work gang" approach commonly used in the employment of unskilled laborers on Lowell's first construction projects. Like Cummiskey's men, many Irish worked in teams supervised by Irish foremen or by Yankee overseers. Although these Irish laborers had lived in North America for some time and were well acquainted with American work habits, they brought with them to Lowell personal loyalties nurtured in previous work as well as traditional Irish ancestral loyalties. These ancestral loyalties did not interfere with their work; moreover, clan associations aided a sense of camaraderie which, perhaps even more important, the Irish carried with them beyond their work experiences. Within Lowell's unskilled labor market, the pattern of employment illustrated to individual Irishmen that clan loyalties worked directly to their

benefit, whether in making application for employment to men like Cummiskey or in obtaining a patch of land upon which to build a crude hut. In
Lowell, the Irish were hardly uprooted European peasants nor were they
deliberately negotiating relationships to their advantage.[36] Rather, they
were immigrants who used what worked in the marketplace and at home
to their benefit because life in the paddy camps made them feel comfortable with each other and with their past.

Both the outlook of these laborers and the Yankee attitudes encouraged
them to identify as Irishmen, particularly in their private lives. Although
their work required a measure of discipline in order to conform to Boott's
time schedule and to his expectations of them, after hours they were free
to develop accommodations on their own, and the development of an Irish
district reflected Irish cultural traditions, including clan associations. The
Irish district which emerged beyond the factory village boundaries looked,
smelled, and felt "Irish." Since they assumed that the Irish would leave
when work dried up and since they noted the high rate of transiency
within the squalid Irish district, initially Lowell's officials never interfered
with what happened there. As a result, the Irish were American laborers
by day, perhaps even enjoying friendships on the job with other transient
laborers, but they remained distinctly Irish apart from this experience.

The Yankees' "leave them alone" policy promoted haphazard growth.
At first, Irish men were the majority of residents in the new district and a
rough, rowdy series of paddy camps arose on unused corporation land
convenient to early construction at the main dam, canal system, and
mills.[37] In the early 1830s, the Boston Associates developed the Western
Canal, a branch of the Pawtucket, to bring water to a series of new mills
north of the Irish settlements.[38] The proximity of this new construction
sparked additional growth in the paddy camps and, as the pace of construction quickened, a number of Irish came to view Lowell as a permanent home. Soon some of them were joined by their wives and children.
While no record of marital status was found among the declarations, the
pattern in the Irish neighborhood once the Irish were firmly settled in
Lowell indicated that most Irish brought their families with them. In the
early days, however, many like Cummiskey left their families behind in
other American communities as they sought temporary employment in
Lowell.[39]

Also, as Lowell was accessible to other mill sites under development
throughout New England, the number of Irish who lived in Lowell and
worked as unskilled laborers on nearby projects increased.[40] By the early

1830s, several hundred Irish lived in Lowell.[41] Except for a few scattered houses, the area upon which the camps were built was open land which lay beyond the boundaries of the mill village. Locks and Canals officials, who were land and general development agents, held title in the name of the company.[42] The region around one Irish camp, for example, was a low swamp covered with maple trees which was used by local farmers for partridge shooting. The Irish scattered their camps over this unused land.[43]

Within the developing Irish district, the most impressive form of organization was the faction, which in the early nineteenth century was fundamental to Irish social structure. The family was at the heart of most factions. While family honor was an important breeding ground for faction feuding, specific complaints over such issues as land use also encouraged fighting. In addition, the faction served a variety of useful purposes. It provided an organizational framework sensitive to traditional forms of Irish social structure long after formal tribal relationships ended, and it unified the Irish regionally, building loyalties in a way otherwise impossible. It also provided leadership, which British bureaucrats considered undesirable and disruptive. In its own way, the faction enforced a kind of order, although the British saw Irish "order" as chaos plaguing nineteenth-century rural Ireland. Still, the Irish understood the purpose of the faction and the rules which governed it even if the British did not.

At the same time, factions encouraged the Irish to turn inward. Within Irish society, most people had little knowledge of the world beyond the farm neighborhood. The average Irishman seldom traveled more than a dozen miles from his land. There was no broad-based Irish nationalist spirit before O'Connell urged all Irishmen to think larger thoughts as a prelude to the fight for independence. Hence, an Irishman's view of the world was colored only by what he saw around him. Loyalty was to family or, more generally, to faction. Variations in speech, tradition, and practice added to the distance which separated one Irishman from another. In a fundamental way, an Irishman had little in common with anyone beyond those who shared his narrow tribal, parochial outlook. Even in Lowell, a Corkonian considered an emigrant from Tyrone as foreign as the Yankees who lived around both of them.

Transplanted to America, factions were attractive forms of social organization and had already proven useful during the Atlantic crossing and in the original decision as to where to live in America. Within the paddy camps, they provided order as well as a sense of continuity and stability. Although Lowell's Yankees viewed the paddy camps as chaotic and volatile, their actual development reflected traditions in rural Ireland. To an Irishman living in Lowell, there was no disorder; no other form of social organization would seem so natural to him. While the Irish were unable to recreate the complexity of Irish factions in Lowell, the very presence of factions there encouraged organization on a larger scale. Although Irishmen near Cork City might have fought those in West Cork in Ireland, in Lowell they banded together in a way which stressed their common traditions. Corkonians certainly had more in common with one another than with anyone else. New associations grouped around family/clan which emphasized a regional identity quickly assumed old forms.[44]

Since employment drew the Irish to Lowell, much of this shift in mentality from "West Cork" to "Corkonian" arose from the work experience. Loyalties developed to specific foremen based upon personal as well as older clan/family/regional ties transferred to America. Beyond the work place, each camp maintained a separate work identity and a distinct physical presence, as camps representing most regions sprang up. This new, broader regional grouping indicated that the size of the Irish community in Lowell precluded a reproduction of the complexities of clan loyalties in Ireland, which even established Irish communities such as Boston were too small to permit. In their place were regional groupings of Corkonians and Connaught men.

In the late 1820s, there were two major paddy camps. The first, called the Acre, developed around Cork (now Marion) and Dublin streets in an area lying just west of the Western Canal and north of Broadway Street. This camp was the larger of the two and contained migrants who came originally from the southwest sections of Ireland.[45] The smaller camp arose to the north and west of the Acre. This "Half-Acre" or Lowell (now Market) Street settlement grew up in the general region of Lowell and Lewis streets. It became home to the Connaught or "West Country" Irish.[46] These camps preserved their own identities and members of each viewed one another with traditional hostility, often aggravated because they competed directly for jobs in Lowell. Periodic battles raged between the two settlements into the 1850s.[47]

Several accounts survive which describe conditions in these ramshackle Irish settlements. They were known collectively as the "paddy camp lands," although other local names such as "New Dublin" persisted well into the 1830s.[48] John McEvoy recalled fifty years after their creation that the Irish in the paddy camps pitched their tents and rough camps using whatever material was available. These early Irish homes were functional

An Irish shanty in the Merrimack Valley in the nineteenth century. Courtesy of the Museum of American Textile History.

and designed to protect the occupant from wind and rain.[49] In the 1880s, George Hedrick recalled that the paddy camps resembled "an Irish village, with the real Irish cabins and shanties, built of board, sod, and mud—such as can be seen in Ballyshannon."[50] In 1831, a visitor described the settlement for the Portsmouth, New Hampshire, *Journal*; the article was later reprinted in *Niles Register*:

> In the suburbs of Lowell, within a few rods of the canals, is a settlement, called by some, New Dublin, which occupies rather more than an acre of ground. It contains a population of not far from 500 Irish, who dwell in about 100 cabins, from 7 to 10 feet in height, built of slabs and rough boards; a fireplace made of stone, in one end, topped out with two or three flour barrels or lime casks. In a central situation, is the schoolhouse, built in the same style of the dwelling-houses, turfed up to the eaves with a window in one end, and small holes in two sides for the admission of air and light. . . . In this room are collected together perhaps 150 children.[51]

The *Niles Register* account depicted conditions in the Corkonian "Acre" camp but the description also applied to other Irish settlements. A. B. Wright recalled that in 1826 the "Half-Acre" or Connaught camp contained a score or more of rude huts built of slabs, stones, and turf. Their open fireplaces conducted smoke through headless lime casks "towards the shining stars."[52]

Within the Irish district, a crude street pattern of narrow alleys emerged and, by the early 1830s, Cork, Dublin, and Lowell streets appeared.[53] Within this ramshackle collection of huts, there stirred the beginning sense of community which drew the paddy camps together. The district retained its native Irish flavor, noticeably in such features as the piggeries attached to most cabins. In the evening when all of the pigs were routinely let loose, the narrow streets were just wide enough to allow them to roam freely throughout the neighborhood. After a while, children were sent to retrieve the pigs, which caused "some lively music in that district."[54] In one of the few examples of American customs intruding upon Irish tradition, Charles Cowley recalled in the 1880s that "although some of the first settlers shared their shanties with their swine . . . ere long a great collection of piggeries was formed behind the shanties, and a peremptory standing order was issued, 'Pigs to the rear.'" According to Cowley, "there was a pig-headed, contrary-minded minority that resented and resisted this Saxon innovation, and that resolved in hog Latin, *stare semper super antiquas vias*, to stand forever on the ancient ways."[55]

While Lowell's Irish recreated Ballyshannon free from Yankee intrusion, their dependence upon Yankee employers forced them to conform to American work habits. Nevertheless, the Yankee expectations for unskilled Irish laborers were clearly different from the factory discipline imposed upon their daughters and sons twenty years later. Still, there were some rules which every Irish laborer came to undertand. Among them was a kind of "pyramid" employment system. At the top of the pyramid was Cummiskey and near him were men like Michael Connolly, a stonemason from Cork who competed directly with Cummiskey on construction of the foundation for the first Catholic church. Initially the Irish applied to Yankee supervisors as teams, and the Irish foreman and the Yankee supervisor negotiated an agreement on their behalf. Cummiskey's team even had a general supervisor, Patrick McManus, who served as Cummiskey's superintendent in imitation of the pattern of authority in the Yankee labor system.[56]

As Locks and Canal's agent, Kirk Boott oversaw both Lowell's power system and the development of the mills, including the Merrimack Company where he served also as agent. Boott's responsibilities were enormous. He delegated authority on land development to two field supervisors, Elisha Ford and Moses Shattuck. Ford built the main dam on the Merrimack River and the Pawtucket Canal's head gates, while Shattuck supervised all outside work performed for the Locks and Canals Company.[57] Ford reportedly ruled "with stubborn firmness over his workers." Shattuck was a "large man, broad-shouldered with very big arms" who was conspicuous in a "blue dress coat, with brass buttons, over which he wore a short farmer's frock, tied about his waist with a big knot in front," with a "red bandanna neckerchief" completing his attire. While the Irish might obtain work from other sources, for instance, as haulers for local teamsters like the firm of Wood and Tapley or on smaller projects undertaken by the Town of Lowell, Ford and Shattuck controlled the large construction projects in Lowell. It was to them that the Irish chiefly applied for work.[58]

Boott hired the first group of Irish laborers for the revitalization of the Pawtucket Canal. Although the Boston Associates had originally hoped to complete it within a year, the project took seventeen months. Cummiskey's men started in April, 1822. Peak construction on the Pawtucket be-

Kirk Boott. Courtesy of the Lowell Historical Society.

gan after 10 July when five hundred men worked to enlarge and deepen it. The revitalized Pawtucket Canal cost $120,000 and measured sixty feet wide by eight feet deep.[59] Other construction projects followed quickly. By 1830, laborers had completed the Pawtucket, Lowell, Merrimack, and Hamilton canals as well as the first buildings at the Merrimack, Hamilton, Appleton, and Lowell mills. Workers laid out streets while also constructing handsome public buildings. A small commercial district and the first private residential neighborhoods arose.[60] The sheer size of the undertaking ensured that work for unskilled laborers was relatively steady throughout the 1820s.

The availability of work on Locks and Canals' projects underscored the increasing importance of Hugh Cummiskey in the pattern of employment. Cummiskey shared a common County Tyrone ancestry with some of Lowell's Irish laborers, but he skillfully depicted himself as the friend of all Irishmen. He was also Boott's contact with the paddy camp Irish, since Boott avoided direct contact with the workers. If the Irish were necessary to speed construction in Boott's mind, they were hardly equals. Cummiskey was the only Irishman who included Boott among his "dear . . . friends." (Others on his list included powerful Lowell officials such as Moody and Lawrence.)[61] An analysis of Locks and Canals records confirms Cummiskey's importance in the pattern of Irish employment in that he was the only Irishman to whom large direct cash payments were ever made.[62] In August, 1828, for instance, Cummiskey received payment of $250, and he was paid an additional sum of $300 in September, with two payments of $743.14 and $300 the following November.[63]

The curious absence of other foremen such as Michael Connolly indicates that some Irishmen obtained work at least occasionally through Cummiskey. Still, even with these payments the Irish remained one small group within a much larger pool of unskilled labor. Cummiskey, apparently, was successful in organizing Irish workers and bringing them into the system of unskilled labor in Lowell. His need to employ Patrick McManus, his superintendent, reinforces this assertion. While Irish work gangs formed the nucleus of the paddy camps, personal relationships among various Irish foremen and Cummiskey often determined who obtained work, at least for a brief period in the late 1820s.

Cummiskey's success in attracting Irish labor and the willingness of Boott to use Irish workers encouraged further structuring within the system of unskilled labor. A second method which consisted of a direct cash payment to individual Irish laborers became common practice. In August,

1828, for example, James Casey, Edward O'Neil, Morris Fielding, Thomas Connelly, and Timothy Raggen were listed in the Locks and Canals payroll register. These Irish worked as members of Moses Shattuck's team of "out-of-door" hands. Locks and Canals paid them monthly and they worked, with slight variation, much of August. In September, men like Raggen remained with Shattuck's team. They earned, on average, 83.3 cents per day and this wage rate remained unchanged before the Civil War.[64] Their presence as members of Shattuck's team at the same time as large cash payments were made to Cummiskey demonstrated that, for a time, both the work gang and the individual payment patterns of employment existed simultaneously, although direct individual payment predominated by the early 1830s.

The Locks and Canals employment of Irish laborers reflected both need and time of the year. Irish laborers were employed en masse during the summer months when the greatest building activity occurred, generally from April to about November. If a particular project, such as the Northern Canal in the late 1840s, required speedy construction, however, Irish might be employed throughout the year. During the winter months, the Irish were usually idle, although many worked sporadically as spare hands. The maintenance crews on already completed projects were almost invariably Yankee.[65] When construction halted, therefore, Irish laborers and their families faced a difficult winter. A few Protestant relief organizations, such as the Charitable Fuel Society, alleviated some of the distress.[66]

When they were employed, the Irish were usually haulers and diggers on the various projects, especially when the high level of construction activity offered winter work. Moses Shattuck's work schedule in 1826–28, for instance, illustrates the Irish laborer's work experience. Shattuck divided his men into ox and horse teams. In order to complete projects quickly, they concentrated upon one or two contruction sites. In December, 1826, Shattuck's ox teams carried gravel almost exclusively to the Merrimack Manufacturing Company's yard, while his horse teams carted gravel to the "new Crofs St.; and sand and bricks to the Merrimack Manufacturing Company's Factory #5." In March, 1827, unskilled laborers guided ox teams hauling wood, stone, and gravel to the Merrimack Print Works, a brick stable, and Factory #2, while his horse teams hauled wood and gravel to the same location and carried cotton from Boston to Lowell. By July, 1828, Shattuck's men had moved to the Lowell Manufacturing Company's canal and buildings, where they worked on puddling.[67]

The degree of on-site segregation which may have existed at the early construction projects is unclear. The work gang approach, the pattern of segregation in housing, and Dublin's discussion of discrimination in the mills after 1850 point to discrimination against the Irish on a grand scale.[68] Yet much of this discrimination was imposed either by the transience of Irish workers or by the after-hour patterns of the Irish themselves. No separate "Irish" listing ever appeared in the payroll records of the Locks and Canals in the 1820s, with the exception of the lump sum payments to Cummiskey, when the Irish were a minority of Lowell's general population of unskilled laborers.[69] While individual Irish may have worked together as an "Irish" team on particular projects, nothing indicates that they were physically separated from other laborers in the work place.

Rather, work proceeded efficiently on these projects because discipline was imposed from above. Yankee foremen seldom thought of the Irish as more than itinerant day laborers throughout the 1820s; indeed, Locks and Canals officials frequently refer to their laborers as "out-door hands."[70] Constance Rourke has noted that Yankee perceptions of Irish laborers were impressionistic until the emergency of the "b'hoy" known by "his swagger, his soaplocks, his firemen's red flannel shirt . . . impudent, full of racy and belligerent opinion" embodied in the character of the "stage Irishman" which appeared in the late 1840s.[71] At Lowell, that humor which appeared in Yankee newspapers before 1850 characterized Irish workers as affable simpletons who needed constant supervision. "An Irish tailor, making a gentleman's coat and vest too small, was ordered to take them home and let them out. Some days later, the gentleman enquiring for his garments, was told by this ninth part of an Irishman, that the clothes appeared to fit a countryman of his and he had let them out for a shilling a week."[72] In another example, one might well imagine Ford or Shattuck nodding in amusement in 1832 at the description of "two honest Hibernians" from Lowell discussing "the subject of working evenings": "One of them exclaimed, 'Bad luck to the man who first invented working by the dirty light iv a lamp, when the blessed light iv heaven is enough for any man!'—'Musha bad luck,' rejoined the other, 'to the dirty sowl of him who first invented wor-r-king at all, at all!'"[73]

Competition among Yankee and Irish unskilled laborers for employment with Locks and Canals was keen. Throughout the 1820s, the Irish were a small percentage of the total number of workers employed in construction by Locks and Canals. The paddy camps were a constant reminder of an Irish presence in Lowell, but their presence, much like the physical look of the camps, seemed impermanent and fleeting. Itinerant gangs of Yankee laborers formed the largest group of workers. Undoubtedly, the agricultural depression in northern New England in the 1820s, the high level of construction activity, and the promise of cash wages were attractive incentives to Yankee farmers and their sons. Still, the Irish maintained a toehold in the unskilled job market. With the construction of a Catholic church in 1831, the Irish provided an important symbol of their presence among Lowell's unskilled workers.

Reaction among Yankee laborers was swift. In May, 1831, they rioted against construction of St. Patrick's Church. The riot was fueled by the nativist undercurrent in America, by the passions stirred by local Protestant evangelists, and, most important, by a conviction among Yankee laborers that the hiring of Irish hurt their own employment opportunities. The presence of an Irish community in Lowell sufficiently large to warrant construction of a Catholic church only increased anti-Irish feelings among Yankee laborers. Joined by a small group of townsmen, they attacked the church. A "Spectator" in the Lowell *Mercury* reported that "the rioters, particularly the leaders, were Idlers, who wandered here professedly in search of employ."[74] The Irish withstood the assault.

The attack on the new Catholic church was important because it indicated that there was considerable friction between Irish and Yankee workers. It seems quite reasonable that tensions among these itinerant work gangs may well have encouraged Locks and Canals officials to abandon single cash payments to foremen in favor of direct payments to individual workers in an effort to break the power of these gangs, to control wages more effectively, and to promote order in Lowell. By the 1830s, what held the unskilled labor force together on a given project was the company supervisor's exercising his power as a representative of the Locks and Canals Company and controlling the work atmosphere. His orders were obeyed, especially when men like Ford "ruled with stubborn firmness." It is significant that the only rioting among laborers which was reported occurred outside the work place and that even the rowdy outbreaks among Irish clans were confined to "after hours" in the Irish district.

The paddy camps were largely a man's world. As late as 1827, a Catholic priest reported that they contained fifty-two men, only twenty-one of whom had families.[75] While the number of Irish women was increasing steadily, it appears that their numbers were not large enough to have a direct impact upon Lowell's general employment. There were almost no Irish women in the mills in the 1820s and the pleasant middle-class

Yankee residential neighborhoods in which Irish women might find employment as housekeepers developed mainly after 1830. In addition, the
highly transient Irish population undoubtedly made many of Lowell's
Yankees skeptical about employing Irish women who could not guarantee
long-term service. Yankee Lowell gave little thought to Irish women; in
fact, they became the butt of Yankee humor only in the 1840s, when Irish
women were characterized as either bad wives or inept housemaids.[76]

By 1830, the paddy camps had become a permanent part of Lowell. Although they remained outside the pristine mill village, the growth of both
settlements brought the two even closer together. By then, what had
been rowdy, ramshackle immigrant camps on Lowell's outskirts had become a cause for concern among Lowell's officials and a blot upon Lowell's
developing urban landscape. With the paddy camps, the Irish recreated
something akin to their ancestral home without outside interference, but,
as the camps grew, so did tribal factional differences transmitted from
Ireland but largely separate from the American work experience. In
short, Lowell's Irish laborers worked as Americans but they lived as Irish.
At first, none of Lowell's officials really cared. Around 1830, however, the
impetus to mold the future of the paddy camps came both from within
and from outside the Irish district.

CHAPTER 3

The First Years
1830–35

By 1830, the Irish population of Lowell had risen to nearly five hundred.[1] These first settlers, largely men, created a turbulent Irish district within Lowell. There were only a few year-round Irish residents, but their numbers were enlarged periodically as itinerant Irish laborers gravitated to Lowell in search of work. Not surprisingly, the paddy camps in which the Irish resided were seen collectively as an impermanent shantytown, although with each year a few more Irish made them home. As their numbers grew, women and children joined them and, in the 1820s, local Irish residents even briefly established a number of short-lived schools.[2] By then, it was clear to everyone that the Irish would be a permanent addition to Lowell's population of resident Yankees and its increasingly famous Yankee factory women.

As Lowell grew, the mill village expanded in the direction of the paddy camps and finally encircled them. In 1831 the Boston Associates constructed the Western Canal, a branch of the Pawtucket, to supply water to a series of mills built in the 1830s immediately north of the paddy camps and adjacent to the profitable Merrimack Manufacturing Company.[3] This new burst of canal and mill construction also undoubtedly stimulated the growth of the paddy camps through which most of the Western Canal passed. In addition, a pleasant residential neighborhood developed along Pawtucket Street to the west and south of the "Fardowner" camp in the area of a colonial tavern, the Old Stone House. The popularity of this district grew when Kirk Boott literally relocated his agent's house to Pawtucket Street from its old location nearer the mills.[4] Within a decade the paddy camps, which had stood apart from the mill village, were near the heart of an expanding Lowell.

This growth, both in the paddy camps and in Lowell generally, posed a dilemma for Lowell's officials. When the paddy camps were on the outskirts of the mill village, town officials never interfered with their development and made no attempt to integrate them into the mill village.[5] Once Lowell's expansion made such benign neglect impossible, town officials moved to extend their authority over the camps. They had no intention of interfering directly with traditional Irish customs, but they did wish to impose order and stability. In achieving this, town officials benefited from the assistance of Boston's bishop, Benedict Fenwick, an emerging Irish middle class, and circumstance. Kirk Boott took the initial step personally when he met with Bishop Fenwick.

Fenwick was descended from a Catholic family in Maryland. Before coming to Boston, he had served as coadjutor in New York. He replaced Jean Cheverus, who had been appointed first bishop of Boston when the diocese had formed in 1808. While in Boston, Cheverus was personable and charming and enjoyed excellent relations with its Protestant elite, who even petitioned the French government against his appointment to the diocese of Montauban in order that he might remain with them.[6] When Fenwick became bishop, he wisely adopted most of Cheverus's policies toward Boston's Yankees, though he did not socialize as actively with them. Fenwick knew that Boston's wealthy Protestants had supported Catholic causes and had even contributed generously to the construction of Boston's Church of the Holy Cross, and he understood that their assistance was essential if the Catholic church was to prosper in Boston.[7]

Fenwick also faced other problems. By the late 1820s, New England experienced an increase in immigration and, as in Lowell, a number of these settlers were Catholic. As late as 1825, however, the Boston diocese supported only one strong parish, Holy Cross, and Fenwick guided a staff of only five priests to serve the entire diocese.[8] They occasionally visited scattered communities throughout New England. The quality of the priests who served Fenwick varied widely; moreover, at the time he arrived in Boston, most American bishops found themselves facing the harsh reality of having to design the foundation of a parish structure with such staff. In addition, Fenwick was determined to avoid the pattern of trusteeship controversies which had historically impaired relations among bishops, priests, and parishioners in Philadelphia, Norfolk, Charleston, and elsewhere. Many of these controversies were over property rights. Fortunately for him, Fenwick held title to church property within his diocese, which he used to good advantage when the need for new parishes arose in towns such as Lowell.[9]

In the summer of 1822, Bishop Fenwick instructed Fr. Patrick Byrne, an Irish missionary priest, to visit Catholics around Middlesex Village at East Chelmsford. Such irregular visits continued until 1827, when Fenwick authorized a permanent priest stationed at Lowell, in response to several letters from Lowell's Catholics requesting that a priest make at least occasional visits to them.[10] They claimed that Lowell's Catholic population had increased sufficiently to warrant a permanent priest. Fenwick instructed Fr. John Mahoney "to visit them the following Sunday, to preach, to give them Mass [and] at the same time ascertain their real number."[11] Mahoney, another missionary priest, had emigrated from County Kerry and spoke Gaelic. Fenwick accepted his credentials and assigned him to Lowell. Mahoney was instructed to divide his service between his Lowell congregation and the more established Catholic community at St. Mary's in Salem.[12]

Mahoney reached Lowell in October, 1827. He said Mass in the small hall of the Merrimack Company schoolhouse, indicating that his appearance had Boott's approval, and preached to Lowell's Irish in Gaelic. When he reported to Fenwick that almost half of Lowell's Irish men had families with them, Fenwick postponed a decision on a permanent priest and ordered Mahoney to return to Lowell periodically.[13] Later that month, Fenwick met Mahoney in Lowell, where they preached to an overflowing crowd of Catholics and curious Protestants.[14] As Merwick has suggested, Fenwick used his Boston Protestant connections, such as the Boston Associates, dining with their Lowell agent, Boott, "in the hope of obtaining from the Company a lot of land sufficient [upon which] to build a church."[15]

Undoubtedly Boott, whose duties included overseeing the general development of the mill village, was well aware that the paddy camps were about to become encircled with new development. He viewed the influx of Irish with considerable alarm, and one legend suggested that a message from Boott to Bishop Fenwick in 1827 was among the "several applications from Lowell to have a Priest . . . visit them at least occasionally." During his visit, Fenwick was met "with uncommon attention by Mr. Boots [sic]" and obtained Boott's promise to donate company land. Boott granted an 8,410-square-foot lot located near the Western Canal bordering Adams Street on the west and Fenwick Street, named for the bishop, on the east.[16]

Fenwick withheld information of Boott's largesse from Lowell's Irish Catholics, however, "until he had regulated matters respecting the possession of the ground" with Boott. After Fenwick obtained clear title, he returned "to Lowell and open[ed] a subscription for the church."[17] Fenwick worked quickly to construct the church, which took shape through-

Benedict J. Fenwick, Bishop of Boston, 1825–46. Archives, Archdiocese of Boston.

St. Patrick's in 1831. Courtesy of the Lowell Historical Society.

out the winter and spring of 1830–31. At the same time, the Irish worked on the adjacent Western Canal. Fenwick maintained an active interest in the church's construction, returning to Lowell to visit in October, 1830.[18] The Irish responded generously; many worked in competing crews supervised by Hugh Cummiskey or Michael Connolly to lay the foundation. Called St. Patrick's, the church was dedicated on 3 July 1831.[19]

St. Patrick's was made of wood and measured seventy by forty feet. It was designed in Gothic style, with a gilded globe and cross surmounting a central tower. The crude huts scattered in the vicinity of the church made St. Patrick's seem an imposing structure.[20] Fenwick dedicated it before "an immense concourse of people . . . of all denominations." The diocesan vicar-general, Very Rev. Dr. O'Flaherty, preached a sermon, while Father Mahoney celebrated Mass. Two or three thousand people, one hundred of whom who had traveled with Fenwick from Boston, attended the dedication, including volunteers from the Boston Cathedral Choir who provided musical accompaniment. The day was very warm, but Fenwick proceeded with the ceremonies and confirmed thirty-nine people. He also delivered a sermon.[21]

The Fenwick-Boott agreement had met the needs of both men nicely. Boott was concerned with the incessant quarreling of rival Irish factions which regularly disrupted the work camps and recognized the value of the Catholic church's presence among Lowell's Irish. Boott therefore placed one condition upon his land grant—that either a school or church would be constructed upon the land within three years.[22] Fenwick left the location, "from motives of delicacy," to Boott, who chose a site equidistant between two rival Irish settlements, the Fardowner and Corkonian camps.[23] Boott saw that the location of the church would play an important peacekeeping role, which would make his own job easier.[24] Fenwick, on the other hand, obtained his goal of legal control of the donated land by using his friendship with Protestants like Boott to get it.

Fenwick indicated in his journal that he was extremely pleased with the arrangements in Lowell. He retained title to St. Patrick's, yet had satisfied Lowell's Catholics by providing them with a priest.[25] The Lowell Irish had financed the construction, even participating in much of the building themselves. Fenwick's accommodationist policies toward Boston's Protestant elite had paid off in that Boott, who represented them, had donated corporate land for the construction of the church. Like Boott's plans for the village, Fenwick's strategy to enhance Catholicism in New England benefited from the growth of an Irish district in Lowell and this common goal cemented the alliance between them, even if their motivations were quite different. Shortly after the dedication, Fenwick appointed Mahoney as pastor of St. Patrick's.[26]

At the time of the dedication, there were probably one thousand Catholics living within St. Patrick's parish. The church attracted Catholics from an area stretching from Nashua, New Hampshire, in the north to Billerica, Massachusetts, in the south, or a distance of about twenty miles, but most of the parishioners lived in Lowell's paddy camps.[27] While many Irish Catholics living there were unskilled laborers or their families, a new class of merchants and craftsmen appeared after 1830. This Irish middle class joined foremen like Cummiskey and Connolly and, in time, they dominated local parish affairs. They did not depend directly upon Locks and Canals for employment but only upon a large Irish community residing in Lowell who needed their services. They provided goods and services for Lowell's Irish in the absence of these services in the mill village.

The importance of the Irish middle class to the creation and nurturing of St. Patrick's parish cannot be overstated. Bishop Fenwick depended upon local parishioners for the building and upkeep of St. Patrick's, including the expense of Mahoney's salary. The highly transient character of much of Lowell's Catholic population, the sporadic nature of Locks and Canals' employment, and the possibility that Lowell's building boom might end precluded much assistance from most of Lowell's Irish laborers. The few foremen who might have been of real help could not support a new church by themselves. As a result of their importance to parish affairs, Irish middle-class support for the Boott-Fenwick land agreement meant ultimately that St. Patrick's parish would fail unless Fenwick's philosophy on the role of the Catholic church in Lowell and the expectations of the Irish middle class were the same.

There were several dozen families who were the nucleus of the Irish middle class at the time of St. Patrick's dedication in 1831.[28] Whether in parish affairs or, more generally, in Lowell, the term "middle class" reflects more the perception shared by them of their place among Lowell's Irish than their economic status. They were the middle class because they saw themselves differently. Like the Irish laborers and their families, they had been in America for some time. Unlike them, however, they abstained from factional feuding; and their interests in things Irish quickly evolved into something more national than narrow ancestral clan loyalties. The middle class had sufficient income to support Repeal and Famine relief, and the financial backing for the construction of a Catholic church had come primarily from among them.

The middle class also were less transient than Irish laborers, because they were shopkeepers and the like who had more of a stake in Lowell. Given the personal nature of employment, the middle class held the loyalty of Lowell's Irish laborers by counting foremen like Cummiskey as members. Still, the middle class lived among the laborers. They provided services with dry goods stores, saloons, and blacksmiths' shops. Put in other terms, the middle class were the most "American" of the Irish in Lowell. They were sufficiently entrepreneurial to live successfully by their wits and personal contacts. Their future in Lowell was largely independent of the construction boom, although the employment of Irish laborers did provide them with opportunities in service and trade. By the mid-1830s, their numbers had risen to about one hundred.[29]

While the dedication of St. Patrick's marked the appearance of an Irish middle class, other evidence such as records of land ownership also supports its formation after 1830. Although Locks and Canals sold off some land as early as 1826, the first sales to Irishmen occurred in the early 1830s. In the first recorded transaction with an Irishman, in 1830 Locks and Canals sold Hugh Cummiskey land at Merrimack and Lowell streets, near where he would live for over forty years. Between 1831 and 1837, Cummiskey added land to his holdings on or near Lowell, Fenwick, Merrimack, and Thorndike streets. Others such as dry goods dealer Charles M. Short and West India goods salesmen Owen McOsker and Patrick McCaffrey also purchased land. While a few laborers also acquired Locks and Canals' land by the late 1830s, the majority of Irish landowners were shopkeepers.

Most Irishmen, however, rented housing.[30] Around Lowell Street and in the vicinity of St. Patrick's Church, many of the initial transactions were not land sales but rather long-term lease arrangements. By this method, an Irishman leased land, sometimes for up to ten years, upon which he then erected a home.[31] Some leases included housing already constructed upon the land. Michael McCarthy, for instance, rented a tenement on Lowell Street "being the second from the Main Road of four tenements" just completed by an Irish carpenter, James Barry, in December, 1832. McCarthy held the tenement "for ten years . . . yielding and paying therefore, the rent of thirty dollars for the year." He then rented accommodations to other Irishmen but he agreed under the original contract not to "permit any riotous or disorderly persons to occupy said tenement, or permit any riot, tumult, or disorder to be made or committed therein." In a second example, T. W. Churchill, a Yankee speculator, negotiated leases along Fenwick Street, near St. Patrick's Church, in return for a thirty-dollar annual payment. In April, 1832, John Sullivan, Michael McCarthy, David Whelton, James Campbell, and Michael Doyle signed agreements with Churchill.[32]

While many of the early leases and/or purchases were near St. Patrick's or in the Fardowner camp along Lowell Street, leases were also popular in the Corkonian camp.[33] Like other Irish, Corkonians had squatted on unused corporation land, apart from their countrymen. A few obtained short-term leases and built crude houses, and in time the Corkonian camp became one of the largest in the Irish district. In the early 1830s, Boott recognized that he had no need for the land and offered it for sale. Speculators quickly purchased the land and evicted many of the Corkonians. One newspaper editor noted: "I presume almost everyone is familiar with scenes there played off in ejecting those unfortunate beings from their houses. The screams of mothers, with infants clinging to their breasts, are still ringing in my ears."[34]

The question of legal title to the land developed into a protracted legal battle argued in several courts. All efforts to purchase clear title failed and the case degenerated into a series of suits and countersuits. Eventually, out-of-state litigants brought the battle before the United States Supreme Court as the *Paddy Camps Lands* case.[35] The corporations won and reopened land sales to speculators. A few Irishmen, including Fr. James T. McDermott, purchased lots. In time, the Corkonian camp took on a more permanent appearance. The proximity of the district to St. Patrick's Church, the Lowell Machine Shop, and the new railroad depot made it especially attractive. Still, fewer Corkonians purchased property there than in the rest of the Irish neighborhood before 1840.[36]

By the early 1830s, the paddy camps had begun to merge into an Irish neighborhood. One local historian noted that about this time Dennis Crowley became "the first Kelt in Lowell who applied whitewash to his shanty," while Timothy Ford and Nicholas Fitzpatrick built frame houses which they painted, so that "the practice soon became common" throughout the paddy camps.[37] Of more importance, the flurry of leases and land purchases promoted the development of a rudimentary street pattern. In the Corkonian camp, Cork and Dublin streets appeared, with Cork Street eventually extended to reach the new St. Patrick's Church.[38] In the area immediately west of the church, Fenwick Street became popular after

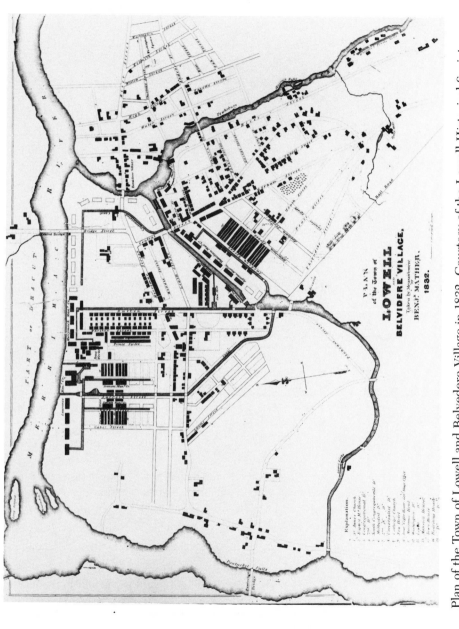

Plan of the Town of Lowell and Belvedere Village in 1832. Courtesy of the Lowell Historical Society.

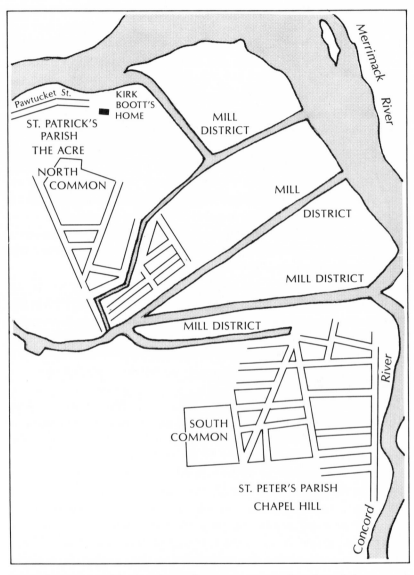

Lowell's Irish neighborhoods in the 1840s. From the Plan of the City of
Lowell, Massachusetts, *City Atlas*, 1879. By Craig Roscoe and Marie Rose
Roderique.

Churchill leased to Irishmen in 1832. The heart of the Fardowner camp lay along Lowell Street, which ran parallel to Merrimack Street, Lowell's principal thoroughfare, and was apparently laid out before the first land sales in 1831. Lowell Street extended from the Lowell Manufacturing Company, constructed in 1828, and facilitated construction of the Western Canal in 1830.[39]

The development of Lowell Street increased Irish visibility in Lowell, with mixed results for the town. Most of the early Irish shops sprang up along it and the first Irish land speculators amassed their holdings on or near it. Lowell Street also linked the mill village to the paddy camps. By the 1840s, it had become a congested tenement district of wood and some brick construction.[40] Lowell's Yankee residents complained periodically throughout the 1840s that Lowell Street was notoriously unsafe and that travelers on it were accosted regularly by stone-throwing Irish youth. While Lowell Street integrated the paddy camps physically into Lowell, it also exposed a seedier side of Lowell and tarnished the town's cherished reputation as an industrial showcase.[41]

The pattern of property holding, much like Boott's munificence toward St. Patrick's Church, indicated a shift in his attitude about the Irish as permanent residents around 1830. Undoubtedly foremen like Cummiskey and the small group of Irish shopkeepers appreciated the new opportunity to purchase land from Locks and Canals. They were Boott's allies in the paddy camps and his goal of peace and stability reflected their own desire to protect their property. Still, there were limits to the accommodation worked out between Boott and Lowell's Irish. Irish ownership of property, for example, never extended into Yankee neighborhoods or into the mill village, where Boott maintained tight-fisted control over land ownership and deliberately kept the Irish out.[42]

With the appearance of an Irish middle class exercising growing influence in the paddy camps, the old clan associations weakened. New relationships based upon their American experiences developed without regard to ancestral origin. The factional feuds continued but the Irish middle class generally remained neutral and, with time, came to view such narrow prejudices unsympathetically. As early as 1832, for example, Hugh Cummiskey petitioned Lowell's officials for constables to patrol the area around St. Patrick's Church to prevent factional feuding during Sundays and, more generally, to discourage fighting too close to the church.[43] Although the Irish middle class acknowledged their ancestral ties, allegiance to them decreased almost imperceptibly and they focused on themselves as "exiled sons of Erin." They showered praise upon the benefits of American citizenship, although relatively few Irishmen in Lowell were naturalized Americans. They also accepted Lowell's special purpose as an industrial showcase and took pride in their part in its development.[44] As their tribal allegiances lessened, the Irish middle class took a more national view of Ireland. Yankee fascination with O'Connell's Repeal campaign added to this feeling of camaraderie.[45]

In 1833 the first Irish society appeared, when "three or four energetic Irishmen" organized the Hibernian Moralizing and Relief Society. Over one hundred Irishmen attended the first meeting. In June, town officials granted them use of a room for their monthly meetings.[46] Their largest celebration honored St. Patrick and the records of their toasts reprinted in nineteenth-century newspapers tell us much about the philosophy of the Irish middle class, who made up most of the membership. Prominent in the organization were shopkeepers such as Richard Plant, Patrick Powers, and Daniel Connell, although a few laborers such as Thomas O'Sullivan also participated actively in meetings.[47] In their toasts, society members characterized the Irish in America as a "firm prop for the American Constitution" and they idolized Andrew Jackson, whose father had been banished from "his dear, native Erin . . . [by] Anglo-Saxon tyrants."[48]

In succeeding years, the Hibernian Society, whose members renamed themselves the Lowell Irish Benevolent Society in 1836, spoke occasionally about their presence in Lowell. They accepted the view of Lowell as an industrial showcase which combined profit, humanitarianism, and a serious effort to avoid the horrors of England's Lancashire. They described Lowell as a place "where the stranger finds a home, the mechanic employment, and the laborer a living."[49] Members expressed the hope that Lowell "as she now stands—her literary institutions, public schools and extensive manufactures" would become "the brightest star in the Union."[50] Although society members accepted the Yankee mill women who dominated the labor system and who precluded them from an important source of employment, one member suggested somewhat slyly that "the powers of Cupid or some good power from above, send each and every one of these fair maids their own best beloved fellow to co-operate with them."[51]

By the mid-1830s, the Benevolent Society became more active among Lowell's Irish, particularly during the presidency of dry goods dealer Charles M. Short. Although laborers were never excluded, the society became a haven for the Irish middle class.[52] They socialized with no real attempt to transform the society into a powerful political advocate for Irish rights nor did they make any effort to develop it into an organization which actively assisted needy Irish. The society did contribute to the assistance of "indigent Catholics" through an $82 gift to the Protestant Lowell Fuel Society in 1835 but only at the insistence of a local Catholic priest, Fr. Peter Connolly.[53] The Benevolent Society was a social club in which the honored guests at St. Patrick's Day dinners were usually local Yankee officials ranging from politicians to the editor of the Lowell *Courier*, William Schouler, who was regarded generally as a spokesman for the corporations.[54]

This alliance between town officials and the Irish middle class raises important questions as to the role of the vast majority of Irish, who were transient unskilled laborers, in the alliance. The explanation lies in the combination of external and internal factors which governed the Irish presence in Lowell. Much as Stephan Thernstrom has suggested for late nineteenth-century New England, Lowell's unskilled laborers were part of a much larger pool of unskilled Irish laborers who roamed throughout New England seeking employment.[55] Although Lowell's building boom ended with the Panic of 1837, new construction projects opened up with the development of Manchester (1838) and Lawrence (1845).[56] Even Hugh Cummiskey, who by the late 1830s had acquired considerable property in Lowell, worked at projects in both cities.[57] This constant movement of Irish through Lowell and the failure of most Irish to advance beyond their jobs as unskilled laborers precluded a workingman's philosophy from developing among Lowell's Irish. In Lowell, the unskilled Irish laborers confined their interests to day labor employment. Willingly or not, these laborers upheld the unwritten rules which governed the pattern of their employment because they participated in that employment. The effort consumed all of their time and, moreover, any efforts toward radicalism would have been blocked effectively by the Irish middle class, who benefited directly from maintaining the status quo in Lowell.

Pleased with the level of opportunity available to them in Lowell, the Irish middle class in Lowell loyally supported the position of the Boston Associates. These shopkeepers, foremen, and traders were the successes among Lowell's largely indigent Irish. The Irish middle class understood that they derived much of their success from their acquiescence to the wishes of the Boston Associates. In 1835 they offered a toast to "Kirk Boott, Esq., and the other liberal and independent gentlemen of Lowell—true and generous friends to industrious Irishmen—remember the gratitude we owe them all."[58] For the Irish middle class, the Boston Associates were benevolent paternal capitalists who allowed them the opportunity to improve their quality of life while holding out the promise of even greater rewards. In 1835, the opportunities in Lowell for the Irish middle class knew no bounds. Even if these opportunities were confined to the paddy camps, they did represent more than the Irish had achieved on the Boston docks or as indigent day laborers in the New England countryside.

In a sense, there was a real division between the middle class and the mass of Irish laborers. If it is surprising that no friction arose between the two groups, it must be remembered that the "middle class" as defined here represented a relatively small group of Irishmen whose shops, schoolteacher's pay, or foreman's wages allowed them to live slightly above the unskilled workers who were their neighbors. The Irish middle class was not wealthy; in fact, the few who made any money generally did so only after 1850.[59] They did demonstrate, however, that Lowell offered some hope for improving one's circumstances, and it was such optimism which precluded envy from the less fortunate Irish. In addition, the Irish middle class did not deny their Irish heritage even if they moved away slowly from the narrow clan loyalties which characterized the early paddy camps. Most middle-class Irish still lived within their regional camp. In 1833, for instance, Bishop Fenwick complained that differences arose within St. Patrick's parish "between those from the North and those from the South of Ireland," and journeyed to Lowell to lecture personally against such disputes.[60] Finally, within the Irish middle class were foremen who, until the early 1830s, could offer employment with or recommend unskilled Irish to Locks and Canals. In short, the Irish middle class shared the experiences of all of Lowell's Irish and lived among them. At the same time Lowell was a place where "the laborer [finds] a living."[61] For most of Lowell's unskilled Irish laborers, finding work was quite enough, without devoting much time or energy to envy of those who were doing somewhat better.

From this perspective, it is not surprising that no Irish political organization appeared and no Irish candidate arose to challenge Yankee dominance, if only at the ward level. Lowell had an Irish mayor in 1882, but by then the position of the Irish had changed enormously.[62] In the 1840s, Benjamin F. Butler, congressman, future governor, Civil War general, and Greenback party presidential candidate, represented Lowell's Irish and received support from them as a Democratic candidate.[63] With the exception of Butler, no local politican ever successfully represented Irish interests, although James J. Maguire, briefly Democratic editor of the Lowell *Advertiser*, had a little success in the 1850s.[64] The failure of the Irish to mount an effective political campaign was the result of several factors. First, as suggested earlier, internal and external factors precluded unified political thought among the Irish and what unity might have existed was exploited effectively by Butler. Second, the paddy camps were divided into wards One and Five, which minimized the strength of Irish voters at the ward level. Third, most of Lowell's Irishmen were not naturalized citizens; in fact, among the several thousand potential Irish voters in the mid-1850s, only about six hundred Irishmen voted. Their votes were split about evenly between Whigs and Democrats.[65] Fourth, in the absence of the secret ballot, Irish voters were intimidated by the corporations. In the mid-1840s, for example, the Hamilton Company warned that "whoever, employed by this corporation, vote[d] the Ben Butler ten-hour ticket . . . will be discharged."[66] Finally, the middle-class alliance with town officials dampened any chance that a charismatic leader might arise among the Irish who was not directly responsible to the corporations or who hoped to profit either from them directly or from the economic vitality which they brought to Lowell.

Despite the failure of Lowell's Irish to organize politically, there were a few Irish who served at ward level. In 1833–34, Hugh Cummiskey and another Irishman, Samuel Murray, served as town constables.[67] Owen Donohoe, who ran the Exchange Coffee House, also became one.[68] St. Patrick's pastor, Fr. James T. McDermott, ran unsuccessfully throughout the 1830s and 1840s for a position on the school committee.[69] Generally, those few Irishmen who served were Whigs who supported accommodations with Yankee Lowell. Most held positions in which their jurisdiction extended only over other Irishmen in the paddy camps. Those Irish active in politics were also members of the middle class; none were unskilled laborers.

Of all Irish political activity, participation on the school committee was most significant. Education was a concern among the Irish middle class, and they negotiated a fascinating compromise with Lowell's Yankees in 1835. This was crucial because it strengthened the alliance between the two groups, giving each side something it wanted while demonstrating the benefit of close collaboration. Historically, the role of education in assimilating immigrants has received considerable attention since Cubberly proclaimed the "public school triumphant" in the early twentieth century.[70] Revisionists usually explain the growth of education in terms of group conflict in which the dominant American culture used education to impose its social, political, and cultural patterns upon immigrants.[71] Other recent studies have warned of the need to separate formal bureaucratic institutional development from increasing school enrollments, arguing, for example, that education, infused with republican virtue and evangelical Protestantism, was an important mechanism in local community building.[72]

Lowell is an excellent place to examine the arguments of these revisionists, particularly because of the history of early education there. When Kirk Boott arrived he found a sparsely attended district school system.[73] As a practical business manager, Boott saw no need to extend education when his labor force consisted of transient Yankee farm women. He certainly did not initially connect the need for education with the Irish, who theoretically had access to the district schools. Boott did provide two corporation schools for permanent employees. He steadfastly maintained, however, that town officials "had done for the public schools what was required; they were proper and sufficient for the poor, but they would never serve for the better sort."[74] Boott opposed the philosophy of the Irish middle class and also of Rev. Theodore Edson, whom Boott had personally brought from Boston to Lowell in 1824. An Episcopalian minister, Edson served not only Boott and Lowell's resident Yankees but also its transient Yankee mill women, many of whom changed religious affiliation at whim as Lowell attracted an increasing number of Protestant sects. As education was popular among all religious groups, including Catholics, Edson's support for it enhanced his own stature, reflected his personal beliefs, and made Episcopalianism attractive to those who might ordinarily have joined more evangelical sects.[75] Edson emerged as Lowell's leading middle-class reformer when, shortly after he obtained a seat on the Lowell school committee, he attacked Boott's support of district schools, calling instead for a townwide graded system.[76]

Edson remained the guiding force behind Lowell's public schools for over fifty years, and his viewpoint closely reflected the majority opinion on the school committee during that period.[77] In the late 1820s, Edson vigorously defended the graded system on two levels. First, he argued that district schools suited small villages but that Lowell's spectacular growth had made them ineffective. Second, he reasoned that Lowell's educators would exert considerable discipline through a graded system which would create larger and more efficient schools. Such schools would be more manageable and orderly. They would also effectively incorporate increased school enrollments as Lowell prospered. Edson reflected that, despite Boott's complaint that Lowell was already in debt with large appropriations for public services, Lowell would profit in that the schools would serve as a bulwark of morality and stability and foster a sense of community. Edson won the debate.[78]

The funding controversy illustrates the importance of understanding the drive for public education as an extremely complex development. Lowell's early industrialists opposed Edson's school expansion program as an extravagance from which they derived no direct economic benefit; indeed, Boott even sniped that "ministers were not suitable to manage the expenditures of the town."[79] In an important sense Boott had missed the point that Edson was, above all else, "of the town." Edson represented Lowell's resident Yankees and understood the need to create a sense of community in what had been an artificial economic experiment.[80] As Meyer et al. have suggested, Edson and men like him fought for school expansion as a means of creating "purified citizen members of a redeemer nation."[81] Education, by merging republican virtues with Edson's brand of evangelical, reform-minded Protestantism, helped to create a moral, disciplined, orderly, and productive America.

Edson succeeded in establishing a townwide graded system but the Irish remained outside his control. Local parish priests and some interested laymen periodically offered Irish children a rudimentary education in the 1820s, but the parish schools lacked funds and held classes irregularly.[82] In 1830 the school committee extended the graded system to include a new school exclusively for Irish children from throughout Lowell, to be located in the paddy camps. The committee appropriated fifty dollars, but the new public school was not a success.[83] It was not that local Catholic priests disapproved of educating Irish children. In the early 1830s, for example, they adapted the basement of St. Patrick's Church to house a number of overcrowded classes. Rather, the priests expressed considerable anxiety over possible Protestant proselytizing if Irish children entered the public schools. Their suspicions kept Irish children out of local public schools or, more usually, away from education altogether.[84]

The situation called for a compromise which would alleviate the priests' fears and achieve the school committee's goal of bringing Irish children into public schools. Curiously, the solution came when a Catholic priest, Fr. Peter Connolly, approached the school committee in June, 1835, for financial assistance for his bankrupt parish schools. The school committee recognized that their own efforts were unsuccessful because the Irish

public school had sufficient money but few students and frequently sus-
pended operation, while the Catholic school had numerous students but
no money.[85] The compromise which arose represented an unusual alliance
between church and state.

Under the 1835 agreement, the school committee appointed and examined instructors, prescribed and regulated books, exercises, and studies,
and operated the proposed Irish school as an integrated part of Lowell's
public system. Connolly had struck a bargain, however, which gave the
Catholic church a large measure of authority over Irish education. The
school committee agreed to appoint only Catholic instructors approved by
local Catholic priests. In addition, its texts would contain no slander on
Catholicism; in fact, the school committee presented the texts used in
Lowell's other public schools to Connolly, who approved their content.[86]
Connolly undoubtedly knew that the school committee had adopted a
curriculum which stressed reading, grammar, spelling, arithmetic, and
geography based upon a nonsectarian program acceptable to all Protestant sects. In addition, his Catholic teachers would interpret any ques-
tionable material within each Irish classroom. In 1835 the compromise
became school policy, and the school committee set up two classrooms in
St. Patrick's Church basement and one in the new Irish "Chapel Hill"
neighborhood.[87]

The 1835 agreement also explains how Irish children entered Lowell's
public schools—the Irish requested and negotiated for their admission.
Obviously, not all Irish parents voluntarily sent their children to public school. Generally, however, those Irish who were also Catholic supported the education agreement negotiated by their priests. Their support raises two questions: (1) why did the priests support the agreement
beyond the obvious financial benefits, and (2) were their motivations similar to those of Irish lay supporters? One development is certain; the
emerging Irish middle class within Lowell agreed with the priests about
the need for Irish Catholic involvement in education but also shared the
school committee's enthusiasm for public education and found the republican rhetoric attached to the drive for public education especially appeal-
ing. Once the religious impediment was removed, these middle-class
Irish openly embraced education as a useful tool to improve their children's position.

Lowell's Irish middle class joined its Protestant reformers in representing the town as an industrial and social laboratory where "liberal" senti-

ments prevailed over narrow prejudice. As the cornerstone of organizations such as the Benevolent Society, Irishmen such as Charles Gorman and the ever-present Hugh Cummiskey warmly praised the agreement. At the 1840 Benevolent Society St. Patrick's Day dinner, Gorman proposed: "May the school committee of the City of Lowell continue to inspire the rising generation with the love of learning and patriotism."[88] At their 1843 celebration, John W. Graves, a Protestant doctor who enjoyed wide popularity with Lowell's Irish, suggested that the public schools were: "A happy expression of the spirit which characterized an age distinguished for philanthropy and liberal sentiments; may we duly appreciate their value, and continue to give them our most cordial support."[89] Theodore Edson might have written the words himself!

Lowell's priests also shared this perspective, as did Bishop Fenwick. In 1836, the school committee congratulated Father Connolly, "to whose zealous and effecious co-operation their [Irish public schools] success may be mainly attributed."[90] In 1840, Fr. James Conway praised "the education of the rising generation of this city. It is conducted upon just and Liberal principles."[91]

In fact, both Connolly and Conway represented Fenwick, who was also a personal friend of Kirk Boott and had met privately with him on numerous occasions. As Merwick suggested, Fenwick ran a small diocese which depended heavily upon Protestant support and in which the Ursuline convent burning in Charlestown had caused considerable tension.[92] The education agreement reflected Fenwick's wishes and had been negotiated by his priests. Undoubtedly, Fenwick viewed the agreement as further assistance from Lowell's social and industrial leaders. He supported their efforts to promote peace, order, and enlightenment since they also enhanced his own position in Lowell.

The education agreement worked well for several years. Within six months, 459 children had enrolled, with 282 students attending regularly. Average daily attendance of 208 students compared favorably with town-wide attendance. The school committee retained the original Irish school-teachers, Patrick Collins and Daniel McElroy, and hired other qualified Catholics. It added a fourth grammar school a year later.[93] In 1838 Collins's and McElroy's schools combined to form the Fifth Grammar School. The attendance figures indicated that, despite high mobility, Lowell's public schools attracted the children of Irish laborers as well as their middle-class counterparts; and Catholics and Protestants alike hailed the education agreement as a noble experiment worthy of emulation throughout America.[94]

The 1835 education compromise demonstrated that a working relationship existed between Lowell's Irish and Yankee leaders. It represented an opportunity for Lowell's Irish children, and it enhanced Lowell's reputation nationally and, undoubtedly, among the local Irish. Despite this advantage, Lowell's Irish remained physically segregated from the mill village. Those opportunities which did arise were generally limited, affecting life only within the paddy camps. The public schools did not offer educated Irish children an avenue to employment in Lowell's mills initially, and public education had little effect upon housing or sanitation within the paddy camps in the 1830s. Still, most Irish were attracted to free public education because it was a tool which might help their children carve a niche in America. For some Irish, support arose because local priests initiated the drive to extend education to the Irish on more favorable terms.[95]

At the same time, the education agreement brought Irish children into Lowell's public schools. Reformers like Edson believed in the republican rhetoric which they articulated and thought that education would uplift Irish children and make them good American citizens, combining, as Charles Gorman suggested, "learning and patriotism."[96] It was not the function of public schoolteachers to train docile mill workers in the 1830s; such opportunities had yet to arise for the Irish. Rather, they were to produce good, well-educated American citizens who were peaceable and orderly, and who nurtured community spirit and the belief in Lowell as an industrial showcase. These were the mutual goals which attracted Edson, Conway, and Cummiskey. In this light, the education agreement was a success because it met individual needs while addressing common concerns.

By the late 1830s, the alliance between Lowell's Yankees and Irish middle class had reached its limit. The successes of the previous decade—the construction of St. Patrick's Church, the formation of the Benevolent Society, and the 1835 education agreement—were considerable, but they masked serious internal dissension within the Irish middle class. At first, these disagreements were confined to issues affecting the paddy camps but, by the early 1840s, the arguments extended to the delicately balanced education compromise. By then, a split had occurred within the Irish middle class and what had been a common strategy deteriorated into petty squabbling. These disputes tarnished the reputation of the Irish middle class among Lowell's growing Irish population. As Lowell recovered from the Panic of 1837, new conditions arose which markedly changed Lowell's social and economic climate. When Lowell changed, the Irish middle class, weakened by internal quarrels, could not safeguard Irish interests or even their own.

CHAPTER 4

Growing Pains
1836–48

The small group of Irish shopkeepers, schoolteachers, and construction foremen who formed Lowell's Irish middle class divided openly over the subsequent development of St. Patrick's parish. They had originally petitioned Bishop Fenwick to organize a Lowell parish for a variety of reasons. First, as recent arrivals from the Boston docks, many were familiar with a Catholic church in their midst. In Boston, for example, the Irish worshipped at the Church of the Holy Cross, which also served as the cathedral for Bishop Fenwick. Second, St. Patrick's was a symbol of the Irish presence in Lowell and represented the Irish commitment to order and stability. In addition, regular church attendance was important to Kirk Boott, who initially deducted 3¼ cents per quarter from the paychecks of Lowell's Yankee mill women to pay for pew rentals at St. Anne's (Episcopal) Church; indeed, "regular attendance at church" was one of the terms of agreement which governed mill employment.[1] If Lowell's Irish accepted the moral environment of Lowell, then attendance at St. Patrick's Church demonstrated their commitment to that environment and to the rules which governed it.

Third, much like the Lowell Irish Benevolent Society, St. Patrick's was a kind of social club and, significantly, one which included all of Lowell's Irish. The church was, in effect, the center of the first stirrings of community among the Irish in Lowell. For middle-class Irishmen, the church was a sign of their prosperity; the "liberal subscriptions" which made church construction possible came from their pockets. For Irish women, church activities were an acceptable outlet for socialization with other women beyond the confines of family. For children, the church offered religious training and, even more significant, provided the framework of an education compromise which brought Irish children into Lowell's innovative public schools in a manner acceptable to Irish custom and Catholic belief. Participation in the activities of St. Patrick's parish, then, was familiar, rewarding, and a uniquely American experience for Lowell's Irish.

Fourth, St. Patrick's also served a religious need. The Irish brought a great deal of religious emotionalism with them to Lowell, but they were not narrowly bound by regulations on such issues as church attendance. The straightforward moralistic religion of institutional American Catholicism did not really affect them until around the middle of the nineteenth century. Rather, the pattern of parish development is similar to that found by Desmond Keenan for the nineteenth-century Irish church. As Keenan found for Irish Catholicism in the same period, St. Patrick's developed in two phases. The first was innovative; parishioners brought a tradition of active involvement and enthusiasm for Catholicism into parish development. They also infused their participation, however, with a spirit of American republicanism. Regardless of their length of stay in America, St. Patrick's Irish believed they had an active role in church affairs. When Fenwick established policy, some followed him; others rejected his authority. Those who scorned Fenwick's policies felt it was their right as adopted citizens in the American Republic. The second phase—consolidation—was a product of forces emerging about 1850. It was only then that St. Patrick's became heavily institutionalized in buildings and in religious practice.[2]

Finally, St. Patrick's defined the Irish presence in Lowell for the Irish themselves. The church was an impressive physical marker and the most visible "Irish" institution in the paddy camps. More important, the church was located at the crossroads of Irish neighborhood life. Though it was originally situated between two major Irish camps, subsequent development in the neighborhood spread toward and then around St. Patrick's. Kevin Whelan noted a similar pattern governing new church construction and village development in Ireland in the first half of the nineteenth century. Whelan found that new chapels were constructed in areas of "outward-looking" farming and merchant families who gave their support to church development. Like Keenan, Whelan argued that the link between new church construction and village life was an important trend during the innovative phase of Tridentine Catholicism.[3] Lowell's Irish Catholics experienced many of these same forces affecting parish development. Fenwick may not have consulted local Irish on the site of St. Patrick's, but the Irish raised no objections to its location, since it was similar to where new churches were constructed in Ireland and elsewhere in New England.

The Fenwick-Boott agreement which made construction of St. Patrick's possible was especially significant not only because it served local Irish needs but also because it enjoyed almost universal support from among all parties affected by its construction. No one stood to gain more than Bishop Fenwick, who held to the same beliefs on accommodation, of course, as the mddle class. This common philosophical outlook marked St. Patrick's from the outset as more "American" than "Irish." Governing its development personally, Fenwick cultivated a cordial, ongoing relationship with Boott, visiting Boott whenever he came to Lowell. After Boott's death, Fenwick built new relationships with his successors. On one trip, Samuel Lawrence, a powerful local mill agent in the early 1840s, took Fenwick on a personal tour of the factories and the surrounding countryside.[4] Through his contacts with such officials, Fenwick procured additional land from the corporations to enhance the general external appearance and expansion of the church.[5]

St. Patrick's also met an administrative goal. The number of Irish had increased sufficiently in Lowell to warrant church construction and the future promised more growth. In 1835 Fenwick called for an addition to the church, claiming that it could hold only one-third of the parishioners. The original church measured seventy feet by forty feet and, one can reasonably assume, could hold about three hundred parishioners at each of its two Masses. Thus, assuming that Fenwick was accurate, Lowell's Catholic population approached eighteen hundred. In a total population of 15,000, Lowell's Catholics were about 12 percent of its citizens.[6] There was also an impressive number of baptisms and marriages. In 1837 local priests baptized 178 children and performed 45 marriages.[7]

At the same time, the Fenwick-Boott agreement gave Fenwick an opportunity to provide for growth in the number of Lowell's Catholics while avoiding the pitfalls which had dominated parish development in other dioceses. With the beginning of parish development in America about 1800, open controversies flared over who held decision-making power over parish affairs. Parishioners often insisted on a locally elected board of trustees to manage church affairs, whose power extended to the appointment of local priests to the parish. These disputes sometimes erupted into confrontations with the bishops; dioceses in Philadelphia, New York, Norfolk, and Charleston were among the most seriously affected. Still, most of these trusteeship controversies were settled by 1820, about the time that the Boston Associates founded Lowell.[8] Bishop Fenwick was well aware of the history of these disputes, however, and wished to avoid a recurrence in the organization of parishes throughout New England. Fenwick's actions during his negotiations with agents of the Boston Associates regarding land use confirmed his intent to establish himself firmly in control of parish affairs.

Unfortunately, not all of Lowell's Catholics agreed with Bishop Fenwick nor did they all understand his perception of the role of parishioners in church affairs. Arguments broke out between priests, among parishioners, and with Fenwick. Fenwick named Father Mahoney as pastor in 1831 and, for a short time, it appeared that Lowell would escape serious bickering. Unfortunately, Fenwick's relationship with Lowell's Catholics was governed by two factors which he could not control. First, he needed their financial support to pay parish debts and to maintain Mahoney in Lowell. Second, the Boston diocese was seriously short of priests and, from Fenwick's perspective, many lacked the professional and personal discipline necessary to represent him successfully at the parish level. As early as 1832, a Lowell delegation approached Fenwick complaining about Mahoney's spiritual guidance and requesting an assistant.[9] Fenwick complied, sending Fr. John Curtin to Lowell, but neither priest exercised enough leadership to prevent what Mahoney described the following May as a "great division . . . between Catholics from the North and those from the South of Ireland." Mahoney reported that "whatever one of the parties propose for the good of the church, the other is surer to oppose let it ever be so proper" and that these divisions made it impossible for any one priest to "do the duty of Lowell."[10]

As the split intensified between rival Catholic groups, the local priests added to the general deterioration in relations by violent personal disagreements. Mahoney's assistants refused to contribute to the rectory's upkeep; the situation worsened to the point that the priests offered Mass on Sundays irregularly. While no detailed account of these disputes has survived, it appears that their intensity drained any popular support for the parish building committee, which Fenwick had organized to enlarge the church. The failure of the local priests to exercise leadership in parish affairs contributed to further breakdown, most noticeably among parishioners who divided into hostile camps, no longer exclusively on the basis of clan allegiance within the paddy camps but rather on their own perception of the development of the parish. One group in particular saw an opportunity to use the disorder to increase their influence in parish affairs, offering Mahoney $1,400 annually, provided they retained control of parish collections. Another faction, which supported Bishop Fenwick, opposed the plan vigorously.[11] In 1836 Fenwick recalled both Mahoney and Fr. Peter Connolly, who had succeeded Curtin as an assistant in 1835.[12]

Fenwick replaced them with Fr. Edward J. McCool, whom archdiocesan historians refer to as an "unfortunate man . . . suffering mental derangement."[13] McCool, a native of Ireland whom Fenwick had assigned previously to Charlestown, soon embarrassed Fenwick by displaying an open and public affection for alcohol. He also failed to push the building committee into completing the St. Patrick's Church addition subscription drive. Despite his personal problems, McCool enjoyed wide support among some of Lowell's Irish—whom Fenwick infuriated by banishing McCool first to a spiritual retreat and then, one month later, permanently from Lowell.[14] The schism among Lowell's Catholics openly drove a wedge between two factions of the Irish middle class, who divided on the basis of their support for McCool or Fenwick, with the rest of Lowell's Irish following into one camp or the other.

The conflict began when Fenwick received a delegation of twelve Catholics carrying a petition "signed by over three hundred persons, male inhabitants of Lowell, requesting that the Bishop will not remove Rev. Mr. McCool from Lowell, stating that if he should persist in doing so the consequence might be afflicting."[15] In a personal letter to their ringleader, dry goods dealer Charles M. Short, who also served as president of that middle-class bastion, the Benevolent Society, Fenwick announced his refusal to comply despite their threat to close St. Patrick's.[16] Instead he appointed a replacement, Fr. James T. McDermott, who arrived in Lowell to find the church doors barred against his entry. McDermott unfastened them unceremoniously by first climbing through an unlocked church window. The McCool faction backed down but continued their opposition to his recall, transforming it into a personal vendetta against McDermott.[17]

Father McDermott, a native of County Tyrone, had arrived in Boston in September, 1831. Unlike the aged and irascible Mahoney or the troubled and eccentric McCool, McDermott was an energetic, eager young priest who had just completed courses in philosophy at Grand Seminary in Montreal.[18] He then applied to Bishop Fenwick for admission into the Boston diocese and Fenwick agreed, providing that McDermott obtained an *exeat*, i.e., a letter of recommendation in which McDermott's Irish bishop freed him to work among Boston's Catholics. McDermott obtained permission and Fenwick assigned him to New Haven in 1832, where he remained until shortly before his reassignment to Lowell.[19]

Despite the opposition of the McCool faction, McDermott did attract some followers. In fact, McDermott was far more decisive than his predecessors and it was clear that he enjoyed Fenwick's confidence and had come to Lowell to implement Fenwick's agenda. His success was especially important because as the fourth priest assigned to Lowell in five years from a diocesan staff of only twenty-four, he was the first one to exercise leadership successfully in the name of Fenwick.[20] While he was there, McDermott's strongest supporters included his brother, Peter McDermott, Daniel McElroy, and Hugh Cummiskey. (The latter had acted as the Lowell agent of the Boston *Pilot* in the late 1830s at a time when the *Pilot's* editor, Patrick Donohoe, vigorously supported Fenwick's approach to the development of Catholicism in Lowell.) Generally, McDermott's supporters included those Irish like Cummiskey who accepted the bishop's authority over parish development. Many of McDermott's most avid supporters were also Lowell's public schoolteachers like McElroy, over whom McDermott held appointment power.[21] Put in other terms, loyalty to Bishop Fenwick brought its reward in the form of influence in parish affairs.

McDermott's initial success over the McCool faction was soon overshadowed by the huge debt left to McDermott and his supporters. The debt also caused Fenwick serious difficulty, especially when many of the disaffected middle class refused to subscribe for pews which would have generated income for parish expansion.[22] When McDermott became pastor, Fenwick had already settled some parish accounts, accepting personal responsibility for many bills; nevertheless, the debt stood at $4719.53.[23] Fenwick faced other less severe but very public nuisances, as, for example, when Mahoney and Connolly appeared in a Concord, Massachusetts, courtroom in a suit filed by a stonemason, Michael Connolly, for payment of wages incurred during construction of the church's foundation.[24] Adopting an austere budget and drawing on his base of supporters, McDermott reduced the debt to $2083.80 by 1840, even spending an additional $1697.20 on badly needed improvements to the church. His resources remained sufficiently limited, however, that McDermott spent most of his time dealing with the parish financial problems.[25]

To supplement what little income was available from pew rentals, McDermott, with Fenwick's encouragement, turned to voluntary subscriptions to improve parish finances. Their task was especially difficult in the business depression which followed the Panic of 1837, but they raised over $2500 in 1838–39. In addition, McDermott received about $75 annually from the sale of burial lots in a Catholic cemetery which St. Patrick's had acquired several years earlier. He also received $200 to $300 annually in Sunday collections and, during this two-year period, $141.09 in interest for money which they held on deposit. By 1840, they had raised a total of over $6000.[26] McDermott's limited success as a local fundraiser nevertheless pleased Fenwick, who could not fail to appreciate the handicaps under which McDermott labored and whose diocese had begun to expand more rapidly, with a growing burden of debt throughout.

With Fenwick's approval, McDermott continued to use most of the money to pay off the heavy parish debt, but he also reserved $500 annually for personal use. He offered small commissions to those who assisted him in collecting voluntary subscriptions and paid a sum of $117.68 to his brother, Peter, for "collection." In addition, McDermott settled a law suit brought against him by unpaid carpenters for $87.50, paid an organist, and hired a sexton to "sweep and light" St. Patrick's Church.[27] His success in reducing the heavy parish debt indicated that, while McDermott may have failed to prevent the factions from persisting among the Irish middle class, he successfully maintained the allegiance of enough parishioners to allow the parish to meet its obligations. In 1841, McDermott received considerable assistance from the Lowell school committee, which advanced $500 for the rental of classroom space in the basement of St. Patrick's Church, in effect using public money to underwrite a portion of the parish debt.[28]

By the early 1840s, McDermott had placed his personal stamp upon parish affairs. The population remained stable, and no well-organized opposition arose from among parishioners.[29] In May, 1838, Father McCool caused a brief stir when he returned to Lowell and "having obtained his dismissal from the Insane Hospital, [went] about, by day and by night . . . scandalizing the Catholics there with his drunken frolicking."[30] Still, if McDermott was generally more effective, he continued to endure sniping from his opponents within the parish, and any project he proposed was effectively blocked by them. Even his success in reducing the parish debt rose principally from the belief shared by all factions that the debt was a blot upon Catholicism in Lowell. Under McDermott, Fenwick succeeded in establishing the viability of the parish but only at the expense of any notions of a unified Catholic community in Lowell.

The dispute in the St. Patrick's Charitable Society illustrates the persistent dissension within the parish. The society had been organized about 1836 and was dedicated initially to "clothing the naked, feeding the

hungry, and ornamenting our church." It languished, however, until Mc-
Dermott's supporters transformed it into the St. Patrick's Charitable and
Young Catholic Friends Society," with a new strategy to care for the religious and social needs of Irish children beyond those met by public education.[31] McDermott's opponents sniffed that "the city authorities of
Lowell provide one grammar school and four primary schools for the sole
use and benefit of the Irish children, and are still willing to go further,"
and they argued that McDermott's supporters were "waging an unpopular
and unsuccessful struggle."[32] The argument went no further but it indicated that Father McDermott faced opposition. The policy of the Charitable Society, if enacted, would have diminished some authority given to
him by the 1835 education compromise. Some of the tension eased in
1839, when Bishop Fenwick appointed an afffable and effective curate, Fr.
James Conway, to assist McDermott.

In 1841 McDermott's opponents renewed their opposition by proposing
a division of St. Patrick's parish. Much of the opposition, including many
members of the Benevolent Society, lived in a new and rapidly expanding
neighborhood called "Chapel Hill," on the far side of the mill district and
inconvenient to St. Patrick's Church, which had always been too small to
serve Lowell's large Catholic population. Undoubtedly, Fenwick vividly
recalled his difficulty when attempting to raise funds from among Lowell's
Catholics, but he also recognized that he could not permit the split within
Lowell's Irish middle class to continue, particularly since it also involved
alienating members of the powerful Benevolent Society. Fenwick appointed Father Conway to supervise construction of a new church and obtain title in the bishop's name. Subscriptions poured in from disaffected
Irish and the new church, St. Peter's, was considerably larger than St. Patrick's when completed.[33] Fenwick dedicated St. Peter's in an elaborate
ceremony in which McDermott played no active role.[34]

Fenwick's pragmatic solution to Lowell's persistent factionalism—to
separate the opposition, who already lived apart, with the explanation
that Lowell's rapid growth mandated it—was tactful; unfortunately, Fenwick failed to consider McDermott's willfulness. McDermott frequently
denounced the Benevolent Society for "not conforming to church discipline," while his supporters accused society members of being "bound together by oaths or solemn promises, and having secret signs and pass-
words."[35] McDermott also attacked society members for their failure to
support temperance, while his supporters lobbied to prevent St. Peter's
construction "by withholding the people from contributing towards it."

St. Peter's Church, 1858. From the Lowell City Directory. Courtesy of the Lowell Historical Society.

Fenwick, siding with those whom he had once opposed, "remonstrated against the unnecessary noise."[36]

In 1843, McDermott went too far when he insisted upon the immediate dismissal of seven out of Lowell's twelve Catholic public schoolteachers. The Boston *Bee* reported indignantly that "the baffled and infuriated man proceeded to blast the characters of these respectable young ladies from the pulpit, their names were publicly called out, their characters villified and traduced." McDermott also attacked the male schoolteachers, reportedly because "one of them . . . publicly lectured on infidelity, or his lectures were crammed with infidel principles."[37] He then ordered every Irish Catholic schoolchild to boycott Lowell's public schools until the school committee complied with his demands.[38] For nearly three weeks, the schools stood empty, although eventually "the strike petered out."[39] When the school boycott failed, Fenwick reprimanded McDermott. Fenwick was reluctant to remove him, however, especially in light of McDermott's role in breaking the McCool schism. In time, McDermott provided Fenwick with an opportunity when, in 1847, McDermott petitioned successfully to establish a new church within sight of St. Patrick's. He justified the acquisition by claiming that an additional church could provide for those parishioners poorly served by the outdated and inadequately sized St. Patrick's.[40]

By this rash action, McDermott had wrecked a highly innovative church-state education compromise and alienated even his own supporters, seriously miscalculating his power at St. Patrick's. His later actions angered a portion of the Irish middle class, including traditional supporters such as Hugh Cummiskey, because all factions had solidly supported the education compromise. At the 1844 Benevolent Society dinner, for example, Cummiskey pointedly proposed a toast to the Lowell school committee: "May their assiduity in promoting the good of that noble cause committed to them never relax, or never again be obstructed by selfishness or ambition."[41] In July, 1844, the Boston *Pilot* publisher, Patrick Donohoe, wrote of the Lowell agreement, in an effort to salvage it, that it was an arrangement "without precedent or imitation," and one in which the school committee "has long since made a separate and most ample provision for the education of Irish children." He also reported that one school committeeman, Ithamar W. Beard, had recently "dwelt upon the unworthy prejudice which had possessed the minds of many in relation to the Irish children, and was proud to say that if they needed confutation of their erroneous opinions, they had but to come into that school."[42] Although no one formally terminated the education agreement, local Catholic influence in Irish public schools decreased rapidly after McDermott's outburst. By 1846 only three of twelve teachers in the Irish public schools were Catholic.[43]

The problems associated with the growth of St. Patrick's illustrate the complex and ever-changing relationships among parishioners, priests, and Bishop Fenwick. The early Irish work camp rivalries continued but they paled before the rivalries within the middle class which exploded during the McCool schism of 1836. Once the opponents' efforts to control the pastor's appointment failed, they submitted to Fenwick's authority to an extent, but they continued sniping at McDermott until the formal parish division. By then, the early factional differences with Fenwick had been replaced by open defiance of his arrogant local representative, McDermott. Fenwick had legal control of St. Patrick's but he recognized that local support was essential. By giving the Benevolent Society St. Peter's and by refusing to support McDermott's whims regarding the education compromise, Fenwick ended the battle and, finally, won a peace which he could accept.

The battle over St. Patrick's also typified the pattern of development in early Irish Catholic communities in the period between the early trusteeship disputes and the more organized, hierarchical church of the late nineteenth century. Living among a transient population of largely unskilled laborers and their families, the middle class developed the customs, traditions, and interests which shaped the early years of the Irish community. They also set the pattern of accommodation which conditioned the response of Lowell's Irish to external forces. The split in the middle class was a telling one because it ultimately affected their claim to unified leadership and because it interfered permanently with the growth of St. Patrick's parish. When Fenwick granted St. Peter's to his opposition within the middle class, all sides submitted to his direction but the damage to any claims to leadership of the Irish community from among the middle class had been done. The growth of St. Patrick's parish in the late 1830s and early 1840s had been painful, with the parish turned into a battleground where it was thought that the outcome determined who held power and status in the paddy camps.

The most obvious loser in the religious struggles was McDermott. The archdiocesan historians referred to him as the "ablest of the early pastors," and for length of service McDermott stood out from his predecessors.[44] He had come to Lowell as Fenwick's representative to break the

McCool faction and had succeeded in destroying its power, although McDermott's opponents remained powerful with their base in the Benevolent Society. In a way, McDermott lost because he could hold a grudge. He had ended the schism and restored parish finances but he could not forgive the opposition nor, undoubtedly, did they let him. McDermott's success was also his liability and it was left to Bishop Fenwick to bring both sides together through the compromise of St. Peter's. His gift to McDermott's opponents finally put the factionalism to rest, at least in regard to his own disputes with them. McDermott's open opposition to St. Peter's during its construction and his destruction of the education compromise had brought him into conflict with Fenwick's policy. McDermott had gone too far and rapidly lost power. Fenwick quietly retired him to St. Mary's, and in 1854, when Fenwick's successor, Bishop John Fitzpatrick, dedicated a magnificent new St. Patrick's, McDermott was not asked back.

McDermott's unwillingness to devise a compromise in the religious struggles together with the inability of the middle class to present a unified claim to leadership among the Irish came at a crucial moment in their history. The 1840s was a period of dramatic economic and social change for them, but whatever feelings of community existed among the Irish were caught up in an aimless drift. If there was any sense of direction, it was manifested in a kind of lip service commitment to the old spirit of accommodation, which had seemed so vital and promising only a decade before. Showing their ongoing support for the principle of accommodation, Irish parents continued to send their children to public school and, on another level, parishioners throughout Lowell faithfully implemented Fenwick's and, later, Bishop Fitzpatrick's directions regarding parish affairs. Still, in retrospect much of the 1840s seems like a deceptively eerie calm—what New Englanders refer to as a "weatherbreeder" day, the time just before a great Atlantic nor'easter blows ashore. In the parishes, all was quiet after McDermott's ploy against Catholic schoolteachers and, among the Irish generally, there was more of a tendency to look for areas on which they might agree. Their search took them across the Atlantic to the dynamic forces affecting Irish history.

On Irish history, all of Lowell's Irish might concur, especially as their views also fit their perception of themselves as "exiled sons of Erin." As Miller, Boling, and Doyle have argued, this image encouraged the adjustment of Irish identity and culture to the harsh realities of urban industrialization.[45] On this level, the Irish middle class might provide some unified direction. Some were literate; all shared a keen interest in the news of Great Britain regularly published in American newspapers and, in part, also carried by Irish emigrants recently settled in Lowell. This national perspective also blended nicely into the climate of accommodation in Lowell, and many Yankee officials joined in support of "national" Irish causes such as Repeal and, for obvious reasons, temperance. Even Father McDermott was an outspoken advocate of national Irish issues. In much the same way as great movements like Repeal and temperance broke down regional and factional barriers in Ireland, so too in America such sweeping changes encouraged Lowell's Irish to break the provincial factionalism and clannish insularity of the early paddy camps. Such movements became a vehicle by which local Irish drew together a progressive and dynamic philosophy of their presence in America from the complexities of Irish culture and tradition.

The first national cause to impact upon the Irish was temperance, which had roots, obviously, that extended deep into American tradition. The first temperance societies appeared in Lowell in the 1820s and, by the mid-1830s, Lowell had several strong societies as well as a number of temperance hotels.[46] At first, Lowell's Irish took little notice of the movement, particularly because it was dominated by Yankees and because the Irish middle class, a portion of whom would embrace temperance, was quite small and a number of them prospered by catering to the local Irish trade in alcohol. In addition, the Irish were preoccupied with the construction of St. Patrick's Church. A report in the Lowell *Mercury* in July, 1830, for instance, noted that the Lowell Temperance Society received support from every group but the Catholics.[47]

In time, however, many Irish embraced temperance openly. Temperance attracted these Irish because the motivation behind the American temperance movement tapped many of the same feelings and much of the rhetoric espoused by the Irish middle class regarding industry, opportunity, and equality. More generally historians have suggested a number of reasons behind the rise of temperance, although most deal with the temperance campaign of the late nineteenth century. Some viewed it as one more campaign in a reform-minded age, while others adopted Hofstadter's position, arguing that temperance was a middle-class reform supported because of deteriorating middle-class status in an age of rapid industrialization.[48] In the most perceptive recent study, William Rorabaugh contended that the temperance movement grew in response to conditions in early nineteenth-century America. He suggested that temperance indicated that American society was inherently healthy and that it was a "building block" which formed part of a new ideology attuned to American industrialization. Intemperance was regarded as wrong because it was morally evil and because addiction was unproductive and a wasteful allocation of resources. Temperance leaders also bolstered religion by fusing it with republican rhetoric, arguing convincingly that intemperance interfered with man's natural rights.[49]

Among Lowell's Irish middle class, this philosophy had real meaning. They stressed the duties of good citizenship and the importance of adhering to laws which governed the American republic and their "adopted homeland." Lowell was, after all, an industrial showcase and the Irish believed in its future and in their part in shaping what was to come. The continual bickering among ancestral factions in the paddy camps had given Lowell's Irish an unsavory reputation as boisterous, rowdy, and unmanageable, contributed to by their affection for cheap whiskey and beer. The Irish appeared in overwhelming numbers on the docket of the police court for drunkenness. Lowell's newspapers also regularly carried such stories as the one concerning "an Irishman by the name of Ryan, aged almost 40, who was found dead yesterday morning, in the floom at Mssrs. Hale flour mill—supposed to have been intoxicated, and fell in."[50] With their growing reputation for drunkenness in Lowell, temperance was a movement by which the Irish could prove themselves worthy of America.

By 1840, the leader in the movement among Lowell's Irish was Father McDermott. In June, McDermott organized the Lowell Catholic Temperance Society. Five hundred people pledged abstinence at the first meeting. McDermott's took his lead from events occurring among Catholics in other cities. Catholic temperance societies had been organized in Boston several years earlier but they failed to attract membership. But in 1840 a new society appeared in New York, followed in quick succession by societies in Boston and, soon, Lowell. By 1841 the Boston Society had nearly ten thousand members, while New York claimed over eleven thousand, and Lowell about two thousand.[51] The leaders among the American Irish were the middle class and Catholic priests. The priests made an important connection between their work in America, which aimed to reform intemperate tendencies acquired in Ireland, with the work of the great Irish missionary priest, Fr. Theobald Mathew, who had converted five million Irish to temperance by the early 1840s.[52] With this connection, temperance was not only a movement arising from a more general effort to convince the American Irish that it fostered productive and useful American citizens but also one which emerged from the general reform spirit sweeping through Ireland. In this sense, temperance tied Ireland and America together in the minds of individual Irish.

In 1841, McDermott participated in a temperance ministers' lecture series at Lowell City Hall. His speech, based upon the text "be not drunk with wine," touched upon the motivations which attracted many American Irish to the temperance campaign. McDermott opened his address by placing the activity of the Lowell Catholic Temperance Society in an international perspective, equating local efforts with Mathew's temperance campaign in Ireland. He noted that when Mathew began his temperance campaign in 1838 "everybody felt obliged to drink—everybody drank— priests and people." McDermott claimed that the international success of temperance, "seems, like Christianity, to be the work of infinite wisdom and goodness." He stressed the moral value of doing "what is right" while linking it to "co-operating with the friends of temperance in promoting the greatest and most important reformation known since the days of the Apostles," and also warning about "its [alcohol's] terrible effects upon the drunkard, here and hereafter." [53]

McDermott's speech was well received. The *Courier* reported that "all true Americans rejoice in the reformation of Irishmen, everywhere." It lavished praise upon Father Mathew, claiming that "no man, since the days of the Apostles, has done more for the cause of religion and morality than Father Mathew . . . [who] seems to have been raised up for the express purpose of reforming his countrymen." The *Courier* argued that under Mathew's guidance, Ireland, "emancipated from the curse of intemperance," would enjoy the "civil liberty [which] will follow her moral freedom." It urged the reform effort to continue among Irish "until Irishmen shall be everywhere what God and nature designed they should be, intelligent, independent, and free, because temperate, religious, and moral." [54]

The Lowell Catholic Temperance Society was applauded because it proposed moral reform as a prelude to civil liberty for Irishmen. That philosophy, which stressed the link between temperance and good citizenship, appealed to many Irish who saw temperance as a principle by which they might demonstrate themselves worthy to seek the opportunities open to them in America. In the moral environment of Lowell, many unskilled Irish undoubtedly pledged temperance and wore their temperance badges as a sign that they understood that environment or, for some, that they understood what causes were important to Father McDermott. [55] Further, the link between moral reform in Lowell and moral reform in

Ireland undoubtedly appealed to American Irish with strong emotional ties to Ireland.

McDermott supported temperance because, despite the split among Lowell's Irish and his alienation from some of them, he believed in the values outlined in his text, pointedly ending his presentation by thanking his Yankee lecture series organizers for the opportunity "to co-operate with them."[56] The temperance movement, with its stress on moral reform, also contributed to McDermott's power over Lowell's Irish Catholics. He used the opportunity to denounce traditional opponents within the Benevolent Society for their opposition to temperance, ignoring the position of many Benevolent Society members as shopkeepers whose livelihood depended upon the sale of alcohol. Finally, McDermott's efforts regarding temperance reflected trends throughout the Boston diocese which were reported dutifully in the Boston *Pilot*. The *Pilot's* editor, Patrick Donohoe, was a staunch supporter and urged his Catholic readership toward the same values of moral reform and good citizenship which marked both the national temperance effort and the philosophy of the Irish middle class in Lowell.[57]

The temperance campaign continued to attract supporters from among Lowell's Irish throughout the 1840s, although much of the enthusiasm generated initially was shifted to Repeal and, later, to Famine relief. Temperance did enjoy renewed popularity among the Irish during the visit of Father Mathew to Lowell in September, 1849, but the enthusiasm was short-lived. A "Committee on Arrangements," made up of influential Lowell Yankees, organized Mathew's reception. Mathew returned their hospitality by penning an acknowledgment in which he praised the "rapid growth of Commercial enterprise and Industry, for which Lowell is so preeminently distinguished."[58] He marveled at Lowell's rapid development and praised the quality of Lowell's mill workers, who included a great many Irish by 1849.

> You have proceeded far in the solution of a most difficult social problem. You have proved to a demonstration, the important fact, that the busiest operations of industrial activity, are perfectly compatible with a high standard of Christian morality, of intellectual refinement, and conscious self-respect. Your factory operatives, amounting to nearly fourteen thousand, may fairly challenge comparison on these points with any similar class in the world. The air of comfort, happiness, and health, so visible in the appearance of the men, and the taste, industry, and intellectuality, which characterize

the female assistants in those busy hives of National wealth and industry, are features as novel as they are interesting, to the friends of
human progress.[59]

Mathew's praise represented a cogent articulation of the philosophy of the
Irish middle class and of the place they hoped to make for themselves in
Lowell. Mathew was aware that Irish had obtained entry into Lowell's
mills and his thinly disguised sentiment also expressed the hope that
these Irish, filled with "the high standard of Christian morality," would
find a home there.[60] This strategy, after all, had been the plan of the Irish
middle class since they came together in the forging of the education compromise fourteen years earlier. It had always permeated local Irish support for the temperance campaign, although mill employment had not
been anticipated in the early years of their quest for a home in Lowell.

   With the blessing of Lowell's Yankees, its Catholic priests, and the Irish
middle class, Mathew administered the temperance pledge to Irish
throughout Lowell. He visited St. Patrick's, where seven hundred pledged
their support, and spent the following morning at nearby St. Mary's. Despite a persistent cold, Mathew left St. Mary's to address an immense
crowd at Lowell City Hall. By the time he reached St. Peter's, Mathew
had devised a technique whereby whole groups recited the pledge simultaneously while he "passed among them and invested them with the sign
of the cross" before dismissing each group. Over four thousand Irish,
roughly 40 percent of Lowell's entire Irish population, took the pledge
during his three-day stay.[61] Enthusiasm for temperance among the Irish
died quickly after he left Lowell, although several temperance societies
reappeared among Lowell's Irish in the late nineteenth century."[62]

   Like temperance, the movement for Repeal generated a growing sense
of nationalism among Lowell's Irish, although unlike temperance, with its
roots in American tradition, support for Repeal emerged directly from
events in Irish history. The union of Great Britain and Ireland, which had
gone into effect in January, 1801, granted Ireland one hundred members
in the imperial Parliament while mandating that the Irish assume two-
seventeenths of British expenditures. More significantly, it also dissolved
the historic Irish parliament. The Act of Union brought Irish problems to
the floor of Parliament, but it did little to help the majority of Irish. In
response, Daniel O'Connell launched the Repeal movement in the 1840s
with a demand for the restoration of the Irish parliament. His actions nurtured the flame of Irish nationalism at home and among those Irish abroad

who shared a nationalistic perspective. O'Connell's movement found considerable support in Lowell.

That support emerged after O'Connell organized a series of mass meetings throughout Ireland.[63] In Lowell, Repeal was discussed widely. The subject even arose in Yankee humor: "'Mickey,' said a pious Irish Catholic to his son, whom he had just met in this 'land of the free'—'Mickey, my boy, do you go to confession regularly, like a good child of the church?' 'Why, no, Father,' replied Mickey, 'but I attend all the mass meetings.'"[64]

Local support for Repeal arose from many of the same motives which had characterized the enthusiasm for temperance. Lowell's Yankees perceived the political turmoil as a wrong to be redressed and characterized it as an undemocratic denial of political rights. Josiah Abbott, a liberal-minded corporation lawyer, for instance, wrote that Irish independence "will most surely be accomplished; seven millions of true-minded Irishmen cannot always be held in bondage."[65] His sentiments were echoed even by President John Tyler: "I am a decided friend of the Repeal of the Legislative Union between Great Britain and Ireland. I ardently and anxiously hope that it may take place, and I have the utmost confidence that Ireland will have her own Parliament in her own capital in a very short time."[66]

Yankee fascination with Repeal made it an attractive cause for Lowell's Irish, but it was also an Irish movement which tied "Mickey" to his immigrant father and, as a result, appealed to a broad range of Irishmen. The lists of Lowell's Repeal contributors published in the Boston *Pilot* confirmed this tendency.[67] In addition, Repeal was not only an Irish movement but also one which was popular in America and which allowed the American Irish to identify with it proudly. Finally, all of the Irish middle class as well as the Irish Catholic Boston *Pilot*, whose editorial position reflected their philosophy, supported Repeal. They were attracted in part by the same rhetoric which characterized their descriptions of the glories of the American Republic. Richard Walsh, a Catholic bookseller and the *Pilot's* Lowell representative, described Daniel O'Connell in 1843 as "the hero, the statesman and philosopher, that Colossus of learning and wisdom,"[68] while John McGowan, a local Irishman, proposed at a St. Patrick's Day dinner:

> May England's rose wither and die
> And Erin's shamrock be reared on high;
> May Hibernia's harp proclaim the strains

> Of liberty, o'er her verdant plains,
> And as Father Mathew has healed our woe,
> So may O'Connell strike the blow
> For freedom's cause, the union's repeal
> And thus bless old Erin with power and weal.[69]

In the minds of Lowell's Irish, Repeal was a glorious movement for Irish independence which harkened back to the American struggle seventy years earlier:

> May the green banner waving on Erin's shore,
> As Free as our Eagle triumphantly soar;
> May her sons be redeemed from the tyrant and the tory;
> And live in the pride of their ancient glory.[70]

Support for Repeal developed in Lowell as early as 1841. Peter McDermott, secretary of the Lowell Repeal Association and Father McDermott's brother, reported that "though we have been slumbering a little in our good city of spindles, it was only to *spin* with increased action when we commenced."[71] At the association's February meeting, members chastised England for its "intrigue, perjury, infidelity and tyrannical treatment of Ireland."[72] Daniel McElroy prepared the following unanimously adopted resolutions, which emphasized the strong support of Lowell's Irish for Repeal:

> *Resolved:*—That years of sad experience convince us that nothing but the restoration of her Parliament will ever redress the grievances under which Ireland suffers.
> *Resolved:*—That as Irishmen and citizens of America, our sympathies and efforts to accomplish the Repeal of the Union, are due to our injured country.
> *Resolved:*—That as Irishmen and citizens of Lowell, we will use every legal and constitutional means within our reach, to aid the Irish people in their present peaceful agitation for Repeal.[73]

By July, 1843, the furor over Repeal died down in Lowell, although support continued until the movement collapsed shortly after in Ireland. As late as June, 1843, Repeal Association members from Lowell had placed a "bill of exchange" aboard the steamer *Caledonia* to be issued to the Irish Repeal Treasury for use in the "glorious movement."[74] Still, not all Yankees supported O'Connell's view of the economic and social inequities in British rule. Although many were fascinated with Repeal, some undoubtedly agreed with William Schouler, editor of the Lowell *Courier*,

who suggested that Ireland's economic stagnation resulted less from pro-
hibitive policies toward the Irish under the union than from the "*great
skill* and greater wealth of the English merchants and manufactures
[*sic*]."[75] That economic stagnation masked an even greater crisis awaiting
Ireland. By the mid-1840s, the impact of the Famine in Ireland would
change the course of Lowell's history.

About the same time that the Repeal movement collapsed, word that a
blight had devastated the Irish potato crop reached Lowell. The extent of
the devastation slowly became known until, by the early 1850s, over one
and a half million Irish had died of starvation or disease, while another
one million had emigrated.[76] The English government spent huge sums
£8,000,000 in one year alone, to alleviate suffering in the first years of the
Famine, but support decreased sharply thereafter. Landlord-assisted
schemes and individual efforts also swelled emigration, particularly to
America. Emigrants carried their Famine stories with them and American
newspapers reported their distress.[77] In Lowell, for example, the *Voice of
Industry*, a hard-hitting labor paper, described the region around Cork as
"most appalling, starvation being universal, deaths from want of food fre-
quent, and fearfully on the increase, whilst despair has seized upon the
public mind."[78] It generated considerable support by graphically describing Famine conditions, referring to Irish distress as the "Death Cry of
Erin":

> Hark! hark! what is that dismal wail,
> Borne by the broad Atlantic gale?
> That dreadful cry of deep despair—
> Of *human woe*—that rends the air?
> Loudly the ocean-tempest raves,
> And onward driven the surging waves
> With thunder-sound assail the shore;
> But louder than the water's roar
> There comes that wild, despairing cry,
> Which speaks a nation's agony!
> 'Tis Erin's famished voice we hear;
> Its anguished tones appal the ear;
> Fast perishing with Famine dread,
> With outstretched arms she calls for bread;
> For *Bread*—for *Bread* for dying men—
> Oh, shall that piteous cry be vain?
> Like ghastly corpses, all around,
> Her haggard sons bestrew the ground;

Men, women, infants, grasping lie,
For *Bread*—for *Bread*—they faint, they die,
And Erin hears their dying groans,
And fain to save her wretched sons
Through all the land, its length, its breadth,
For aught she seeks, to stay the death.
She seeks in vain, death is not staid.
And once again, she shrieks for aid.
Oh! Earth, canst thou stand coldly by,
Till thou hast heard her last death-cry?
America! 'tis thou canst save
Her starving thousands from the grave.
Much hast thou given, but still thy store
O'er-flows, and thou canst send her more.
'Twas gave thee—and *thou* must *give*,
And bid this dying people live.
Kind heaven, hast thou a pitying ear,
A nation's wail of woe to hear?
And wilt thou spread thy saving hand
O'er Erin's famine-tortured land?[79]

In February, 1847, the Lowell Famine Committee elected Lowell's mayor, Jefferson Bancroft, as chairman, and passed a series of resolutions stressing America's duty to relieve Famine suffering.[80] While Lowell's corporations refused to pledge assistance, two unidentified women approached all boardinghouses attached to Lowell's mills asking for contributions. Contributions were arranged in "five large boxes so nicely packed, [that] I was astonished to see how much a few weak hands could accomplish." At the same time, the Lowell Famine Committee raised $1,919.65 from Lowell's Protestant religious societies, from Boston and Lowell Railroad employees, from hands at the Merrimack Print Works, and from general subscription raised in Lowell's wards. Irish relief efforts in Lowell were concentrated primarily in individual remittances and in relieving distress among poor Famine immigrants within Lowell.[81]

In each movement—temperance, Repeal, and Famine relief—interested Lowell Yankees participated in efforts to ameliorate conditions among the Irish. They saw temperance as a movement to reform human weakness that arose principally from conditions within European peasant life where "everybody drank" and applauded Mathew's efforts to attack the source of the problem. Repeal had the same attraction in that the legislative union between England and Ireland denied Irishmen the natural rights of free men. Famine relief was a humanitarian impulse but it failed to generate the enthusiasm of earlier movements. When the editors of the Lowell *Courier* discovered that the American Irish had assisted the Young Ireland revolt through financial remittances in 1848, they feared that the revolt would spread "to the whole civilized world" and warned Lowell's Irish of a "systematic attempt to gull the Irish in this country, and pick their pockets under the pretence of helping friends at home." By 1848 the fight for Irish independence had become unpopular among Lowell's Yankees, who no longer described the movement in terms of freedom and civil liberty.[82]

The support among Lowell's Irish for each movement is far more complex, reflecting trends occurring within the paddy camps, in Lowell generally, and in Ireland. But whatever the motivation for support, the campaigns of Mathew and O'Connell had ended by 1850. It was the natural disaster of the Famine which had the most pronounced impact upon Lowell's Irish. In the 1840s, the Irish middle class lived under rules which had been worked out with Lowell's Yankees in the 1830s. Kirk Boott died in 1837 and, while the rhetoric of camaraderie continued, with his death the position of the Irish in Lowell changed and these rules no longer applied. As Lowell's Irish population increased with Famine immigration, officials worried less about good citizenship and more about order. If the Irish could not reform themselves and, in fact, if the character of Lowell's Irish population had deteriorated with the arrival of Famine emigrants, Lowell's officials would take whatever steps were necessary to preserve the quality of life and the moral environment of Lowell. In time, the officials would be betrayed, but the force which destroyed Lowell's reputation as an industrial showcase was not so much the Irish as the Boston Associates and their descendants.

CHAPTER 5

The Pattern of Employment
1838–50

In the depression years which followed the Panic of 1837, the total number of Irish in Lowell changed very little. In 1838, for example, Father McDermott baptized 163 children and married 35 couples, while three years later he baptized 179 children and married forty-two couples.[1] At the same time, Lowell's population rose from 18,010 in 1837 to 20,981 in 1840, and to 33,383 in 1850.[2] The Irish contributed so little to Lowell's increase in population around 1840 because of the nature of their work in Lowell and because of increasing opportunities in other New England towns. In Lowell, Locks and Canals had largely completed construction of the mills and power canals before the Panic of 1837, and the panic dampened any enthusiasm for new construction. For many Irish, work in Lowell grew scarce. From this perspective, it is surprising that Lowell's Irish population did not decrease, especially since emigration from Ireland also slowed during these years.

This stability can be explained by both local conditions and those prevailing more generally throughout New England. First, some Irish found employment outside the mills. Enough unskilled Irishmen worked as itinerant day laborers in the area around Lowell that the Lowell *Courier* reprinted humorous stories about the danger of employing them as gardeners and farmhands.[3] Other Irish laborers found work with construction projects in the new residential areas of Centralville, Belvedere, Ayer's City, along Pawtucket Street, or in the growing commercial district along Merrimack and Central streets.[4] The emergence of a resident Yankee middle class in a time of cheap labor also opened employment to Irish women, especially along Pawtucket Street and in Belvedere. In 1847, the Lowell *Courier* recounted a story about one such Irish servant: "An Irish servant girl applied to a druggist a few days since for six cents worth of the 'glory of rhyme.' She had been sent for chloride of lime!"[5] Some Irish were quite successful at specialized trades. Hugh McEvoy, for example, was a tailor who catered to Yankee customers from his shop on Central Street and, eventually, built a successful business and became a real estate speculator.[6]

Also, a few Irishmen had marketable skills sought by the corporations. Some were employed at the Lowell Machine Shop, which boasted five hundred workers in 1845. There were Irish working there as early as 1835, and their employment had become common practice in the mid-1840s.[7] Machine shop officials hired an Irishman, John Holland, in May, 1844, for example, noting that he had "worked here before." Other Irishmen, including Richard Hieland, William Masterson, and Richard Harrington, also were employed there. They worked apart from other employees under specific foremen.[8] It is also likely that Irishmen once employed in the English woolen industry worked at the Middlesex Company after its agent, Samuel Lawrence, sent a recruiter to Lancashire in the late 1830s.[9]

In addition, Lowell's Irish found opportunities outside Lowell. With the decline in construction activity, many Irish laborers rejoined the permanent pool of transient Irish wandering through the New England countryside in search of work. Even Hugh Cummiskey worked briefly on projects in nearby cities. One trend which encouraged migration was the decision of entrepreneurs like the Boston Associates to develop other factory villages. By 1837, the Boston Associates had acquired 15,000 acres around Amoskeag Falls on the Merrimack River in New Hampshire not far from Lowell. They developed Manchester as an industrial city on the Lowell model with even more stringent restrictions than at Lowell. Although Manchester's agents reluctantly employed Irish laborers, they soon made considerable use of them.[10] In the mid-1840s, the Associates developed another textile center near Lowell, naming it "Lawrence."[11] While convenient to these developments, moreover, Lowell was also situated along the paths followed by transient workers searching for employment in other New England river valleys, Boston, Worcester, Providence, and Fall River. The pattern of commerical and industrial development in central and southern New England was sufficient to encourage temporary migration among the Irish in Lowell to other, more promising sites. From 1845 to 1857, for instance, scattered references in Locks and Canals payroll records indicate that employees, among them Irish, were loaned out regularly to the Essex Company in Lawrence.[12]

Lowell's growing importance as a factory village also opened important opportunities for the Irish along the developing transportation routes

Lowell Machine Shop in 1845. Courtesy of the Special Collections, University of Lowell.

linking it with the rest of New England and, especially, to the port of Boston. Irish laborers had assisted in the construction of the Middlesex Canal, which remained a vital link with Boston, drawing cotton to Lowell and facilitating the shipment of finished cloth to the world's markets. Presumably, Irish laborers also worked as teamsters for firms hauling goods overland between Boston and Lowell.[13] Finally, there was the Boston and Lowell Railroad, completed in 1834, which employed Irishmen to handle the freight and passenger traffic.[14] While the number of Irishmen employed along these routes was not especially large, it was sufficient to suggest that the Irish found employment not only in the construction of these routes but also with the companies which serviced them after the construction was completed.

When the economy revived after the Panic of 1837, the mills expanded production and agents sought extra hands. Their actions were taken in response to a number of conditions affecting employment in Lowell's mills, chief among them the dissatisfaction of the Yankee factory women with their working conditions. As Dublin has shown, these women felt that their sense of community was endangered by the rapid expansion of production, which caused a deterioration in working and living conditions.[15] That sense of community, of course, had been shaped largely by the image which the Boston Associates held of Lowell. As one of them, Nathan Appleton, commented: "Ours is a great novel experiment in politics and civilization. Whatever the result, it is our destiny to make it. It is our mission—our care should be to understand it and make it succeed. It is an attempt to amalgamate, equalize, and improve the whole mass of population, by elevating the lower portions from their usual abject state and depressing the higher, in dispensing with a privileged aristocracy. The process consists in a higher reward and higher estimation of labor, with the assurance of enjoying its own fruits."[16] Appleton's words expressed the feelings of the Yankee factory women who, in response to a decline in their quality of life, formed the Lowell Female Labor Reform Association, organized under the banner of the ten-hour day. Led by Sarah Bagley, union leaders took their grievances to the Massachusetts legislature, but legislative leaders were, in the words of these women, "tools of corporate agents."[17] The movement for labor reform collapsed soon after but, with its demise, there rose unprecedented opportunities for Lowell's Irish.

These opportunities developed slowly at first. There had always been a few Irishmen employed by Lowell's mills, usually in unskilled positions.

Boott Mills in 1845. Courtesy of the Lowell Historical Society.

As in transportation and overland shipping, a few found work after the
initial construction had been completed. Some were employed hauling
cotton "in the yard" or with maintenance crews. A number worked in the
Bleachery or at the dyeworks. With the exception of those few Irish working in specialized trades in companies such as the Lowell Machine Shop,
the pattern of their work was similar to what the Irish might historically
expect with the construction crews which had recently completed the canals and mills. In a sense, the relative scarcity of such employment in
Lowell indicated a narrowing of opportunity for the Irish around 1840.[18]
Still, there were enough Irishmen in the mills in 1842 for Samuel Lawrence, a mill agent who was running as the Whigs' congressional candidate, to solicit votes from among his Irish employees in an unsuccessful
campaign, asking them pointedly: "Who is it, fellow citizens, that gives
you employment?"[19]

The first sign of change in the pattern of employment which opened
Lowell's mills to the Irish coincided with the business revival and, significantly, with a change in the pattern of Irish emigration to the Northeast
which predated but foreshadowed the routes eventually taken by Famine
emigrants. In the early 1840s, several years before the first Famine emigrants reached Lowell, American seaports such as Boston and New York
became major debarkation ports for Irish emigrants for the first time.
Boston attracted emigrants after Enoch Train initiated regular packet service to Europe about the same time that the Cunard line named Boston as
a terminus.[20] Lowell, which had the second largest Irish community in
New England, was connected to Boston by the Boston and Lowell Railroad, the Middlesex Canal, and the carriage trade. This expanding transportation network also linked it to New York via the railroad and the Fall
River ferry.[21]

In Lowell, transportation agents prospered under the new transportation network and a number of regional and national firms, such as Barr
and Company, stationed representatives in Lowell.[22] The most successful
local agent was a Catholic bookseller, Richard Walsh, who ran a shop at
Lowell and Worthen streets. Walsh represented New York and Boston
shipping agents and sold prepaid passage tickets to Lowell's Irish, then
forwarding the tickets to relatives and friends in Ireland who were prepar-
ing to emigrate to America. He advertised in local newspapers in 1844, for
example, that he could bring Irish "from all the principal towns in Ireland
direct to Boston, or by way of New York." At the time, Walsh was an agent
of "the old established line of Packet ships belonging to Joseph McMur-

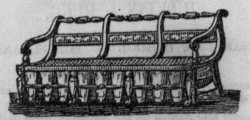

FURNITURE, FEATHER, AND
CARPET WARE-HOUSE.

B. H. WEAVER,

KEEPS constantly for sale, at the lowest prices, 'wholesale and retail, a large and select assortment
OF FURNITURE,
FEATHERS AND CARPETS,
COMPRISING EVERY VARIETY OF PATTERN
and style,—at the old stand, corner of
CENTRAL AND MERRIMACK STREETS.
N. B. Particular attention paid to putting up feather
beds in large or small quantities.

LOWELL CATHOLIC
BOOK & PERIODICAL STORE
CORNER OF LOWELL & WORTHEN
STREETS, ... LOWELL, MASS.
Where will be found an extensive assortment of
Standard Catholic Works, of the most approved character.
Prayer Books, Bibles, Testaments, Histories,
Discussions on Religion, School Books, Stationery, &c.
☞ SUBSCRIPTIONS receceived for the BOSTON
PILOT, an excellent Family Newspaper, published weekly in Boston, at $2,50 per year. RICHARD WALSH.

DR. I. W. SCRIBNER,

Has removed to the office lately occupied by DR. H.
PILLSBURY, in the
BANK BLOCK, MERRIMACK STREET.

Advertisement in the Lowell City Directory, 1844. Courtesy of
the Lowell Historical Society.

ray, Esq., of New York," guaranteeing his remittances to Ireland and even refunding money on unused tickets "after deducting five percent for postage and other expenses." He also ran a profitable mail-order business in passage tickets.[23]

Walsh was successful because, shortly before Lowell's economy revived, the number of Irish in Lowell suddenly rose. In the early 1840s, its Irish community was large enough to attract emigrants directly from Ireland, especially those whose Lowell relatives provided them with prepaid passage tickets, the promise of a place to stay, and stories of their own experiences. It appears that the number of Irish remained stable through 1841 and began rising thereafter, although the sporadic and seasonal nature of their employment makes it difficult to estimate the precise number of Irish living in Lowell between 1837 and 1841. We do know that in 1837 Bishop Fenwick estimated Lowell's Catholic population at eighteen hundred and that most of Lowell's Catholics lived in the paddy camps. If they also belonged to St. Patrick's parish, as seems likely, then something like twenty-five hundred Irish lived in Lowell in 1837.[24] That number, as measured by baptisms and marriages recorded at St. Patrick's, remained fairly constant through 1841.[25]

In 1842 the increase in the number of Irish in Lowell began. At St. Patrick's, McDermott baptized 145 children and married 50 couples, while at the new St. Peter's Conway baptized 70 children and married 10 couples. If the baptisms and marriages at both churches are combined, they represent increases of 17 and 30 percent respectively from the numbers in 1837. These figures are particularly interesting in that Lowell offered little employment to unskilled laborers before a brief building boom in the late 1840s.[26] By 1843, however, the number of Irish had doubled from six years earlier. Walsh, writing to the Boston *Pilot's* editor, Patrick Donohoe, in May, 1843, noted that Lowell had a population of five thousand Irish.[27] The surprising increase in Lowell's Irish population just prior to Famine emigration suggested that Lowell had been tied effectively to the new emigration routes passing through Boston and New York as early as 1842 and that something about Lowell beyond the presence of a large Irish community attracted emigrants to it.

The Famine emigrants arrived in Lowell in full force in 1846. In two years, the number of baptisms at Lowell's Catholic parishes rose from 228 in 1844 to 353 children in 1846, or an increase of over 54 percent, while the number of marriages nearly doubled, rising from 60 to 109 couples.[28] By Walsh's estimate in 1843, Lowell's Irish formed about 20 percent of the general population. In the Massachusetts state census of 1855, when the flood tide of Famine emigrants had ended and Irish emigration to America fell off sharply, the number of foreign-born Irish in Lowell amounted to 27.6 percent of the general population. Irish children and native-born of Irish parentage swelled the number further so that the Irish were perhaps half of Lowell's general population by the Civil War. In addition, the Irish outpaced all other immigrant groups, with the combined percentage of all foreign-born in Lowell other than Irish only 9 percent in 1855. Many of these non-Irish foreign-born had come as skilled English craftsmen to work in the dyehouse and in specialized mill trades.[29]

The Famine emigrants arrived immediately after the Lowell Female Labor Reform Association's unsuccessful fight for the ten-hour day. They also came at the moment at which Lowell began to lose its preeminence among textile cities (although in some technological areas it had lost out as early as the mid-1830s). By 1846, Lowell was twenty-five years old and its investors would be required to take major steps to upgrade aging equipment if it was to regain its reputation as an innovator in the textile industry. The labor system, with its complex of boardinghouses and other amenities, was also expensive. In addition, some of the new cities throughout New England developed with advantages which Lowell's agents could not match, especially in the use of steam power and in geography—Fall River, for example, lay south of Cape Cod and much closer to the developing cotton market and banking system in New York. To make Lowell competitive, its investors would have to make major changes affecting Lowell's economic and social development.[30]

Some of these changes were welcome. James B. Francis, a brilliant hydraulic engineer who served as agent at Locks and Canals after 1843, persuaded the Associates that a number of physical changes would have to be incorporated into the power canal system. In particular, Francis responded to the need for more water as the mills revived and expanded production. Lowell's power system had suffered from a drought in the early 1840s. In order to draw more water into the system, Francis obtained permission to construct a new power feeder, the Northern Canal, and to make improvements in the existing system, at a cost of about $650,000. He also shifted from breast wheels to more efficient turbines, after tests in 1846 on Uriah Boyden's outward flow turbines convinced him that turbines were more practical and efficient.[31]

Francis needed to complete construction of the Northern Canal quickly, and the combination of speed and the size of the project increased employment for Lowell's unskilled Irish laborers significantly. Although a few Irish found permanent employment with Locks and Canals, the company had generally maintained a policy of retaining Yankee employees at the expense of the Irish, who were hired in large numbers only during major construction projects.[32] The Northern Canal represented such an opportuniy. In January, 1846, just before the project began, most of the twenty-three outdoor employees who operated the canal gates, tended flashboards, worked on an agent's house, and assisted the Essex Company in Lawrence were Yankees. Six months later, Locks and Canals employed 792 men, many of them Irish, who worked on the Northern Canal at the "Dracut Ledge," "River Wall," embankment spilling, guard gates, dam, ledge near the guard locks, and at a boardinghouse on the Dracut side of the Merrimack River.[33]

Irish laborers appeared on company payroll lists more frequently as the work intensifed and working conditions became more dangerous. Over four hundred workers toiled throughout the winter of 1847, despite company practice which usually limited outdoor work to warmer months.[34] Construction continued hurriedly and by August, 1848, the Locks and Canals employed 838 men. By then, the clear majority were Irish. Names such as Harkins, Murphy, Daily, Sullivan, Crowley, Fitzpatrick, and Harrington predominated. Many of the Irish in these work teams toiled in dangerous, backbreaking jobs excavating at the Dracut and Guard Locks ledges.

The difficult work caused numerous accidents, although only the most gruesome found their way into print. On 9 July 1847, for instance, two workers died "from drinking an excessive quantity of cold water."[35] Many of the injuries and at least two deaths were attributed to the danger of the work undertaken by these laborers. In October, 1847, Thomas Ducy received a serious head wound when a small temporary building, which workers had erected over a steam engine, blew down and struck him.[36] On the previous day, another Irishman, Michael Reefe, had died in a rockfall: "Workmen had by means of a derrick hoisted a huge rock (weighing a ton and a half) out of the bed of the canal, and raised it as far as the wall, when the chain got unhitched, and the rock fell and struck Reefe below, cutting off one of his arms, and otherwise injuring him so much that he died in about half an hour."[37]

The wages paid these Irish laborers reflected a wage scale for unskilled laborers common throughout Lowell. Since the 1820s laborers had received about 83.3 cents per day for their work.[38] In the early years, Locks and Canals had experimented with lump sum payments to foremen who then distributed the money among their men. When Locks and Canals instituted the practice of hiring individual Irish laborers in the late 1820s, lump sum payments were discontinued and workers were paid directly, once a month. Foremen earned higher wages. Hugh Cummiskey, for example, received about $3 per day, while work team leaders like Nathaniel Hill earned about $1.50 per day for their efforts at the Northern Canal.[39] On this project, which was among the most dangerous ever undertaken in Lowell, Irish laborers also fared a bit better, averaging about $1.00 per day for their efforts.[40]

Francis's improvements to the canal system made further development of Lowell's mills easier, but only several years after the reviving business economy had encouraged expanded production. In an important way, Francis's refurbishing of them was a response to expanded production and the obstacles to it such as drought. As always, Irish laborers benefited from development of the mills as Francis turned to them, in part, as manpower for his projects. That the Irish eagerly accepted is hardly surprising and reflects a continuation of an employment tradition already a generation old. For the first time in the history of the mills, however, additional development had the unintended effect of opening factory employment to Lowell's Irish on a scale unprecedented before the expansion.

Above all else, it was a labor problem forced upon the Boston Associates by the circumstances of Lowell in the early 1840s which prompted them to turn to the Irish. The Associates saw their actions as crucial to the continued vitality of Lowell and gave little initial thought as to how expansion might affect the labor force. There were other issues which conditioned their response—aging equipment, the segmenting of the market for cotton cloth, and maintaining dividends among them—but the most troublesome was labor. The labor system had been based upon the use of temporary Yankee female operatives recruited from the hill farms of northern New England, but it also required a large physical plant with boardinghouses and other amenities which were expensive to keep up. As Dublin has shown, the effect had been to produce a sense of community among the operatives, but that sense of community was fragile and easily disrupted. As the working and living conditions for them deteriorated in the early 1840s, it became more difficult to sell the traditional image of Lowell to new farm recruits. Many of the lowest-paying jobs required no special skills anyway and improvements in mechanization simplified some of the more difficult phases of production. Finally, there was the need for additional workers; a need which was constant and pressing in an era of high turnover, labor agitation, and steadily increasing production.

The pre-Famine Irish were a logical choice from among the pool of additional workers which the Associates might tap. There were large numbers in Lowell and a few of them already worked in the mills. Many of the potential workers among the Irish were also recent products of Lowell's much-touted public schools and could be expected to understand what would be required of them. The Boston Associates also enjoyed excellent relationships with many of the men who were influential among the Irish, such as Hugh Cummiskey, Bishop Fenwick, and Father McDermott, men who believed in accommodation with Yankees and who would see mill employment as a triumph of accommodation policy. It was to groups like the pre-Famine Irish whom Nathan Appleton referred in 1844 when he spoke of a duty "to elevate them from their abject state." Historically, the Associates saw nothing especially exceptional about employing them; rather it was a continuation of a policy, perhaps unintentionally encouraged for several years. Once hired, the Irish worked in a relatively few rooms and in the lowest-paying jobs.[41] Irish workers returned to their families in the paddy camps at night, shunning boardinghouses with the tacit approval of all parties.[42] Still, the type of Irish worker to be employed was of some concern. As one Yankee operative warned her co-workers: "As long as our mills are wrought by operatives from the country, or from the common schools of Lowell, they will not be filled with a depressed and ignorant class."[43]

Viewed from this perspective, the opening of the mills to Lowell's Irish was gradual and reflected a need for extra hands to increased production. The pattern of employment which governed the first years of Irish mill employment was similar to that faced by unskilled Irish workers on Lowell's construction projects. In both cases, the Irish worked together with little chance of promotion into skilled positions. Their presence in the mills, therefore, must have seemed fairly traditional based upon the history of their employment in Lowell. The most distinctive feature of Irish mill employment, especially to the Irish, was the hiring of Irish women, particularly young Irish women educated in the public schools. These women, of course, were the most Americanized Irish, the best examples of accommodation policy, and the most acceptable to Yankee operatives.

The 1850 federal census, the first to report women's occupations, supports the assertion that unmarried young adult Irish women were the largest group among Irish mill workers and demonstrates that married

Irish women worked in far fewer numbers.[44] For single adult women, we do have some idea of the range of occupations in which they were employed. From May, 1844, to May, 1846, Father McDermott recorded the occupations of both adults when he performed marriages at St. Patrick's. Of the ninety women recorded by McDermott, seventy-one listed their occupations. Of these seventy-one women, only ten (14 percent) were servants. Of the remaining 86 percent, an overwhelming majority were employed by the mills.[45]

When these figures are compared with the percentages of female servants in other cities with large Irish populations, an interesting pattern emerges. The percentage of Lowell's Irish women working as servants was lower than in Boston, Poughkeepsie, Milwaukee, or London in the mid-nineteenth century.[46] It appears that while Lowell had a middle class who could afford some servants, it lacked a wealthy upper class who might employ large numbers of them. As a result, there were historically fewer Irish servants in Lowell than elsewhere. As the mills opened another employment option to Irish women, the percentage of Irish servants decreased still further, to only 3.7 percent of Lowell's adult Irish women, although some servants undoubtedly lived with those who employed them instead of in Irish neighborhoods.[47] Even with their addition, however, the percentage of servants among Irish women was small. The limited employment opportunities for Irish women in Lowell in traditional occupations might well have encouraged the Associates to consider them for employment.

Dublin's analysis of immigrants in the mills suggests that mill agents turned quickly to Irish women to meet their labor needs. He noted that the Irish were 8 percent of the Hamilton's work force in 1844. Since the decisions reached by the Hamilton's agents reflected the approach adopted at all of Lowell's mills, we can assume that the percentage of Irish in Lowell's mills was somewhere near the percentage of those employed at the Hamilton. If such is the case, there were about six hundred Irish employed in the mills in 1845 in a total work force of seven thousand workers.[48] At that time, Lowell's Irish population was about five thousand, indicating that perhaps as much as 12 percent of Lowell's Irish worked in the mills. If we exclude young children, the elderly, married women not working, and such, the percentage of Irish working there was considerably higher.

The opening of the mills to them had a major impact upon the Irish, especially upon the family. The change in the pattern of employment from

Yankee farm women to Irish immigrants indicated a shift from an individual to a family wage economy. The earnings of Irish mill workers, especially Irish daughters, were crucial to family income. Avoiding the boarding-houses, they lived at home and contributed their pay to family income, important in a situation where a father provided only 60 percent of a family's support.[49] Such contributions were common and reflected Irish traditions of family support which had been carried to America. Their brothers also contributed, although most young Irishmen in the 1840s continued to work as unskilled laborers.[50] Word of the range of opportunities available in Lowell spread quickly in letters sent with remittances to relatives and friends elsewhere.

In the mills, Irish women used family and neighborhood ties to obtain work and to ease their way into the world beyond the paddy camps. Harriet Hanson Robinson, who worked in Lowell's mills from 1836 to 1848, offered the best account of the movement of the first Irish women into the mills. She noted that "before 1840, the foreign element in the factory population was almost an unknown quantity."[51] The first foreign employees were Englishmen hired as skilled craftsmen for the dyeworks, but the Irish followed quickly. Robinson noted that the first Irish women worked as scrubbers and waste pickers. In her description of Irish mill workers, Robinson combined the same curiosity which surfaced in other early accounts by Yankee mill women of the Irish in Lowell, and which reinforced the gulf between Yankee and Irish cultures, and an acknowledgment that the Irish soon adapted to American ways: "They were always good-natured, and when excited used their own language. . . . These women, as a rule, wore peasant cloaks, red or blue, made with hoods and several capes, in summer (as they told their children), to 'kape cool,' and in winter to 'kape warrum.' They earned good wages, and they and their children, especially the children, very soon adapted themselves to their changed condition of life, and became 'as good as anybody.'"[52]

Once the first Irish women were employed in the mills, more followed in an unorganized migration in which the Irish obtained jobs individually and without active solicitation by the mills. They applied when vacancies occurred or when the mills hired extra help. With the high turnover rate and expanding production, entry was fairly easy. Many Irish women found employment through an extensive network of relatives and friends who recommended them to particular overseers: "First, whenever any vacancies occur or more help is, for any reason, required, every foreign operative has a sister, cousin or friend, standing nearby, whom she wishes to introduce. No people are more clannish, none will work harder for their particular friends than the Irish."[53]

This network of relatives and friends increased the percentage of Irish in the overall work force. At the Hamilton, for example, one-third of the employees were Irish in 1850, up from the 8 percent employed there in 1845. By the late 1840s, then, employment practices had shifted. With expanded production, moreover, the number of workers increased and the mills employed over ten thousand workers.[54] In addition, a business recession in 1848 threw hundreds of operatives out of work and many Yankee women returned home. When the mills revived, labor was in some demand and, in that "Irish girls already form[ed] a large proportion of the female mill laborers," the corporations turned to a "local, dependent class" who worked for whatever terms they could get.[55]

In 1851, the Prescott Corporation institutionalized the practice of employing Irish women when it not only abandoned recruitment of Yankee women but also hired Irish women permanently to replace Yankee operatives "who were visiting their friends at home during the warm season." The Prescott's agents justified their decision on the assumption that "the Irish girls, having no friends to visit in this country, would remain at their posts at all seasons."[56] Their decision sparked enormous criticism because, whereas before Irish women had filled vacancies or moved into newly created jobs, Lowell's mill agents now turned their back on the labor system which had made Lowell famous by substituting Irish women permanently for Yankee operatives.[57]

By the late 1840s, the pre-Famine Irish who had obtained mill employment were joined by Famine emigrants. Responding to the hopelessness of their situation in Ireland, they fled to cities like Lowell. It was the steady flow of these immigrants which provided a constant, almost inexhaustible source of labor. By 1850, there were twice as many children baptized in Lowell's parishes as had been baptized in 1844.[58] By the 1855 state census, the foreign-born Irish living in Lowell exceeded the total number of Irish, whether foreign, naturalized, or American-born, who had lived in Lowell in 1843.[59] Although there were small numbers of other immigrant groups living there, especially English, Scotch, and French Canadian, to be "immigrant" and working in the mills meant to be Irish. (The next great wave of emigrants awaited the close of the Civil War when train routes linking Boston and Montreal provided an avenue for French Canadians.)[60]

The shift to the employment of Irish immigrants had an effect on Lowell which extended far beyond the mills. More than anything else in Lowell's history, the extensive use of Irish labor called into question the generation-old pattern of accommodation between Irish and Yankees. In 1845, Rev. Henry A. Miles, a Protestant minister who served the Yankee middle class, wrote of his vision of Lowell, in a book significantly titled *Lowell As It was and As It Is:*

> The great experiment of Lowell is an experiment of another kind: it is an experiment whether we can preserve here a pure and virtuous population; whether there are no causes secretly at work, and to be developed in the course of thirty or forty years, to lower our standard and to sink our character; whether we can run a career of half a century free from the corrupting and debasing influences which have almost universally marked manufacturing cities abroad. And a great experiment it is. We are deciding the question, not for ourselves alone, but for numerous other places around us—indeed, for New England itself.[61]

There had always been limits to how far either side was willing to go regarding accommodation. It must be stressed that the Irish in Lowell, like the Irish throughout New England, experienced pronounced segregation. The Irish lived apart from Lowell's Yankees and the opportunities available to them in employment, housing, secondary education, and health care were limited. Almost no Irish attended coeducational Lowell High School, for instance, and the Corporation Hospital treated only mill operatives.[62] Despite these limitations, however, a level of opportunity existed in an air of social tolerance. In some cases, particularly housing, such segregation was not even perceived as a limitation, as Lowell's Irish derived economic, social, and psychological benefits from their close association. In addition, there were actually two groups of Irish in Lowell, a distinction made even more obvious when Famine emigrants poured into the city. The first was a highly transient population of unskilled laborers, many with families, for whom Lowell was not a permanent home. They maintained many of their clannish associations and lived precariously in the rented flats of speculators' tenements before moving on. The second, a much smaller group, was the resident Irish who included the successful middle class and those whose jobs in Lowell were permanent. Increasingly, this group included Irish mill workers and their families. It was to this group that Lowell's officials had always directed such policies as accommodation.

Unfortunately, the internecine warfare which marked relations between these Irish destroyed the tradition of compromise which had characterized the mid-1830s. Additionally, it showed that the Irish middle class was in disarray at precisely the moment at which the Irish made their first inroads into the mills. The inability of the Irish middle class to represent Irish interests, the massive influx of Famine emigrants who compared unfavorably with the pre-Famine Irish population of Lowell, together with shifting employment patterns, explain the change in policy by Lowell's officials in their relationship with the Irish. By 1850 Lowell had changed from a Yankee mill village into an immigrant industrial city. With this change, the policies of Lowell's officials became more repressive, structured, and rigid.

There had always been some animosity toward the Irish in Lowell. Indigent Yankee day laborers attacked the still unfinished St. Patrick's Church in 1831 to protest the employment of Irish laborers, for example, and various Protestant sects warned of dangers like "secret hiding places" inside St. Patrick's Church.[63] On the whole, however, the spirit of accommodation, tinged with a high level of curiosity, marked relations between Yankees and Irish in Lowell for the first twenty years. Yankees made a sharp distinction between worthy and unworthy poor in dealing with the Irish, particularly in Yankee-backed charitable institutions, but that distinction was shared by the resident Irish. According to their mutual definition, worthy poor received assistance because their need was temporary and because such assistance would allow them once again to rely upon themselves, whereas unworthy poor were incorrigible. Significantly, Lowell's Irish initially were worthy poor. For example, when the slow development of St. Patrick's parish inhibited the establishment of separate Catholic assistance societies, no Yankee critic spoke of the failure of Catholics to take care of their own.[64] In fact, Lowell's Yankees joined the Irish in support of broader Irish concerns which transcended events in Lowell, such as Repeal and Famine relief.

Apart from philosophical or psychological concerns, the growth of Lowell around 1840 had diminished the physical distance which separated the paddy camps from the mill village. By the Panic of 1837, the Lawrence, Suffolk, and Tremont mills had opened to the north of the paddy camps. To their west lay the attractive Yankee residential neighborhood to which Kirk Boott relocated his home. To the east, a small commercial district arose between the Hamilton, Appleton, and Lowell mills and the Boott, Massachusetts, and Merrimack mills along the river. In 1844, tolls were abolished and "suburban" neighborhoods like Centralville in Dracut grew steadily.[65] With the expansion of the Yankee mill village and the appearance of residential neighborhoods around it, the original paddy camps were encircled by a developing network of mills, boardinghouses, businesses, and residential neighborhoods. Within the paddy camps, the lines between the original camps blurred, particularly after the construction of St. Patrick's Church and when Locks and Canals permitted land sales around the church and along Lowell Street. By 1845, the old Fardowner Camp had become a congested tenement district.

By then, the paddy camps were more commonly referred to as the Acre. As the Acre filled in, it also expanded, particularly to the south. The purchase of property declined throughout the Acre in the Panic of 1837 but, in the early 1840s, land sales to Irish rose again. By then, the *Paddy Camps Lands* case was settled and the area around Cork (Marion) Street enjoyed rapid growth. Even Father McDermott purchased property for himself in the region.[66] In this area, a cluster of small, gable-roofed detached workers' cottages of wood construction predominated.[67] In addition, Locks and Canals authorized a huge land sale of unwanted lots throughout the Acre. After the land sale, Irish speculators Stephen Castles, Hugh Cummiskey, Owen Donohoe, and Hugh McEvoy were the largest landowners.[68]

While the Acre expanded, Lowell's Irish also moved into other areas. By 1845, a large Irish neighborhood developed on Chapel Hill in the outskirts of Lowell but in the vicinity of the Hamilton and Appleton mills. In 1842, Fenwick dedicated St. Peter's parish to accommodate the Chapel Hill Irish, many of whom were originally opponents of Father McDermott and claimed membership in the Benevolent Society. Like the Acre, Chapel Hill was attractive to Famine immigrants and the parish grew rapidly. Between these neighborhoods, especially in Lowell's commercial district along Market and Middle streets, many Irish also lived in tenements. In his study of family structure among the Irish of nineteenth-century Lowell, A. Gibbs Mitchell confirmed the existence of Irish here and throughout Lowell. By 1845, the settlement pattern reflected heavy concentrations of Irish in the Acre and on Chapel Hill with the remaining Irish scattered throughout the city.[69] This was hardly surprising since, despite Lowell's considerable growth, it remained a small city physically. The enormous wave of Famine immigrants, when concentrated in a congested city, much of which had been already given over to mills and boardinghouses, made the Yankees feel that the Irish were everywhere.

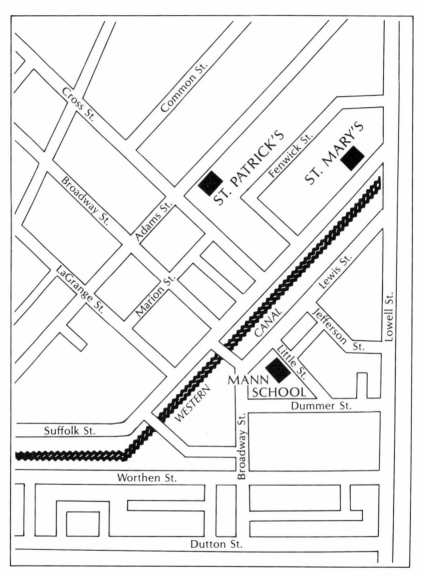

The Acre in the 1850s. Plan of the City of Lowell, Massachusetts, 1850.
By Craig Roscoe and Marie Rose Roderique.

One nativist critic noted: "When we see respectable and wealthy American families driven out from tenements that they had erected for their own use, and convenience, rather than endure the nuisances created by their Irish neighbors; when we see whole streets deserted by their former inhabitants and filled with a low class of foreigners before whose doors are presented constant and disgusting exhibitions of their filthy habits, . . . we wonder that by word or act they should countenance the policy [unrestricted immigration] of which our American citizens so justly complain."[70]

Initially, the policies of Lowell's officials regarding their duty to Lowell's Irish citizens were designed either to incorporate the Acre physically into Lowell or to ameliorate conditions caused by overcrowding, often through the improvement of city services. In the 1830s Lowell's officials tied Lowell Street into the city sewer system and laid out sidewalks along it as part of a general plan to upgrade the neighborhood.[71] In the 1840s, they set aside North Common behind St. Patrick's Church and South Common near St. Peter's Church to alleviate congestion near the heart of both Irish neighborhoods.[72] By 1850, Lowell's officials had paved Lowell Street and laid gas lines into the Acre. They also established a professional fire department, which prevented the use of the rowdy volunteer companies among rival Irish gangs which characterized other cities, particularly Philadelphia and New York.[73] The Irish welcomed most of these improvements, some of which provided employment during construction and operation.

By 1850, the spirit of compromise which had guided the pattern of accommodation between the Yankees and Irish had passed. Lowell's officials criticized the Irish for the scope of their migration into Lowell and for the squalor in which they lived. Horatio Wood, a colorful Protestant minister who ran the nondenominational "Ministry-at-Large" which directed assistance to foreign needy, was especially critical. He charged that New England's seaports had sent Irish paupers to Lowell deliberately to "shift the burthen" by deceiving Irish into believing that Lowell was what its promoters had pictured it to be. He noted that Lowell's officials provided relief to two to three hundred more Irishmen than could be employed locally and recommended "withholding from them charity . . . to scatter them away from Lowell."[74] The Lowell *Advertiser* echoed Wood's concerns, warning that "the Irish are here in Lowell, and they are here in great numbers too . . . and we cannot avoid their being here."[75]

As the Famine emigrants moved into Lowell, they taxed housing severely and conditions deteriorated. Wood wrote of his impressions to Dr. Josiah Curtis in 1848:

> Their rooms are generally not ventilated at all. From six to ten persons frequently sleep in a single room, and sometimes in one bed. This is particularly the case among our foreign population. The air is stagnant, soon becomes poisonous and exceedingly offensive. Often every room in the house has from four to twelve inmates, in a narrow lane, perhaps, crowded close with tenements; the little uncovered ground the receptacle of dirty water, rubbish, and corrupt vegetable matter; and numerous outhouses of necessity near to the windows, sometimes filling every room, and the whole neighborhood with noxious exhalations. Cellars are occupied in very damp locations, where water frequently stands in drops on the walls, and in wet times can be wrung from the sheets of the bed. Two-thirds of the inhabitants of the city, probably, would not deposit their vegetables where not a few families reside, and pay from $1.50 to $2.00 per month for rent. There are many cellars underground, with only one or two half-windows, and a few panes of glass, where the poor are urged to locate themselves, at a cheaper rate—urged to gratify avarice, though they take to themselves fevers, rheumatisms, and consumption. I know of one case, where in two connected rooms in a cellar—and lighted by only three small panes of green glass covered with cobwebs, and where, on entering, I stumbled over the beds, because I could not see them—four families, amounting to twenty-two souls, were living![76]

Curtis responded that housing throughout Lowell demanded attention and that the "worst district, the 'Acre,' specifically which, inhabited exclusively by foreigners, beggars all description." He also noted that "sewage and drainage are in a very imperfect condition in many parts of the city, and many lanes and alleys are without either; the house slops and other refuse remaining on the surface, especially in wet weather."[77]

The poor housing and sanitation characteristic of the Acre contributed to a very different perception of Lowell's Irish. Until the Famine migration, they had been viewed as children who needed only to be taught table manners. Once the Irish had been elevated from their abject state, so the theory went, they would be productive, temperate, and free. The introduction of what Reverend Wood called "swarms of Irish poor," however, precipitated a new division of Lowell's Irish into two classes, at least in the minds of Yankees like Wood. The first were the pre-Famine Irish who had lived in Lowell for some time, educating their children in the public schools and appreciating order, cleanliness, and respectability on a Yankee scale. The second were "Irish paupers," as many of Lowell's Yankees referred to them, who knew nothing of Lowell's promise but who were what Wood called "the causes of poverty and trouble."[78]

These groups were identified in a series of exchanges among the editors of *Vox Populi*, Lowell *Advertiser*, Lowell *Courier*, *American Citizen*, and Boston *Pilot*. Whatever each editor's perspective, all agreed that two very different types of Irish lived in Lowell. The first group was few in number but of sound quality: "'Tis true there are in Lowell some few Irish families that would feel themselves dishonored by being classed with the great mass. . . . We are ready and happy to say . . . that these are families of intelligent, industrious, neat and worthy Irish among us, and such we respect and honor. They are worthy of respect, and none would object to their sons or daughters as associates in the mills or elsewhere."[79] The *Vox Populi* noted that they also existed "in other cities" and it was not "against the patronage which such receive that we protest."[80]

All editors except Patrick Donohoe at the *Pilot* complained, however, about "Irish paupers" who lived in "an *odiferous* region" like "the Acre." Yankee "repugnance to coming in close contact, or living in close proximity, with such a class of human beings" seemed "natural and unavoidable."[81] The *Vox Populi* argued "'tis against these ignorant and filthy thousands who come up among us like the frogs of Egypt, around whose homes gather the filth and stench that invited a pestilence" that it protested.[82] The nativist *American Citizen* picked up the debate three years later when it concluded that "the mass of Irish are just what we have called them, stupid, negligent, and abominably filthy."[83] While it was not surprising that Famine immigrants should be criticized so severely at the height of their presence in Lowell, it was unusual that a sharp division should be scrupulously noted between worthy and unworthy Irish. That worthiness was based upon length of residence is even more striking, particularly in that by this definition some Irish made acceptable mill workers while others did not. By 1850, the Irish presence in Lowell had become less of a curiosity and more of a threat.

These then were the battle lines, with the Irish put into two categories, the "few" and the "masses," almost bystanders and sometimes victims in what would follow. The Irish in Lowell were visible symbols of deteriorating standards affecting employment, housing, education, and health. The Irish, at least most of them, were the causes of "crime and trouble." Lowell's officials determined to arrest this decay if they could and control it if they could not. These officials, it must be remembered, were not mill agents but an array of ministers, lawyers, and doctors. A few still believed in the vision of Lowell but most were appalled at the speed of Lowell's decline. They took the traditional perception of "worthy" and "unworthy" poor and applied it to Lowell's Irish and their poverty culture. For the first time, most of Lowell's resident Irish did not meet Yankee standards and would never make useful and productive citizens. For them, Lowell's officials developed a series of institutions to control their excesses. Still, the Irish were not to blame if they caused Lowell's troubles. The root of these troubles lay in the employment practices of the Boston Associates but, in the early 1850s, it was the Irish who would answer for them.

CHAPTER 6

The Impact of Famine Emigrants
1845–55

By 1850 the position of the Irish in Lowell had changed dramatically. The pre-Famine Irish were joined by Famine emigrants who descended upon Lowell in great numbers, discovering with their arrival that the mills had opened to them. The large-scale employment of Irish in Lowell's mills changed the nature of their presence in Lowell, destroying older patterns of accommodation while encouraging the growth of new rules of conduct which would govern their presence there. The paddy camps, now commonly called "the Acre," had become a teeming Irish tenement district, new Irish neighborhoods had formed, and the Irish could be found throughout Lowell. For the first time, the Irish dominated the look, feel, and smell of Lowell. To many Yankees, the startling increase in the numbers of Irish threatened to turn the city into what Patrick Donohoe at the Boston *Pilot* called "Catholic" Lowell.[1]

Obviously, the most immediate impact of the Famine emigrants was on the existing pre-Famine Irish community, especially upon class and family structure. For the Irish middle class, the decade of the 1850s was a period of prosperity. By 1860, for example, Hugh Cummiskey listed himself as a "gentleman," with $6,000 in real estate and $1,000 in personal property. Stephen Castles, a neighbor and real estate speculator living on Lowell Street, acquired extensive holdings on Lowell, Lewis, and Jefferson streets. Hugh McEvoy, an Irish tailor who catered to Yankee tastes, bought property on Suffolk, Thorndike, and Hanover streets before moving his family to the north bank of the Merrimack River to newly annexed, largely rural and Yankee Centralville. Owen M. Donohoe, who ran the Exchange Coffee House and was once a city sheriff, was less successful but still claimed a $400 personal estate.[2] For these Irish, the arrival of Famine emigrants had meant increased business and new opportunities, especially in real estate, although none achieved great wealth. Still, among those household heads who remained in the Acre throughout the

1850s, there was a 25 percent increase in those reporting real estate holdings. The wealthiest among them continued to be retail merchants, tailors, traders, and real estate speculators, or much of the same group who had been successful since the 1830s.[3] These were the individuals, of course, most likely to remain in Lowell throughout the 1850s. The middle class was still a small group; in fact, only 13.3 percent of the 1850 Acre Irish could be traced directly to the same neighborhood in the 1860 census.[4] It is also significant that the most successful Irish were almost never found in the mills.

While the Irish middle class enjoyed this prosperity, it did not extend much beyond them. There were only a few Irish taxpayers on the assessor's lists in the 1850s and, among those who were listed, none were laborers or mill hands. Despite their absence on the tax lists, however, it is wrong to assume that conditions among the Irish did not improve somewhat relative to their standing in the 1830s. Among Irish laborers, pay scales remained fairly constant, fluctuating slightly upward from 83.3 cents per day in 1830 to as high as $1.00 per day in 1860. These scales were adopted throughout Lowell and applied at Locks and Canals, with the Boston and Lowell Railroad, and at the Lowell Gas Company.[5] At the same time, the opportunity for Irish laborers traditionally employed in Lowell decreased, although it improved in other rapidly developing centers like Lawrence. A number of Irish laborers left in the business recession of 1848 or with the opening of the California gold fields, when Lowell's population dropped by about fifteen hundred.[6] Although it is impossible to estimate how many Irish laborers moved elsewhere, it is likely that many left families behind, particularly with the growing opportunity for the employment of their children in the mills.

An examination of Irish households in 1850 suggests an interesting relationship among employment, family structure, and migration patterns. Although the number of nuclear families was lower in Lowell (62.4 percent) than in London, Milwaukee, or Hamilton, in 1850 83 percent of all Irish households in the Acre had at least one child living with them.[7] Lowell was a logical choice for young adult Irish emigrating to America, especially as word of mill employment spread along emigration routes. Lowell's Irish made excellent use of the prepaid passage ticket, sending $12,000 in passage money to Ireland in 1866.[8] For those young adults already living in Lowell, mill employment was an opportunity, especially to contribute income vital to family support. Whereas sons might be expected to contribute their laborers' earnings, for the first time daughters found in the mills an employer of a scale comparable to that which their brothers historically enjoyed with such firms as Locks and Canals. A number of factors in Lowell, then, including economic growth, the existence of a large Irish community linked by informal but effective kinship networks to news of vacancies in the mills, a transportation system linking Lowell to Boston and New York, traditional patterns of a family wage economy, and a history of Yankee tolerance tied family structure to employment and migration patterns in identifying Lowell as an especially attractive Irish settlement. Together these factors also made the family an important institution among the Irish in Lowell.

Although the percentage of nuclear families among Lowell's Irish was lower than in other cities, the nuclear family was the most common type of household. For these Irish, the opening of the mills reinforced the dominance of a family wage economy. Dublin demonstrated that Lowell's Irish did not enter into Yankee boardinghouses, while A. Gibbs Mitchell indicated that the Irish did not form separate boardinghouses in large numbers in Irish neighborhoods. Instead they lived with families before marriage and generally formed separate households when they married.[9] Widows were the most likely to take in boarders, contributing to family income as housekeepers while their children sought mill employment. (This practice among widows upheld the traditional pattern among Lowell's Irish, in which women did not work outside the home once they had children.)[10] This reinforced traditional Irish family structure.

Thus as an Irish father's ability to provide for his family decreased in Lowell, except among those laborers who now worked at unskilled occupations in the mills, his declining opportunities had less dramatic effect upon his family, who now depended increasingly upon the wages of adult children living at home. By combining his income with that of his children, an Irish father often improved his family's circumstances, especially if the employment of his children in the mills was steady. In this sense, the father maintained a kind of influence, although that influence reflected traditional emotional and psychological rather than economic ties:

> In Ireland every son was "a boy" and every daughter "a girl" till he or she was married. . . . they considered themselves subject to their parents till they became parents themselves. . . . In America, in consequence of the newness of the soil, and the demands of enterprise, the boys were men at sixteen. . . . They all work for themselves, and pay their own board. They either live with the boss "governor," or "old man," or elsewhere, as they pleased. They may have

respect,—they must have some natural deference for parents, but the abstract Irish reverence for old age is not yet naturalized in America. . . . Over half a dozen of these keen, hard, worldly young Yankees, an Irish father is to preside.[11]

Since the shift in employment patterns affected primarily wages, it strengthened the family as an institution, changing economic but not emotional relationships among family members.

As Hasia Diner has shown, the cornerstone of an Irish family was "herself." An Irish mother managed family income and, on payday, children turned their wages over to her. Lowell-born Cardinal O'Connell of Boston noted upon return to his mother's Irish birthplace that "the place where my mother was born is a sacred place to me." Diner also noted that an Irish mother, faced with high rates of male mental illness, desertion, alcoholism, and periodic unemployment, became the center of decision-making as well as of respect. She provided continuity within family life and held the family together. An Irish mother was often an opinionated and determined woman, controlling her children not only through love but also by guilt. By contrast, an Irish father emerged as a much weaker and more ill-defined figure who commanded parental respect from his children but not much else.[12]

Of the 499 male household heads who listed their occupations in 1850, 64 percent were laborers, including those who worked in the mills. About 6 percent held skilled jobs such as dyers, printers, operatives, and engineers. The remainder worked either in construction or in the service occupations which traditionally belonged to the Irish middle class.[13] Among Irish women, however, the pattern was quite different. As shown in the 1860 census, the mills were three times more likely to employ Irish women than men. The employment of Irish women was also important for its composition. While a few married Irish women, usually childless or recently married, worked in the mills, most married women did not, suggesting, as in Milwaukee, that marriage was a way out of the mill. Among Irish women in the mills the median age was twenty-one. Since most Irish women who married did so in their mid-twenties and remained at home until then, these Irish daughters provided an important source of income.[14] Many of these daughters entered the mills in compliance with the certificate statute, indicating exposure to Lowell's public schools. The link between public schools and the employment of their children in the mills was not lost upon Irish parents. While Irish parents used public schools in this fashion, the decision of young Irish women not to live in Yankee-operated boardinghouses goes well beyond the segregation that Dublin suggested.[15] The impetus to this segregation came from within the Irish family, to whom boardinghouses would have been an intrusion upon Irish family structure, especially family income and traditional patterns of authority.

The relationship among various members of an Irish family was also strengthened by external forces. Upon arriving in Lowell, immigrants used kinship connections to ease their transition to their new environment. While Lowell's Irish did not take in large numbers of boarders, new arrivals did live temporarily with relatives or, more likely, nearby.[16] Harriet Hanson Robinson, among others, commented on the value of kinship ties in the employment of new Irish mill hands where mill workers introduced their relatives to foremen as new jobs opened up.[17] This pattern, in which individual Irish or small groups of them were employed as vacancies occurred, was the most common until the mills turned to the employment of large numbers of Irish as permanent replacements for Yankee operatives in the late 1840s.[18] Once again, the relatively small size of Lowell and its concentration upon textiles made this approach particularly successful. This kinship network, based in the Irish family, emphasized the importance of strong family ties to successful employment in the mills.

By 1850 the sharp increase in Famine emigrants not only affected class and family structure but also disrupted the delicately balanced relationship between Lowell's Irish and Yankees and introduced real problems affecting health, education, and crime. When they observed "swarms of Irish poor" in the mills, Lowell's resident Yankees concluded that the Boston Associates had sacrificed Lowell to profit. In the process, the Famine emigrants who brought their poverty with them threatened to undermine standards in the mills and, more generally, to engulf Lowell. Despite the 1848 business downturn, Lowell's mills were general profitable, especially after the passage of a higher tariff in 1844. Still, in the midst of an expanding prosperity fueled by the increase in production, Lowell was a city in decline, especially when measured by the rigorous standards established by the Boston Associates at its incorporation regarding Lowell's physical appearance and its moral environment. While no one ever suggested seriously that Lowell was an industrial utopia, many in Lowell believed that the "Lowell Experiment" was far superior to those efforts to industrialize which had preceded it.

Among this group were most of Lowell's resident Yankee middle class, for whom Lowell's decline was a rude awakening, particularly since it seemed to occur almost overnight. By 1850 the signs were everywhere. Like Boston, Lowell had been a healthy city before 1845. Lowell's officials had recognized early that unsanitary conditions bred disease. They argued for the construction of a sewer system in 1837, for example, claiming that "the cleanliness of the city and the health and comfort of the inhabitants cannot be secured without them." They met with limited success.[19] The major justification for the sewer projects was that the same water was also used for bathing and drinking by many of Lowell's citizens, including the Irish. Finally, in 1851 James B. Francis ordered all the drains emptying into Lowell's canals closed.[20] Shortly after Francis's order, city officials began to pump Lowell's water directly from the Merrimack River, providing a slightly cleaner drinking supply, but they constructed a filtration system only in 1870.[21] These conditions generated particularly high rates of tuberculosis, dysentery, cholera, and typhus, especially since some of Lowell's residents continued to take water from its polluted power canals throughout the period.

As expected, tuberculosis caused the most disease-related deaths in Lowell. It killed 25 percent more of Lowell's residents than the next major killer, dysentery, between 1841 and 1860.[22] There were two major reasons for the prevalence of tuberculosis. First, the lint-laden air at the mills was unwholesome, especially because the mill windows remained shut to achieve the desired humidity in the production process. The mill workers breathed this air during the long work hours and then transmitted disease in the congested boardinghouses and tenements to which they returned at night. Second, the Irish suffered chronically high rates of tuberculosis in Ireland and carried the disease with them to Lowell. In 1842, for example, tuberculosis was responsible for about one-third of the disease-related deaths among both Lowell's Irish and the general population, although the Irish comprised only about 16 percent of the citywide deaths from tuberculosis. By 1849, tuberculosis caused about 43 percent of Lowell's disease-related deaths. Significantly, about one-half of these deaths were among Irish and tuberculosis accounted for about one-half of the total disease-related deaths among them.[23]

In addition, Irish deaths from tuberculosis increased markedly after 1845, when Famine emigrants reached Lowell and as many of them found employment in the mills. After 1845, the Irish increased rapidly among Lowell's mill workers and the unhealthy working conditions aggravated the already chronically high tuberculosis rate among them. Tuberculosis rates dropped off sharply, for example, in 1848, when hundreds were dismissed from the mills in a business downturn. In the 1850s, however, the Irish were well entrenched in Lowell's mills and tuberculosis rates remained high throughout the period.[24] The high tuberculosis rates, nurtured by conditions in the mills and the filth within Irish neighborhoods, suggested that the arrival of Famine emigrants had made Lowell a less healthy place in which to live. This belief was substantiated further by outbreaks of dysentery, cholera, and typhus.

Dysentery was particularly troublesome for the Irish who lived in overcrowded tenement districts. Much of the problem stemmed from Lowell's use of the Merrimack River for its drinking water, a practice encouraged by the belief that the Merrimack cleansed itself of impurities from upstream cities as it traveled south. Outbreaks of dysentery were especially irksome in that it had been a relatively minor health problem before 1847 and cases which were reported before then had come almost invariably from Irish neighborhoods. After 1846, however, dysentery affected residents throughout Lowell, who undoubtedly viewed it as an Irish malady which had infected them. In 1847, for example, the Irish accounted for only about one-third of all dysentery-related deaths, whereas five years earlier all dysentery-related deaths except one had been Irish.[25] It is small wonder that Lowell's Yankees complained about the personal habits of the Irish with whom they worked and lived.

At the same time, Lowell shared epidemics which swept through seaports such as Philadelphia, Boston, and New York. In 1847, Lowell experienced an outbreak of low-grade typhus which took seventy-five lives, fifty-two of them Irish. The typhus epidemic spread throughout Lowell with the flood of Famine emigrants and was referred to more generally as "ship fever," a term which fixed blame effectively upon them.[26] Two years later, Lowell suffered a serious cholera epidemic which claimed seventy-three lives, most of them adult Irish. Most of these deaths occurred in the summer of 1849. By September, of the seventy-one cholera victims fifty-one were interred "in the Catholic burying ground."[27] The percentage of cholera-related deaths during the 1849 epidemic agrees with Handlin's findings for Boston. In both cities, about three-quarters of the cholera deaths were Irish, indicating that it mattered little whether infected Irish lived in debarkation ports or in inland manufacturing cities.[28] The high mobility of Famine immigrants in the late 1840s ensured that the epidemic spread throughout New England.

The accuracy of the inhabitants' perception that Lowell was becoming less healthy and that the responsibility for the decline lay with the newly arrived Famine emigrants can be shown by a comparison of death rates per thousand in specific diseases among the Acre Irish and the general population of Lowell. In 1843, before the Famine emigrants arrived, the deaths per thousand for Lowell's Irish and the general population coincided roughly for consumption, which was the most common disease in Lowell in the 1840s. In fact, the Irish rate for a disease like typhus was lower than that of the general population. By 1849, however, the health of the Acre Irish had decreased substantially in comparison with the rest of Lowell. Consumption killed 4.34 persons per thousand in the general population, while it took 5.6 lives per thousand among the Acre Irish. The death rate for dysentery was also higher among the Irish, rising to 3.1 per thousand versus 2.5 per thousand in the general population. The rates for typhus were roughly comparable in 1849, but the Irish had been responsible for the 1846 "ship fever" epidemic and the memory of their role in the outbreak remained strong.[29] The Irish were less healthy than they had been six years earlier and less healthy than the general population. They had also caused a statistical decline in the health of the general population of Lowell.

By 1850, it was clear that Lowell had become an unhealthy city in which to live. If it was no more unhealthy than Boston, that knowledge offered little comfort to Lowell's residents, who believed that Lowell should be better. As late as 1841, Dr. Elisha Bartlett, who was serving as Lowell's mayor, wrote an elaborate defense of factory conditions in which he strove to dispel the unhealthy image which besmirched Lowell's reputation by comparing its death rate with those of other New England cities.[30] Within several years, the Famine emigrants made such a defense impossible, as Lowell suffered from high tuberculosis rates and waves of dysentery, typhus, and cholera epidemics. Since the worst effects of these outbreaks were felt in Irish neighborhoods, it was easy to place blame upon them. City officials had made some progress with the construction of a water system, in sewerage and drainage, and in the expansion of charitable agencies, but this progress failed to offset the feeling among many in Lowell that the city had been overwhelmed by problems on a scale unimagined only a decade earlier.[31]

Just as Lowell was less healthy, it was also less safe, and the rise in crime could be traced directly to the increase in Irish immigrants. This time, however, Lowell's officials could take steps to ensure community stability. For the first twenty years, they had largely ignored paddy camp disorders and concentrated instead upon street improvements, sanitation, outdoor relief, and education. The Irish were left to settle differences among themselves. Until the late 1830s, moreover, the paddy camps and the mill village were continents apart culturally, as well as separated physically, even if technically joined by Lowell's incorporation as a town. In addition, Lowell, like most American cities, had no modern police force but relied upon an ineffective system of constables and night watchmen. Even after Yankee Lowell physically engulfed the paddy camps and a few Irish moved into Yankee neighborhoods, it was assumed that there were good and bad Irish much as there were worthy and unworthy poor.[32] It was also assumed that the good Irish needed only to be shown how to be productive citizens and their rowdy clan outbreaks would fall before Yankee order and respectability.

Of course, the Irish middle class led the way by adopting these standards. It was Hugh Cummiskey, after all, who requested constable patrols around St. Patrick's Church to diminish squabbling among the Irish on Sundays. They also openly embraced movements such as temperance, a stand against crime since Irish crimes were often alcohol-related.[33] All were dangerous because they demonstrated that Lowell's Irish had carried unsavory features of their poverty with them to America. While it was impossible to correct these tendencies among many adult Irish, city officials saw the real danger in the effect that these tendencies might have upon Irish children and the long-term threat to the moral environment of Lowell. In this sense, the spirit of the original education agreement was the same one which prompted Lowell's officials to turn increasingly to institutionalization to control the Irish threat to peace and stability and also to Lowell's endangered reputation.

The need for this effort was obvious. Before the Famine migration, the moral environment of Lowell precluded much serious crime. Irish squabbling was a persistent nuisance and travel along Lowell Street through the heart of the Acre was ill-advised but these problems were relatively confined. The most serious disturbance occurred during an Irish riot in September, 1849, at the end of the cholera epidemic. On 6 September, fighting broke out between the Acre "Corkonians" and the Lowell Street "Connaught men" over unspecified "old national prejudices." The fighting continued sporadically until Sunday evening, 9 September, when hundreds gathered on either side of the Western Canal, which historically separated the old paddy camps. At the height of the disturbance, Irish women were seen "working like beavers, lugging bricks and stones in their aprons for the contending parties."[34] The mayor called out the city guard, who quelled the riot, and Lowell's mill agents supported its elected officials by dismissing any Irishman at the mills, Lowell Gas Company, or Boston and Lowell Railroad who had been involved in the incident.[35] After the riot, Lowell's officials placed the blame upon alcohol: "There ought to be some way to stop these disgraceful riots. They almost universally commence over a glass of liquor. *Rum* is the prime mischief-maker, and under its influence the sectional differences of the old country are magnified into hugh proportions. Is there no way to put down the reign of rum among the Irish population?"[36]

The 1849 paddy camps riot illustrated that, while the temperance movement made some strides among Lowell's Irish, it was primarily a middle-class, church-sponsored phenomenon. The riot, which occurred only hours before Father Mathew, the great Irish temperance crusader, arrived, demonstrated that while most of Lowell's adult Irish population took the pledges, theirs was little more than lip-service commitment. Brian Harrison has shown that the saloon was an important locus for socialization among the Irish, and, in a culture where alcohol was readily available, it mattered little what Father McDermott said or what the middle class did in support of temperance.[37] It was significant that the riot broke out in the midst of Famine emigration, when "old national prejudices" were reinforced by the mass of Famine emigrants for whom individual paddy camps still had real meaning long after they ceased to be important for Lowell's "Americanized" Irish middle class. It was also noteworthy that the riot broke out just after the worst of the 1849 cholera epidemic had subsided. That the riot coincided with the epidemic was undoubtedly noticed by many Lowell Yankees, who saw a connection between deteriorating health standards and a rise in crime. One obvious sign to them of this connection was in the use of alcohol among the Irish.

In Lowell, very few Irish listed their occupations as saloonkeepers in the city directories of the 1840s and 1850s. The transient character and the increasing poverty of Lowell's Irish in the late 1840s inhibited the development of large numbers of saloons. Rather, the Irish obtained their liquor in unlicensed "common dram shops" which flourished in the front rooms of tenements throughout the Irish neighborhoods.[38] The problem reached such proportions that Lowell's board of aldermen passed a resolution in 1846 designed to suppress "the numerous unlicensed drinking places that are now scattered all over the city."[39] Even Father Mathew's visit barely affected the practice. Horatio Wood reported that "some stepped in and were saved . . . a few shops were closed . . . [but] things remain much the same."[40] In 1849, Wood estimated that the Irish ran over three-fourths of the unlicensed saloons in Lowell.[41] In the early 1850s, a halfhearted effort was made to close the saloons when Massachusetts passed the so-called Maine Law, which forbade the sale of alcohol. The illicit nature of the saloons and the Irish practice of making poteen at home, however, doomed these efforts.[42]

If intemperance was "the source of a great portion of the poverty, crime, tax, trouble, tears, and anxiety of the city," Lowell's officials argued that the root of the problem lay in the nature of Famine emigrants.[43] Within a decade, the Famine emigrants had made Lowell more Irish than Yankee and the speed with which they arrived prevented their assimilation into Lowell under the terms which had accommodated the pre-Famine Irish. The nature of the Irish presence in Lowell had changed since the mills turned to them for workers, and the feelings of Lowell's Yankees were now quite different as well. The figure on arrests for drunkenness in the late 1840s indicated that city officials were overwhelmed with problems which had been confined to the paddy camps in earlier years but which they now faced directly as the Irish spread in large numbers throughout Lowell. Horatio Wood compared two five-month periods (February-August) in 1847 and 1848 and found that arrests for drunkenness had increased by 89 percent. In August, 1848, 234 arrests were reported, which was as many as had occurred for an entire year in the early 1840s. Wood noted that when the figures were adjusted for repeat offenders, the Irish represented an overwhelming 92 percent of these arrests.[44] Drunkenness remained a particularly Irish problem. The only other major crimes in Lowell around 1850 which were committed by them were assault and battery and larceny, and these were usually alcohol-related. Other crimes in which the Irish participated included burglary, malicious trespass, "rescuing prisoners," disturbing the peace, rioting, violation of the license law, fornication, adultery, and vagabondage.[45]

While the crimes committed were not heinous, they represented a real threat to the order and stability of Lowell. Even if the mill owners were less interested in Lowell's moral environment, local elected officials were quite concerned. Unfortunately, they lacked the resources to handle what must have seemed a bewildering breakdown of order. Increasingly, city officials turned to institutionalization to arrest the decline in Lowell's environment. It was not that they dropped the concept of elevating Irish from their abject state; it was rather that fewer Irishmen were seen as worthy of such effort. Faced with a lower class of Irish plaguing Lowell, its officials adopted institutionalization as a way to enforce Yankee standards.

This turn to institutionalization demonstrated that city officials felt that the old approach to the assimilation of Irish immigrants must be modified and that new methods must be employed. One reason lay in the obvious failure of existing institutions. The Irish had already wrecked the 1835 education agreement and the increase in Irish paupers undermined private and public relief efforts. The old constabulary and city watch was ineffective to quell neighborhood riots; in 1849, the mayor called upon the city guards during the Acre riots. After the riots, the editor of the *Vox Populi* criticized the "*miserable inefficiency in the Lowell Police Court*" which had become a "standing joke," releasing "desperadoes" for "$2 and $3 and costs—for the payment of which they have a regular organization and standing fund."[46] Since existing police, educational, and judicial systems were inadequate, Lowell's officials turned to new and more repressive institutions to enforce at least a veneer of moral and social order.

At Lowell's first town meeting in 1826, residents had pledged over $400 for pauper support.[47] Ten years later, the figure had risen to $3000 annually.[48] Residents also approved construction of a city poor farm or almshouse. By 1850, city officials spent almost $16,000 annually, or over five times what they had spent fourteen years earlier.[49] By 1850, they established a house of reformation for juvenile offenders at the poor farm. Both the house of reformation and the almshouse were designed to correct deficiencies in human conduct among their inmates through well-enforced regulations governing work, living accommodations, education, and personal hygiene. If low-class Irish could not learn by the example set by the larger community, they would be taken from that community to be shown the necessity of Yankee standards of conduct. Through this process, Lowell's officials would reform the criminal and assist the poor, who were overwhelmingly Irish. When "O" reported in the Lowell *Courier* on his visit to them in the Lowell almshouse in 1849, for example, he found that nine-tenths of the inmates were Irish. "O" insisted that the almshouse was a "source of gratification to the American citizen," who now had "a sufficient answer" when "appealed to as a nation to help the Irish in their calamity [the Famine]—if we point to the millions, that were contributed to the support of improvident foreigners here with us."[50] Even after Massachusetts assumed care of nonresident aliens in 1852, the expenditures for Lowell's almshouse rose quickly to their former levels. The predominance of Irish in other almshouses in New England indicated that the problem had become a major regional concern.[51]

The removal of paupers, criminals, and delinquent children did not assure that Lowell would be free of crime and poverty. There were simply too many Irish in Lowell. Wood's suggestion that they be scattered away by withholding charity expressed the view of many of Lowell's residents, since the Irish presence in Lowell had cost its taxpayers considerable money. This was especially true because the poor farm was only one area which drained city services. In the 1840s, Lowell's officials organized a professional fire department, spurred, in part, by fears of a serious conflagration in crowded Irish neighborhoods which might spread to the adjacent mill and boardinghouse district. In the 1850s, they disbanded the old constabulary and city watch and organized a professional police department which could also be reinforced from the state militia headquartered in Lowell.[52]

Of all the institutions designed to enforce Yankee standards, the one which underwent the most striking metamorphosis was the public school. Local Catholics and Protestants had hailed the education agreement as evidence of growing cooperation among them and as a mechanism to bring the benefits of American citizenship to local Irish. Many Irish parents sent their children to public school and, despite the high mobility of unskilled Irish laborers, Irish attendance compared favorably with citywide trends. In addition, the school committee provided liberally for their education.[53] McDermott's willful destruction of the agreement in 1843 was more a catalyst than an underlying cause of the metamorphosis in education. The people who organized the compromise were still there but conditions had changed in Lowell. City officials faced a deterioration in standards when the floodtide of Famine emigrants descended upon them.

The school committee gradually shifted its educational philosophy in recognition of the changes governing the condition of the Irish in Lowell. Public education became increasingly institutionalized as Lowell's officials appointed a truant officer, opened a house of reformation, designed "intermediate" schools for older Irish children with no formal education, and enforced a "certificate statute" to ensure that older Irish children who obtained mill employment had received at least some public education.[54] Behind this bureaucratic expansion, however, there also existed some of the same goals which had characterized the earliest drive for public education among Irish immigrants, particularly a demand that education promote peace, order, and good citizenship. When St. Patrick's pastor, Fr. John

O'Brien, opened Notre Dame Academy for Girls in 1852, for example, the school committee vigorously attacked sectarian schools:

> That any sect has a perfect right to establish schools of its own, none can deny. . . . But if it shall be found that the children withdrawn from our Public Schools, and sent to places of religious instruction, are not properly educated in those branches which make successful men and women, then it becomes a matter of interest to the public mind generally. . . . Whosoever refuses to educate his children is a foe to the community, for a single generation of ignorant children would endanger all our future history. For its own safety society is bound to educate its youth, and if children refuse to be educated, the law comes in to enforce the claims of society.[55]

In Lowell, the rates of attendance were higher than in other American Irish communities. After the 1835 education compromise, for example, over 60 percent of the Irish enrolled in public school attended regularly, with average daily attendance reaching 45 percent. These figures compared favorably to townwide attendance.[56] Almost 90 percent of the Irish children in Number 12 Primary School on Lewis Street in the Acre attended daily in 1840. Three years later, 85 percent of the older children enrolled in the Mann Grammar School nearby attended regularly, with daily attendance reaching 52 percent.[57] The appointment of a truant officer shortly after ensured that Lowell's schools continued to show high attendance rates in comparison with other cities throughout the 1850s.[58] It should also be remembered that much of the discrepancy between the number enrolled in Lowell's public schools and those attending daily resulted from the highly transient character of its Irish.

From another perspective, the relatively high percentage of those enrolled in public school can be attributed to the widespread support which these schools enjoyed and also to the passage of the certificate law. Still, the school committee pointed proudly to its success in attracting Irish children into public school: "From inquiries made respecting the bearing of the common school system upon the Irish population in other cities and large towns, the committee has devised new evidence of the wisdom of the plan adopted in their city, and which is believed to be peculiar to ourselves. No other place, it is supposed, can exhibit the same proportion of this class of children in the common schools."[59] Ten years later, the secretary of the Massachusetts Board of Education, a Doctor Sears, found the same tendency, commenting on the Mann Grammar School: "I have

seen no school of the kind to equal it, with all my visits to schools." The
school committee added: "It may well be that similar remarks were made
by Dr. Sears, in regard to some of the Primary Schools which he visited,
composed entirely of Irish children."[60]

The school committee's praise for the percentage of Irish children enrolled in the public schools who attended regularly accurately reflected
Lowell's standing among other cities with large Irish populations in 1850.
Over one-half of all potential students attended the Mann Grammar
School and even larger numbers attended many of the Irish primaries. By
contrast, only about one-third of the Irish children in Hamilton attended
school regularly in 1850. In London, even fewer attended, with only
about one-quarter returning daily. There were some similarities among
these cities. In Hamilton, London, Milwaukee, and Lowell, slightly more
boys attended regularly than girls. In addition, most enrolled at five years
and, as the age of schoolchildren increased in Milwaukee and Troy/Co-
hoes, the percentage attending dropped, much as at Lowell. Only at
Lowell, however, did the percentage of Irish children attending regularly
compare favorably with the percentage for the native-born. In Milwaukee, for example, the Irish were less likely to place children in public
schools than native-born or English immigrants, although more likely
than German immigrants.[61] In addition, only at Lowell did the Catholic
church encourage Irish support for public schools.

Although the Irish attended primary school and most also went to
grammar school, almost none went on to Lowell High School. The school
committee insisted that Irish "children are admitted to the high school,
and to all other schools when their parents desire it, on the same terms
with other children" without any "prejudice or exclusiveness."[62] The absence of Irish students in the high school, however, indicated that Irish
parents did not see higher education as an avenue for their children. Significantly, among those attending Lowell High between 1852 and 1859,
only nine received certificates which allowed them to leave Lowell High
and enter the mills, despite the fact that 263 children were employed
in the mills in compliance with the certificate statute in 1859 alone.[63] Of
the four Irish who sought admission to Lowell High in 1850 from the
Mann Grammar School, three scored sufficiently low to be rejected.[64]
This pattern was similar to trends found in Poughkeepsie, Milwaukee,
and Troy/Cohoes, where children left school usually before their thirteenth birthday.[65]

There were obvious benefits to public education. For Lowell's Irish, the public schools were an avenue to mill employment. It was known that Lowell's mill agents sought students educated in public school, believing that educated help was consistently more productive. The school committee's justification for intermediate schools demonstrated the value of public education to the Irish. In 1855, it offered a warning to "every intelligent foreigner" advising that their "sons will never be able to successfully compete in the active business of life with our sons, unless they are trained side by side with them." The message was not lost on Irish parents and the daily attendance rate of their children in the intermediate schools frequently surpassed that of students in Lowell's grammar schools.[66] That the Irish middle class also sent their children to public school and that public schools enjoyed the support of local Catholic priests were also noted by Irish parents. The public schools gave Lowell's Irish the advantage they needed, with a certificate of attendance serving as a letter of introduction when Irish children approached the mills. What had started out to be education aimed more generally at assimilating the children of Irish immigrants had become training for mill workers.

This became the greatest advantage of public school education for Lowell's Irish by 1850. For this reason, both Lowell's resident Yankees and its mill agents supported public schools. Lowell's elected Yankee officials still believed in the link between learning, patriotism, and good citizenship, but increasingly they also aimed to keep immigrants in line. In a society of declining health standards and rising crime, the movement to extend public schools to Lowell's Irish went beyond the institutionalization of criminals, paupers, and delinquent children by enforcing Yankee standards upon the next generation of Irish. While some mill agents applauded their efforts, all of Lowell's business and political leaders were generally more interested in promoting peace and stability and, by the mid-1840s, in educating immigrants as productive workers. Homer Bartlett, the agent of the Massachusetts mills, wrote to Horace Mann in 1859 of the value of public schools: "From my observation and experience, I am perfectly satisfied that the owners of manufacturing property have a deep pecuniary interest in the morals of their help. . . . I believe it will be seen that the establishment, other things being equal, which has the best educated and most moral help, will give the greatest production at the least cost per pound."[67]

By the time Bartlett wrote, public schools had become the most institutionalized of all the new agencies organized to deal with Irish immigrants on a large scale. When Lowell-born William Cardinal O'Connell wrote of his experiences as a child in the public schools of St. Peter's parish in the late 1850s, it was as an outsider looking in.[68] By then, the 1835 education agreement was a historical footnote and the schools of O'Connell's day exhibited a kind of rigorous segregation never seen by the pre-Famine Irish, for whom segregation had been much more informal if as effective. That the Irish turned against public schools was not surprising. As Vincent Lannie argued, Catholic priests like Fr. John O'Brien and his brother Timothy, who developed Lowell's Catholic schools through personal contributions to their construction and maintenance in the early 1850s, opposed public education as godless.[69] With the construction of these Catholic schools, any discussion of the "noble experiment" in public education ended.

The success of the Irish as they applied for mill employment made them obvious targets for nativist aggression. The introduction of thousands of destitute Famine immigrants into Lowell precipitated an immediate Yankee reaction in response to declining health standards and rising crime. The root of Lowell's Irish problem lay far deeper in the minds of Lowell's resident Yankees, however, than with the problems associated with Irish living among them. Lowell's officials experienced problems handling Famine immigrants which were common throughout the industrializing Northeast. As the Irish became not only "hewers of wood and drawers of water" but also a permanent American industrial working class, local control over the regulation of Irish within a given community passed out of the hands of elected local officials.[70] In many cases, these elected officials shared power with the new industrialists who had been responsible for growth and prosperity.

This was particularly the case in Lowell. Before 1845, the Boston Associates and its resident Yankees had shared a common perception of Lowell. There were differences concerning early expenditures for public schools, for example, but these differences never interfered with a common outlook on the future and promise of Lowell. Lowell had sparkled as the pretty sister of American industrialism. Many of its social, physical, and psychological characteristics spread elsewhere as the "Lowell Plan" received wide recognition, especially since the Boston Associates turned Lowell's profits into capital used in developing ventures elsewhere. The fuel behind their enterprising spirit, however, had always been profit. By 1845, problems plagued Lowell and the Boston Associates and their descendants questioned the expense of the humanitarian impulse which had always been a part of the Lowell experiment. Faced with a loss of profit or a modification to their approach, profit won out and they turned to Irish labor.

As a result, three groups had emerged in Lowell at mid-century which were concerned with the shaping of Lowell's future: the Boston Associates, the resident Yankees, and the Irish. As the Boston Associates changed the balance of the relationships among these groups by offering the Irish mill employment, they also lost support among Lowell's resident Yankees. Characterizations of the Boston Associates as "benefactors" disappeared from local literature as the Boston Associates suddenly became "capitalists."[71] Many in Lowell now argued that the ultimate blame for the overwhelming numbers of Irish in Lowell lay with the mill owners. The Boston Associates had introduced the Irish into the mills and, in doing so, they had ignored the implications of their new employment patterns upon Lowell's social structure and its moral environment. Lowell's resident Yankees had been among the Boston Associates' most vocal supporters, and many had been attracted to Lowell originally because of the message which the Boston Associates had sent throughout the world on the strengths of American industrialism. When Abbott Lawrence observed that "a better class" of Irish had emigrated in 1849 than in previous years, his message fell on deaf ears in Lowell, where the new belief among Lowell's resident Yankees was that mill owners like Lawrence had abandoned them.[72]

The debate concerning the power held by the Boston Associates over Lowell's development erupted when the *Vox Populi*, an independent local weekly, opened a series on "Irish labor" in response to the Democratic Lowell *Advertiser's* notice that the Prescott mills had turned to Irish help in 1851.[73] The *Vox Populi* linked the "welfare of the city, and all its best interests" to mills which were filled "with the best American help." It blamed Lowell's decline upon the Boston Associates, who pursued a policy which would "inevitably result in the depression of real estate, of the profits of trade, of remuneration given intelligent labor, of the honor, beauty, respectability and hitherto fair fame of our city."[74] The *Vox Populi* series pointed out to many of Lowell's residents that the shift in employment patterns authorized by the Boston Associates had a debilitating effect upon the social and moral order of Lowell and had diminished its reputation.

The *Vox Populi* absolved the local overseers and agents from responsibility, instead blaming the "capitalists of Boston" who would "sacrifice everything but the cotton interests of Lowell to their love of gain" and who "live not in the midst of the ruin and degradation they are causing." The *Vox Populi* argued that if the Boston capitalists lived in Lowell, "they would have interests, social, political, and domestic, and religious, similar to their own; yes, and pecuniary interests too, that would conflict with their cotton interests, and cause them to adopt a different policy." The *Vox Populi* complained:

> But these men are not citizens of Lowell though in one sense they *are Lowell itself*, and Lowell is theirs. They can mold and fashion it as they please, and all the products of its industry go to increase their hoarded wealth. The operatives *stay;* the mechanics *stay,* the merchants and tradesmen *stay,* if they can do no better, the over-seers live, the agents thrive; but, comparatively speaking, all the money made in Lowell, *enriches* others than Lowell men, or those by whose toil it is accumulated. These men look only to the means by which they shall most successfully and certainly increase their divi-dends; and if it costs the sacrifice of every individual enterprise in our midst, they will, doubtless persist in their unjust and despicable policy. The men who plead for a protective tariff that the manufac-turer might be enabled to pay a higher price for labor, and when this prayer was granted, forgot the operative, and increased their own gains in both dividends and sinking funds, the men who cut down the pay of operatives under the most favorable auspices of manufac-turing companies, oppressing the honest laborer to increase their own profits, have few bowels of compassion for other interests than their own, and their love for Lowell is all cotton.

It warned that "from them we have nothing to hope—from their policy everything to fear."[75]

The opinion expressed by the editor of the *Vox Populi* reflected the perspective of many of Lowell's resident Yankees and, as the debate raged throughout the early 1850s, his opinion was repeated in varying degrees in the pages of the Lowell *Advertiser*, the independent *Lowell Daily News*, and the American party's *American Citizen*. The editor of the Whig paper, the Lowell *Daily Courier and Journal*, remained silent on the shifting employment pattern adopted by the Boston Associates, whom the newspaper had always represented.[76] The debate was significant because of its duration and because of the intensity with which opinions were ex-pressed. By the mid-1850s, the *American Citizen* expressed what had be-come obvious, diminishing slightly the importance of the Boston capi-talists to Lowell from the earlier *Vox Populi* position. It criticized Patrick

Donohoe's defense of Irish mill women in the Boston *Pilot* by chiding
Donohoe for presuming that "manufacturing companies in Lowell are
Lowell itself," although the importance of the shift in the pattern of employment was not denied.[77] Change in the employment pattern may have
been lost on an outsider like Donohoe but Lowell's Yankees understood
the difference. Lowell had become an immigrant industrial city—another
Manchester, England—and the Boston Associates were responsible.

It was inevitable that a reaction should occur. As the political ramifica-
tions of the shift in employment patterns reverberated throughout Lowell,
American politics was also in turmoil. It was clear in the early 1850s that
blind allegiance to old traditions and belief in old promises had produced
chaos and disorder in Lowell much as it had nationally, particularly concerning slavery. In Lowell, the Boston Associates had sacrificed Lowell's
citizens to profit and the recognition was profoundly disillusioning. From
this perspective, the Irish were caught in the middle. As symbols of the
deterioration, they were local and visible, unlike the capitalists who remained in their merchant houses in Boston. If the Irish were not the
cause of the new employment trends, they were the effect, and their
effect upon Lowell spelled disaster for the quality of life there. In addition, the Irish, who had been politically impotent since their arrival in
Lowell, rallied to new leadership with the appearance of a new pastor at
St. Patrick's, Fr. John O'Brien. The O'Briens apologized to no one and,
unlike the old Irish middle class, saw Irish assimilation into American society in distinctly Irish terms. In time, the verbal battles became physical ones.

CHAPTER 7

The Know-Nothing Crisis
1847–55

Father McDermott remained at St. Patrick's until 1847, his final years there undistinguished. He never forgave the members of the Benevolent Society for their interference in his management of the parish. With the exception of his efforts on behalf of temperance, McDermott stood for very little. He enjoyed only halfhearted support among his parishioners and lived constantly in the shadow of St. Peter's, which Father Conway, his former assistant, had molded into a unified congregation, larger and richer than St. Patrick's. After McDermott's disastrous interference with the education agreement in 1843, he lost much of his support as parishioners like Cummiskey turned against him. In the mid-1840s, McDermott petitioned the new bishop of Boston, John Fitzpatrick, for permission to acquire an old Methodist meetinghouse about two blocks from St. Patrick's Church. Fitzpatrick granted his request and McDermott moved there in 1847. Renaming it St. Mary's, McDermott bore much of the redecorating expense personally.[1] He gathered his few remaining supporters around him but never exercised again the influence that he had once possessed.

St. Patrick's Church remained open and Fr. Hilary Tucker succeeded McDermott. Tucker was a thoughtful, pious, and conscientious priest. Arriving at St. Patrick's, he reported to Fitzpatrick that "the Catholics . . . for many years past have been in a very disturbed state and divided into factions." Tucker reported that while "many of them seem to have very little religion or faith . . . the dispositions of the congregation" were excellent.[2] Tucker appealed immediately for support not only to longtime parishioners but also to recent Famine immigrants. He worked diligently at the enormous task of reenergizing older parishioners and accommodating new ones throughout 1847. Recognizing that many had just arrived in Lowell, Tucker organized a retreat in March, 1848, for parishioners who spoke only Gaelic and arranged for two Gaelic-speaking priests to assist

St. Mary's Church, 1858. Courtesy of the Lowell Historical Society.

him.[3] Throughout his brief stay the enormous difficulty of administering St. Patrick's parish weighed heavily upon him. In May, 1848, Tucker requested a leave of absence from Bishop Fitzpatrick to ponder the strength of his commitment to the priesthood. Fitzpatrick granted his request, speculating that Tucker's decision upon his return would be "the will of God." Tucker remained a priest, even serving as rector of Holy Cross Cathedral in the 1850s, but he never returned to St. Patrick's.[4]

Fr. John O'Brien succeeded him. O'Brien was a native of Ballina, Tipperary, and had been educated and ordained there. He had served as a priest for twelve years in Ireland before emigrating to America in 1840. O'Brien settled in Richmond, Virginia, where he joined his older brother, Timothy, a fellow priest who had emigrated some years earlier. In 1848, Fr. John O'Brien moved to the Boston diocese, where Bishop Fitzpatrick assigned him to serve Chelsea, Lynn, and Newburyport. In December, O'Brien became permanent pastor of St. Patrick's.[5] In 1851, Fr. Timothy O'Brien, "an aged priest somewhat infirm," joined his younger brother at St. Patrick's.[6] The O'Brien brothers inaugurated what local Catholic historians have called the O'Brien dynasty, since the O'Briens or their young relatives served as pastors of St. Patrick's parish from 1848 to 1922.[7]

Fr. John O'Brien was an ideal choice as the new pastor of St. Patrick's. A speaker at the parish Silver Jubilee in 1881 recalled that O'Brien was "a man of big frame and bigger heart, the tender father of his people; and the dear friend of all his brother priests. . . . His courtesy, his hospitality, united to every manly, sacerdotal virtue, made him truly loved, and his company sought after." The speaker also called Father O'Brien a "faithful priest and a true gentleman, he had a hearty welcome for all, but he knew how to combine politeness and duty."[8] In short, O'Brien was a successful administrator who knew how to get along with his parishioners while expecting dedication in return. His enthusiasm played off nicely against his brother's stately reserve and old-world courtesy. Fr. Timothy O'Brien supervised St. Patrick's new parish school, which opened in September, 1852. He also served as confessor to the nuns who ran it and who remembered him years later as their "protector."[9] Fr. John O'Brien worked on general parish administration, especially plans for a grand new St. Patrick's Church.

Fr. John O'Brien must have been disheartened at the condition of St. Patrick's parish when he arrived in 1848. St. Patrick's Church was almost twenty years old and in extremely poor physical condition. The parishioners had always been reluctant to contribute to its support and many of

the new parishioners were simply too poor to afford their share of its upkeep. A number of wealthier Irish had moved to St. Peter's since Bishop
Fenwick agreed to a formal division of the parish in 1841. St. Patrick's suffered by comparison. In addition, Father McDermott had drained parish
resources even further by opening St. Mary's Church within the boundaries of St. Patrick's parish, literally within sight of St. Patrick's Church. His
diehard supporters followed McDermott there. Father Tucker's tenure at
St. Patrick's was too brief to spark a resurgence in parish loyalty among
those parishioners who remained at St. Patrick's.

In spite of these difficulties, Tucker and then the O'Briens took some
tentative steps to shape new loyalties within St. Patrick's parish. They recognized that the parish was home to thousands of Famine immigrants who
lived in horribly overcrowded tenements and who had little need for the
kind of parish that St. Patrick's had traditionally been. The early parishioners of St. Patrick's had had a far different attitude toward Catholicism,
shaped largely by the considerable time many of them had spent already
in America. They had never come together successfully to establish a
framework for parish unity and, by 1848, two divisive factions had split to
form St. Peter's and St. Mary's. St. Patrick's had become a parish without a
mission, attracting Famine Irish without serving them. The problem was
compounded by the lack of "institutional" tradition which had characterized the pre-Famine Irish church and which had been carried by Irish
emigrants to America.[10] Tucker and the O'Briens now faced the dilemma
of how to meet the religious needs of Irish parishioners whose immediate
concern was their temporal situation. The question became whether St.
Patrick's priests could generate a local devotional revolution in a parish
noted for dissent and facing enormous internal crises. Put in other terms,
the O'Briens had to nurture historic Irish emotional enthusiasm for religion while developing a new policy of service.

The task before them was great but, by the time Fr. John O'Brien became pastor, these disadvantages masked some real strengths which he
capitalized upon quickly. First, McDermott took his supporters to St.
Mary's while the Benevolent Society dissidents remained at St. Peter's. As
a result of these separations, the old antagonisms were gone and McDermott's successors, particularly the O'Briens, forged new relationships in
their absence. Second, there was no question as to loyalty among Catholics in St. Patrick's parish by 1848. Fitzpatrick received the support and
respect which St. Patrick's parishioners had grudgingly given Fenwick in
his last years as Boston's bishop. Third, the Famine Irish offered a new and

expanding base of parishioners from which new loyalty could be shaped. This became the O'Briens' strategy—to provide leadership by serving all Irish within the boundaries of St. Patrick's parish with a pragmatic program of institutional growth. They would loyally represent Bishop Fitzpatrick, who allowed local priests considerable control over parishes. They would cultivate new relationships with old factions at St. Mary's and St. Peter's as outsiders who had never been involved in the old dispute, and parish unity within St. Patrick's would be molded in their personality.

For the O'Briens, community leadership was a logical extension of their role at St. Patrick's. Since the formation of the paddy camps, there had been an absence of local Irish leadership on a political and religious level. Political loyalties had been split between Whigs and Democrats. Irish Whigs favored assimilation under Yankee standards and included real estate speculators like Hugh Cummiskey, Charles Short, and Stephen Castles.[11] Benjamin Butler, who used the Irish as a political voting base and favored assimilation to Yankee standards, led Irish Democrats.[12] The O'Briens chose to abandon the policy advocated by the Irish middle class of imitating Yankee standards in the hope of obtaining individual success within the perimeters accepted by Yankee Lowell. They knew that the Famine Irish had overtaxed Yankee resources and that traditions such as local educational policy had been modified to meet the shift in employment patterns among the Irish in Lowell. The O'Briens also recognized that, while the transient nature of Lowell's Irish population remained constant, the effect of their presence in Lowell was entirely different. The newspaper debates of 1851 drove such a perception home. Finally, they saw that the Irish had found a sense of permanence in Lowell which was different from their days as unskilled laborers and which reached beyond the narrow interests of the Irish middle class. The mill owners needed the Irish to maintain their profits and, since Lowell's elected local officials were ultimately responsible for order among its Irish, the mill owners cared little how they obtained Irish operatives, although they did favor exposure to public education. With Lowell's officials turning to a policy of institutionalization and the Boston Associates abandoning their interests in maintaining the moral environment of Lowell, the O'Briens were free to ignore past working relationships and devise new ones.

The financial success of the O'Briens' strategy at St. Patrick's rested upon a unified congregation for whom the O'Briens provided dedicated service. That strategy, in modified form, had already worked at St. Peter's and, as the Irish found traditional Yankee institutions increasingly repressive in their reliance upon a philosophy of "worthy" and "unworthy" Irishmen, the O'Brien approach held great promise. It also complemented the policy of Father Tucker who, seeing the Famine emigrants pouring into Lowell, had provided Gaelic-speaking priests to minister to their needs. The O'Briens would lead by example. They were pious, devoted, concerned priests, who were courteous and hospitable yet commanded respect from their parishioners, combining "politeness and duty." The O'Briens never interfered with McDermott and his little group of supporters at St. Mary's, although after construction of the new St. Patrick's Church there was no need for St. Mary's to remain open. They enjoyed an excellent relationship with Bishop Fitzpatrick, recognizing that by submitting to Fitzpatrick's authority they held great power within St. Patrick's parish. The O'Briens were equally friendly with Father Crudden and his parishioners at St. Peter's. They participated at every social function and worked with St. Peter's priests to present a common Catholic front in Lowell.[13] Within St. Patrick's parish, the O'Briens exuded fatherly concern for all Catholics, opening parish facilities to feed and house indigent Irish when the need arose. This concern, for example, even led indirectly to the formation of a highly successful patent medicine company. Concerned with the persistence of "the cough" among his parishioners, Fr. John O'Brien sent them regularly to a local druggist for a patent medicine. In time it came to be known as "Father John's" and led to the formation of a patent medicine company of the same name which operated in Lowell until the 1970s.[14]

Their approach worked beautifully and, for the first time in a history of checkered relations, St. Patrick's was a unified and loyal congregation. The problems faced initially by the O'Briens were enormous but the most striking feature of their success was the speed with which they reformed parish relations and organized parish development. To accomplish these reforms, the O'Briens devised a strategy which not only served the needs of an Irish neighborhood in the throes of social, political, economic, and religious transition but which also demonstrated that they safeguarded the rights of Lowell's Irish. As part of their plan, the O'Briens abandoned the assimilation philosophy of the Irish middle class, arguing instead for a more pluralistic perspective. In the process, they created an Irish identity in Lowell which transcended the "limbo" status of the early unskilled Irish laborers or the later divisions into worthy and unworthy poor adopted by Lowell's Yankees. The O'Briens carefully nurtured this Irish identity, infus-

Father John O'Brien. Courtesy of the Lowell Museum.

ing into it a strong Catholic component. By 1860, Lowell's Irish were Catholic Irish united behind the O'Briens and Bishop Fitzpatrick.

The O'Briens succeeded because it was clear that by 1850 Lowell's Irish were in desperate need of strong political and religious leadership. While Father Crudden pursued a similar policy at St. Peter's, St. Patrick's remained the heart of Lowell's Irish community and the neighborhood into which most Irish settled initially. If strong leadership was to come from Lowell's clergy, it would come from the pastor of the "mother" church of Lowell's Irish. At the same time, St. Patrick's under the O'Briens became a target for nativist bigotry. The original impetus to the more strident separation between Yankees and Irish occurred, of course, as the Irish presence in Lowell increased dramatically, and it came from Lowell's Yankees. If the 1851 newspaper debates signaled anything, it was that the older approach to assimilation had failed. The complaints raised against "low" Irish touched most of Lowell's Irish because the Irish middle class had always been a small if important part of Lowell's general Irish population. The O'Briens' advocacy of the right of all Irishmen to a decent life in Lowell turned what Lowell's Yankees perceived as a roadblock to assimilation into a reaffirmation of Irish heritage in a time of increasing local nativism. If the Irish suffered discrimination in their work, they returned nightly to the familiar confines of their families and to the comfort of their church, where local priests redefined their lives by Irish Catholic rather than Yankee standards. As part of this strategy, the O'Briens tried deliberately to remove their Irish parishioners from Yankee influence, setting up a separate school system for Irish girls in which the psychological and intellectual underpinning was rooted deep within the American Catholic church.[15] In the absence of alternative leadership, the O'Briens quickly attracted a loyal and zealous congregation.

In spite of the proximity of St. Mary's, the number of parishioners in St. Patrick's more than doubled between 1845 and the opening of the Catholic school in 1852. By 1850, nine hundred of these made their First Communion.[16] In addition, O'Brien baptized and married nearly as many parishioners as at St. Peter's and approximately twice the number as at St. Mary's.[17] The parish indebtedness stood at only $35,000 in 1855, with a $15,000 mortgage due in ten years, despite the dedication of the new St. Patrick's Church in 1854. The receipts for pew rent and collections reached $4,500 annually. In all, St. Patrick's parish contained probably about sixty-five hundred parishioners, excluding those who attended St. Mary's regularly.[18] While not as large as some Catholic parishes in New

York, Boston, or Philadelphia, St. Patrick's had become one of the largest Irish Catholic parishes in New England. It still served a large geographic area, which included the central, western, and northern sections of Lowell, as well as most of Dracut, Tyngsboro, and Chelmsford.

Since the O'Briens' strategy linked leadership with service, they moved rapidly to expand parish institutions. According to archdiocesan historians, St. Patrick's would become the most highly institutionalized parish in Lowell by 1900.[19] Its parishioners, like those studied by Dennis Clark in Philadelphia, might go "from cradle to career" without significant non-Catholic contact, within the confines of parishes such as St. Patrick's.[20] The O'Briens left charitable assistance on a formal bureaucratic basis to Protestant relief organizations like the Ministry-at-Large and concentrated upon capturing their parishioners' hearts and minds. To this end, the O'Briens were most concerned with the failure of the education agreement, denouncing Lowell's public schools as "godless."[21] Fr. Timothy O'Brien assumed control of a drive for separate Catholic education and persuaded the Sisters of Notre Dame de Namur to open a girls' school in Lowell.[22] To accomplish this goal, O'Brien paid $4,000 out of his own pocket for land and a house on Adams Street and an additional $600 for the support of the Notre Dame Sisters during their first year in Lowell. He argued that the need for Catholic education among Lowell's Irish girls was particularly pressing because so many of them worked in Lowell's mills and outside the home before they married.[23]

The O'Briens welcomed five Notre Dame Sisters to Lowell from their motherhouse in Cincinnati on 21 September 1852. Sister Desiree, who headed the new girls' school, recalled their reception: "Our arrival was a source of rejoicing for the Catholic inhabitants. The house was surrounded by a great many good persons who came to see us; the next day the Reverend Timothy O'Brien came to bring us the Blessed Sacrament and he continued to say Mass every day."[24] Two days after their arrival, the Sisters opened the girls' school without "having it announced in the church." They called together "all the children who lived in the neighborhood" and enrolled 150 Irish students during the first day. Within three days, the number had increased to three hundred.[25] The Sisters used the small wooden frame house which O'Brien had built for them as a school, but the crowd of students grew so great that the smallest children received instruction in the basement of St. Patrick's Church.[26] The Sisters offered a traditional education, teaching their young Irish charges to use "the rosary, the pen, the broom, and the needle," presumably in order of their importance to each Irish schoolgirl.[27] In 1853, the O'Briens constructed a small schoolhouse to accommodate the Irish students.[28] The success of the new Catholic school was noted that year by the Lowell school committee, who spoke out against "sectarian schools" and the dangerous precedent which they represented for Lowell's public system.[29] The new school demonstrated that the O'Briens' strategy had precipitated an important change in the relationship of the Irish to the rest of Lowell. The founding of the new school set the O'Briens up as leaders and spokesmen for the Irish community.

The Notre Dame Sisters were received extremely well by St. Patrick's Irish. When many of the Sisters took sick shortly after they arrived, for example, local parishioners paid their medical bills and stocked the convent with provisions.[30] The school expanded, and within two years the student population approached four hundred.[31] In July, 1853, the first academic year closed "with a distribution of prizes, a musical and literary program, and an exhibition of the pupils' handiwork."[32] About this time, the Sisters discovered that enough young Irish mothers worked in the mills to create a problem with their youngest children, who remained at home either alone or in the care of older brothers and sisters. As a result, many children were unable to receive religious training and a general education from the Sisters. Perceiving a real need, the Sisters organized a day school for children "from struggling families" for a "small monthly remuneration." The Irish parents gratefully accepted the new school, and some petitioned the Sisters to expand their care to include "children from better homes." In response, they opened Notre Dame Academy as a boarding school in October, 1854.[33]

The new boarding school was as successful as the original girls' school. The children supplied their own bedding and table furnishings and returned home only on weekends.[34] The younger children attended the day school at the same time but were "kept in a large room supplied with amusement and toys, and subjected to a kind of kindergarten surveillance." The Sisters provided cots and nursery swings. Some Irish mothers, "seeing how tenderly their children were cared for, begged Sister Desiree to keep them with those who stayed overnight." The Sisters complied and expanded Notre Dame Academy to incorporate their new charges.[35] The Sisters charged $100 "payable in advance" for full-time boarders and $50 for half-boarders who dined at the academy during a forty-six-week year. There were additional charges for washing, piano and vocal music, guitar, painting, and drawing. French was taught to each child without charge.[36] The creation of Notre Dame Academy in conjunction with the girls' school as well as with the church, rectory, and convent had created a visible presence among Lowell's Irish which the Catholic church had never enjoyed previously.

The construction of the new St. Patrick's Church provided an even more dramatic symbol of the increasing power of the Catholic church in Lowell. As soon as the girls' school opened, the O'Briens commissioned a "most magnificent structure" of cathedral proportions, of stone laid in cement with an impressive central tower in the Gothic revival style. The new church would be among the largest of any denomination in Lowell, and would dominate the skyline for miles around, overshadowed only by the mills. It measured 170 feet long, while the width through the transept was 100 feet, and had a seating capacity of two thousand, eight hundred more than St. Peter's, hitherto the largest Catholic church in Lowell. In his description, a *Courier* reporter noted that "the arch through the nave is the most perfect one we ever saw"; he measured the distance from the floor to the center of the arch at seventy feet. The architect set off the arch with "finely shaded" squares and attached gas burners to the fourteen ornamented pillars which supported it. Magnificent stained glass windows, including a large one behind the central altar which was manufactured in New York at a cost of $1,000, completed the decorations. A local artisan, John Mack, finished the interior in stucco. The new church cost $60,000 to construct, and the O'Briens had raised $25,000 by the time of its dedication.[37]

The O'Briens arranged for an impressive dedication, which was held on 29 October 1854. Bishop Fitzpatrick attended and the new bishop of Hartford, John O'Reilly, officiated. A Reverend Doctor Moriarty of Philadelphia delivered the principal sermon on the unity and identity of Christianity in which he noted, with an eye to the rising intolerance faced by Catholics in America, that "as the son of God whilst on earth had been persecuted, so now, as well as in times past, his religion and his true followers are persecuted." Moriarty congratulated St. Patrick's parishioners for constructing "this beautiful temple" which was "dedicated to the honor and glory of the Most High." The dedication service was extremely well attended. Almost twenty-five hundred people crowded into the church for the afternoon services, and local organizers had to regulate the crowds by issuing admittance cards. A large retinue of priests added to the festive air. In the evening, Bishop O'Reilly confirmed three hundred girls dressed in white and wearing white veils.[38]

The "new" St. Patrick's, 1858. Courtesy of the Lowell Historical Society.

The dedication of St. Patrick's Church had been a carefully staged production meant to demonstrate the power of the Catholic church in Lowell. The timing of the dedication was significant in that it occurred less than five months after a Know-Nothing mob had attacked St. Patrick's and only days before the Know-Nothings would sweep to power in Lowell and throughout Massachusetts. That the Know-Nothing victory was imminent was well understood by the people who attended the St. Patrick's dedication. The dedication also served notice that the O'Briens had become the leaders of the Irish community in Lowell. The sheer size of the new church, the magnificence of the dedication ceremony, and the presence of Lowell's outgoing mayor, Sewall Mack, in the congregation indicated that Lowell's Yankees respected them.

The emergence of the O'Briens as the leaders of Lowell's Irish had gone beyond the notion of service and the displays of fatherly affection for which they had become known. This linking of service and personality explained much of the basis of their support within the Irish community, but their leadership would have been less impressive had outside forces not intervened. The rising intolerance toward Irish Catholics had caused them to turn inward, especially since no leaders had emerged from within the Irish middle class. In fact, the middle class adopted an approach similar to that of Bishop Fitzpatrick, who urged Irish Catholics to remain silent until the persecution from the Know-Nothings passed.[39] In Lowell, Fitzpatrick put aside this approach because the O'Briens had such support that he felt more comfortable displaying the power of the Catholic church. With the construction of the new St. Patrick's, the O'Briens could accommodate almost every parishioner. The persistently high attendance at Sunday Masses illustrated their success at transforming Irish Lowell into Irish and Catholic Lowell. In their task, the Know-Nothing intolerance actually aided parish solidarity by drawing the parishioners closer to the O'Briens, who were such vigorous defenders of Catholicism and stalwart advocates of Irish rights. Lowell's Irish may have experienced segregation in the mills and persecution on the streets of Lowell but they were safe and strong within the confines of St. Patrick's parish. This combination of service, personality, and leadership in the face of Yankee intolerance turned Lowell's Irish community into a heavily Catholic one.

In this manner, the O'Briens redefined the position of the Irish in Lowell. They rejected traditional efforts toward accommodation and forged a new Irish Catholic identity. By the time of the dedication in October, 1854, Lowell's Irish were beset by the persecution brought on by

the rapid rise of the local Know-Nothing party and these new troubles
further strengthened the O'Briens' leadership. There had always been a
nativist undercurrent in Lowell and an American party had been organized as early as 1845. The local Know-Nothing movement, however,
originated in 1851, about a year after the Know-Nothing party was organized nationally. In Lowell the Know-Nothings increased their power
steadily despite suffering a brief eclipse in 1853 before rising with renewed vigor in 1854.[40] In the 1854 general elections, they elected the governor, lieutenant governor, eleven congressmen, every county commis-
sioner and state senator, and 326 state representatives, as well as Ambrose
Lawrence, a dentist, as Lowell's mayor. Patrick Donohoe commented
glumly: "God save the Commonwealth of Massachusetts."[41]

The triumph of the Know-Nothings heralded the collapse of the Whigs'
power both nationally and in Lowell, which they had always controlled,
representing the interests of the mill owners on the local, state, and national level.[42] Weaknesses in Whig support could be found as early as
1849, when a local Democrat, Benjamin Butler, helped to put together
a coalition of Free Soil Whigs and Democrats electing, among others,
Charles Sumner as United States senator.[43] The reason for the collapse of
the Whigs has received considerable attention from historians. Oscar
Handlin argued the view most widely held until recently, claiming that
the Know-Nothings arose after the failure of Butler's coalition to pass reform legislation in 1851. The reform movement lost to Whig and conservative Irish interests and many voters turned to the Know-Nothings to
oppose this voting block. When the Know-Nothings failed to offer a unified national policy, many former Know-Nothings drifted into the Republican party by the late 1850s.[44]

Dale Baum and Michael Holt, among others, have challenged Handlin's
argument and their revisions have significant implications for our understanding of the rise of the Know-Nothings in Lowell. Baum, for example,
suggested that it was necessary to distinguish between the Know-Nothings
as a political force and as a force which had power in politics. He argued
that local antagonisms, especially the presence of a large Irish community, must be separated from the national antislavery issue which caused
the Whig party to deteriorate as Free Soilers joined Democrats in a state
reform coalition.[45] Such was the case in Lowell, where the 1851 debate on
the Irish presence in Lowell signaled the rise of the Know-Nothings.
There had been growing animosity toward the "swarms of Irish poor" who
wreaked such havoc upon the moral, economic, and social character

of Lowell in the eyes of its Yankees. The opening of a Catholic school and the construction of the new St. Patrick's Church only exacerbated local tensions.

At the same time, the large Irish presence in Lowell not only increased local antagonism but also threatened the status of Lowell's Yankees, whose interests were now quite different from those of the mill owners. In this sense, the cultural antagonisms masked far deeper fears among Lowell's Yankees about the rapidity of social change and and the possibility of a "Catholic" Lowell. The rise of the local Know-Nothings must be seen as part of what Michael Holt has called the "politics of impatience."[46] In Lowell, those Yankee voters who feared Irish power, which was being organized with increasing effectiveness by the O'Briens, turned to the Know-Nothing party because the traditional political parties, particularly the Whig party to whom they had always given undivided support, no longer acted upon these concerns. Lowell was a Whig stronghold and the Whigs had catered periodically to Irish voters, more typically splitting the Irish vote with the Democrats as late as 1854.[47] Even more important, it was the Whigs who had betrayed Lowell's Yankees when the mill owners opened Lowell's mills to Irish. As Holt suggested, the Know-Nothings achieved power by magnifying Yankee voter impatience with the traditional two-party system, intensifying local prejudice at a time of indecisive local, state, and national leadership within the American political system.[48]

The O'Briens' position as the leaders of the Irish Catholic community made Irish Catholics a convenient target for nativist aggression. In June, 1854, open conflict broke out between Lowell's Irish and Yankees, principally over the presence of the St. Patrick's girls' school and the danger which it represented to free public education in Lowell. In 1853, the Lowell school committee noted that several public schools had opened "without a single female scholar." It called into question the ability of the Catholic Sisters to achieve "the object contemplated by the laws of this Commonwealth." The school committee concluded that the Catholic school was dangerous because the "avowed object" of such schools was religious training which neglected intellectual development, because Catholic children who left the public schools failed to retain the knowledge and skills which they had acquired there, and because these schools were beyond the investigation of public school committees. The school committee condemned Catholic schools because they "foster bitterness, engender strife, and break down the bulwark which our anti-sectarian free schools have reared around the education of our youth, and the liberties of all," further pronouncing them un-American.[49]

After this, both sides recognized that a clash was inevitable. The catalyst was a speech delivered by a nativist agitator named John Orr, more commonly called the Angel Gabriel because he arrived in each city tooting a tin trumpet while warning of the dangers of Catholicism. On the Sunday before Orr arrived in Lowell, Catholic priests throughout the city urged their parishioners to avoid "riotous manifestations." At the same time, Lowell's Catholics took steps to protect Catholic property and lives. When Orr arrived in Lowell, he spoke to a large crowd on the South Common, near St. Peter's Church, on the evils of Catholicism. The speech passed with only minor disturbances, especially since a large retinue protected Orr from Irish anger. Orr left the next morning for another speech in nearby Lawrence but his eloquence, which even the Know-Nothing *American Citizen* condemned for its harshness, had stirred up anti-Irish, anti-Catholic passions among many of Lowell's Yankees.[50]

On the following evening, gangs of "half-grown boys (full-grown rowdies) paraded through the streets" organizing a spontaneous demonstration in front of the offices of those newspaper editors who had opposed Orr's visit. Shortly after, a Yankee military company practicing their drill march for the upcoming Fourth of July festivities marched along Lowell Street, the heart of the Irish community in the Acre, accompanied by a jeering gang of Yankee boys. The Irish, whom the O'Briens insisted would remain peaceful yet vigilant throughout the Orr visit, retaliated against the military display. They hurled missiles at the Yankees and the city watch responded to the outbreak. During the disturbance, "Captain Mitchell, of the watch, while endeavoring to preserve order, was considerably injured." The crowd eventually dispersed, although, according to the Yankee reporters, "it did not appear to be desirous of doing injury to persons or property, but persisted in groaning and cheering, as the fit came upon them." A few evenings later, another crowd gathered and ignored the attempt by Mayor Mack and his watchmen to "read the riot act."[51] The following morning, Mack issued a proclamation which forbade citizens from "collecting together in the streets and upon the sidewalks in numbers, and as far as consistent with the performance of their regular business, to remain at home during the evenings, as the most rigorous measures will be taken" to prevent rioting.[52]

The Irish version of Yankee hostility in 1854–55 differed significantly from the accounts in Yankee newspapers. Two sources have survived—a

convent diary which the Sisters of Notre Dame kept of their activities in
Lowell and an 1890 version of the encounter written by the last surviving
"pioneer" Sister of the original band who founded St. Patrick's girls'
school. Both reports conveyed the same feeling and the impressions of
the direction of events in Lowell were quite similar. According to them,
for nearly two years after their arrival, the Sisters served St. Patrick's Irish
until "the peace was broken and terrifying rumors came to the ears of the
little community." The Sisters knew that the "lawless marauding of the
Know-Nothings was then rife in Massachusetts," and they had heard that
the Know-Nothings had already forced entrance into their convent school
in Roxbury.[53] When "some of the band [John Orr] came to this city" word
passed that a Know-Nothing attack on St. Patrick's was imminent. To prepare for the expected encounter, the Sisters dismissed their students before Orr arrived, urging them to remain at home. The Sisters gathered
their possessions and "bundled them together . . . each Sister was allo-
cated her portion to carry should she be compelled to flee." Parishioners
from St. Patrick's and St. Mary's organized a watch in the St. Mary's
Church tower, devising a warning signal in which "one peal of the bell was
to let priests, sisters and people know that the godless band was upon
them." Once the church watchman sounded the alarm, the Sisters would
escape though a portion of the board fence which surrounded the convent
which had been conveniently loosened.

"Days passed in this state of suspense," in which the Sisters listened
"from hour to hour for the boding toll." Lowell's Irish Catholics rallied to
their defense; indeed, "after their hard day's labor, the factory girls con-
gregated in the parlour, carrying stones for want of better weapons." The
"good fathers O'Brien" placed a guard of sixty men around the convent
nightly to watch in behalf of the Sisters hiding in the cellar. These Irish
men "in a sturdy way declared that if a finger were laid upon the convent,
there would be hard blows dealt in its defense." Finally, the Know-
Nothings approached St. Patrick's and the Irish who were waiting for them
there:

> Just at dusk one quiet evening, the ominous peal sounded forth from
> the belfry. Fear and consternation were in the many hearts, but
> trustful prayer in the little convent. The self-constituted defenders
> stood with arms uplifted, ready to hurl their missiles at the first as-
> sailant. Yes, the Know-Nothings were approaching the church, but
> they had not counted sufficiently on Irish loyalty and vim. When just
> within sight of St. Patrick's, they were attacked by some strong-

armed Irish men and women,—yes, women for these led the attack. The march became a melee, and the street was completely filled with the motley crowd. They reached the bridge which spans the canal just within sight of the convent. There was a halt, a splash and a ringing cheer—A sinewy matron unable to restrain her indignation had seized upon one of the leaders of the gang, and flung him over the railing floundering into the water below. The rest of the gang made the best of their way out of the mob, and although the Sisters were still in a state of anxiety, yet the attitudes of their assailants grew less and less threatening.[54]

Local Yankees dismissed the incident. The *Courier* reported that "there are certain parties in the vicinity of Lowell Street, who seem to be very much, but very unnecessarily alarmed, lest their churches may be pulled down, their houses demolished, and their heads broken, by the attacks of some anti-Catholic mob." It claimed that "hundreds assemble every night in the vicinity of Lowell St.," explaining that the incident started when an unidentified Irishman whistled about 2:00 A.M. as a warning, prompting the St. Mary's Church watchman to send his prearranged alarm. Immediately "all the Acre was in arms."[55] The *American Citizen* noted that "everyone to be seen was armed; paving-stones, shillelas, brickbats, guns, pistols, knives & c. were brought into requisition and for a few moments there was an 'illegant' display."[56] The *Courier* brushed off the attack, suggesting that "the affair is fit only to be laughed at." It insisted that the night had been among the quietest in Lowell's history and that Lowell's authorities had taken "the keeping of the city and the defense of persons and property into their own hands; they have power enough, military and police, to enforce order; and all further apprehension of danger from a scamp party is only childish."[57] Although the danger of rioting eased, Know-Nothing harassment continued and assumed new forms.

The Know-Nothings continued to focus their attention on St. Patrick's girls' school and expanded their condemnations to include a local Irish militia force, the Jackson Musketeers. Shortly after the Know-Nothings swept to power in November, 1854, five "well-dressed" supporters, led by Know-Nothing Mayor Ambrose Lawrence, arrived on the steps of the Notre Dame convent one noon. They demanded admission and that the premises be opened for inspection. While they stalled the Know-Nothings, the Sisters called upon Fr. Timothy O'Brien, who demanded of the Know-Nothings: "What is your business in this house?" A spokesman for the Know-Nothings replied that they wished to inspect it, to which O'Brien retorted: "You may follow me, and see what is to be seen, but I warn you not to lay a hand upon anything in this holy dwelling." O'Brien then escorted the Know-Nothings through several community rooms but refused them access to the Sisters' private quarters. Shortly after, the Know-Nothings left without further incident.[58] This was about the time when the Sisters organized Notre Dame Academy as a boarding school, and it was to the convent and new boarding school that the infamous "Smelling Committee" of the Massachusetts state legislature made its famous visit.

The legislature had created the Smelling Committee to search for abuses in Catholic convent schools. In particular, committee members investigated charges that both teachers and students had been confined against their will. The Smelling Committee made eyewitness investigations of Catholic facilities throughout Massachusetts, first visiting Holy Cross College in Worcester before moving to the Notre Dame Convent School in Roxbury. In March, 1855, they came to Lowell to investigate the convent, girls' school, and Notre Dame Academy. The "pioneer" Sister remembered the visit vividly:

> for the report reached Lowell that another band of fanatics was making raids upon convents and under the name of "smelling committee" had appointed to themselves the task of dragging dark secrets forward to the light of day. They had already visited the convent of our order in Roxbury succeeding in putting the Sisters to great annoyance. Now they announced their intention of making a thorough search of the Lowell convent. Back to the minds and hearts of the sisters came the terror that had harrowed their very souls just a year before. Their brave defender Father Timothy O'Brien bade them be of good cheer for said he "they shall not harm a hair of your heads, the black-hearted villains." He counseled the Sisters not to let one of them in until he arrived. Soon the expected committee came, twelve in number, headed by no less a personage than the mayor of the city. According to their pastor's instructions, the Sisters refused them admittance until they saw Father Timothy who escorted them through the house, asking them whether they met the extraordinary sights they had expected. They insisted upon all the closets being opened for inspection, which was accordingly done, the children's dormitories were visited, and lest anything should escape observation the worthies raised the counterpanes, and examined the beds. When, however, they were about to enter the dormitories of the religious, the Reverend Father forbade them to cross the threshold as they valued their own safety. The twelve desisted and in taking their

leave expressed themselves satisfied with the result of the visit. Neither mayor nor committeeman made his appearance at Notre Dame again.[59]

The Lowell visit brought the Smelling Committee into serious disrepute resulting from indiscretions committed by a member while in Lowell. When they arrived, the committee members lodged at the Washington House Hotel where their leader, Joseph Hiss, charged his liquor bills and the hotel bill of a Mrs. Moody, alias Mrs. Patterson, with whom he had spent the night, to the Commonwealth of Masschusetts! Boston newspapers learned of his impropriety and published vivid accounts of the scandal. The Massachusetts legislature set up a special investigating committee to examine the charges raised against Hiss. The investigators called a battery of witnesses, and the evidence mounted against him. Finally, Hiss took the stand in his own defense but failed to provide a convincing explanation of his actions or his relationship with Mrs. Patterson.[60] The Boston *Pilot* noted that "his answers were incoherent and confused. He could not answer simple questions, and floundered in his answers—replying 'yes' and 'no' to the same question. He 'didn't know' very conveniently." After his testimony, the Massachusetts legislature censured Hiss and he died in obscurity several years later. The Smelling Committee retired in disgrace. The final report concluded that "from the evidence that has been presented to the committee, and from what we have seen of the institutions themselves . . . we do not feel sufficient cause to warrant legislation in reference to them as convents."[61]

After the Know-Nothing activity against the Catholic school died down in Lowell, nativists turned their attention to the local Irish militia company. In this instance, the reason for nativist opposition was less Catholic and more cultural and political in nature. With the collapse of the Whig party in Massachusetts, the Know-Nothings moved against potential opposition. In Lowell, the most serious opponent was Ben Butler, who had always received considerable support from Lowell's Irish and was a colonel in the Irish militia company, the Jackson Musketeers. In 1855, the Know-Nothing governor, Henry Gardner, ordered all Irish militia companies throughout Massachusetts to disband. Gardner's motivation on a state level had been cultural but his actions locally undercut Butler's traditional power base. As their commander, Butler refused to comply, insisting that he be formally court-martialed and arguing that Gardner had issued an unconstitutional edict. After some debate over strategy, Gardner reorganized the Massachusetts state militia in a manner which left Colonel Butler without troops at his disposal. Butler skillfully manipulated the election procedure by which officers were chosen in the militia and emerged from his battle with Gardner as a general. There was nothing Gardner could do.[62]

The Butler-Gardner dispute illustrated the cultural basis of nativist opposition to the presence of a large Irish community in Lowell. The Know-Nothing *American Citizen* defended Gardner's actions, publishing a letter from "Corazon," who argued that Lowell's Yankee population was large enough to support a local militia company without Irish participation. While the *American Citizen* reproached Corazon for his fiery denunciations, it echoed his fears about foreign military organizations, describing Ben Butler's refusing to accept Gardner's edict as "sullen obstinacy."[63] The Lowell *Advertiser*, a Democratic paper briefly under the control of James J. Maguire after 1854, supported Irish participation in the state militia, arguing "ought not American citizens of foreign birth . . . have the same rights, and the same privileges as other citizens?" Maguire asked if the admission "of an adopted citizen into any company is to be the signal for depriving that company of the bounty of the government," asking Gardner's supporters "if, in their conscience, they believe that an equal number of native American, or Yankee companies, can be found, in the Commonwealth, whose conduct, *under precisely similar circumstances*, would have been more military, more pacific, or more patriotic?"[64]

The dispute over the disbanding of the Jackson Musketeers demonstrated the change both in the perception of how the Irish should be assimilated and in the nature of political power in Lowell. For the Irish, the dispute illustrated that they no longer wished to be assimilated within the narrow confines of Yankee provincialism; rather, they wanted the changing nature of the Irish presence in Lowell to be shaped by their dual identity as Irish and as naturalized Americans. The Irish were now Irish Catholics with strong kinship ties and the leadership of the O'Briens, but they also held to the traditional belief that as "adopted citizens" they were entitled to the rights of full citizenship and to the obligations which these rights placed upon them. The Jackson Musketeers disbanded because, under federal and state law, it was their duty to do so.

For Lowell's Yankees, the disbanding of the Jackson Musketeers demonstrated once again that cultural antagonisms and their impatience with the existing political system were inexorably tied together but, as Butler's triumph indicated so well, they were powerless to slow the speed of the socioeconomic change occurring in Lowell or to alter its direction. Lowell had changed from a Yankee mill village into an immigrant industrial city and the Know-Nothings had created deep scars locally. They had been discredited by the leadership exercised by the O'Briens, by the Hiss scandal, and by Butler's triumph. More generally, they failed to provide leadership in Massachusetts because their concentration upon cultural antagonisms precluded the development of a well-intentioned state or national platform. In this sense, the struggle in Lowell reflected the narrowness and parochialism of the Know-Nothings' appeal on a state and national level; the Know-Nothing party would be a transitory phase between the collapse of the old political system and the emergence of the new Republican party, which reflected more accurately the interests which shaped American economic, particularly industrial, development.[65]

In Lowell, the philosophy of the Irish and the development of the Irish community had also been changed by the dramatic events of the Know-Nothing era. The verbal, physical, psychological, and intellectual attacks of the Know-Nothings had drawn Lowell's Irish together under the leadership of the O'Briens. The corporations never challenged their authority because the O'Briens had always seen mill employment as an opportunity for their parishioners and, even more basic, because the corporations needed workers drawn from the permanent Irish working class in Lowell. While the rates of persistence among Irish were low throughout the 1850s, the local power base, centered in the Irish family and the Catholic church under the O'Briens' leadership, remained strong. Even if naturalized Irish voters and their children could not exercise enough political power through their voter strength to control local politics for another quarter-century, the Irish were still an important force in politics. In addition, the O'Briens' leadership provided Lowell's Irish with enormous potential, if only implied, power in Lowell. Paradoxically, the Know-Nothings had strengthened many of the Irish institutions which they wished to see diminished, forging a new Irish Catholic identity in Lowell. By the late 1850s, Lowell's Irish had carved a niche for themselves. Perhaps more significant, while the niche was extremely limited when measured, for example, by their social mobility, their position was secure, their institutions were strong, and their potential power in local politics was well understood.

CHAPTER 8

Aftermath:
The Meaning of Community
1855–61

With the Know-Nothings in disgrace locally and their power decreasing nationally, Lowell's Irish entered into a new relationship with its Yankees. That relationship reflected the strengths of the Irish community within Lowell and was built upon three factors: the family, the new pattern of employment, and the leadership of the Catholic church. Generally, the Irish rejected assimilation on Yankee terms. The controversy sparked by the activity of the Know-Nothings further eroded the old agreements and called attention to the implications of their presence in Lowell. There would be no more talk of "elevating" Irish to their rightful place as adopted American citizens. Now that the Irish were a majority in Lowell's mills the city had become what nativists had warned it might be—a "Catholic" and "Irish" manufacturing city with no pretensions any longer to set it apart from England's Lancashire. Mill employment did not advance the Irish in Lowell socially, however, nor did it offer great material rewards to Irish employees. The Irish were in Lowell's mills because they worked cheap, and the mill owners had no illusions about their duties toward Irish mill workers.

The availability of cheap Irish labor was important to Lowell's mill owners because, although an economic revival began in 1844 which continued until the Civil War, growth was spotty and unspectacular. In 1855 Lowell's population stood at 37,490 but it decreased slightly to 36,867 by 1860.[1] There had been two business recessions, from 1848 to 1851 and from 1857 to 1861, which threw hundreds of employees out of work, many of them Irish.[2] In the same period, the work force employed in Lowell's mills rose by less than nine hundred workers, increasing from 12,630 in 1848 to about 13,500 in 1860. About 65 percent of the new positions went to men.[3] In addition, much of the expansion of production stemmed from increased mechanization and speedups. The total number of looms rose from 8,749 in 1847 to 12,188 shortly after the Civil War.[4] From an Irish perspective, their position did not improve much during the 1850s. While Irish replaced Yankee mill women, Dublin has shown that the Irish generally went into the lowest-paying jobs.[5] As they had become dependent upon mill employment, the Irish also suffered more in the business recessions. In addition, the mill owners were encouraged by the cost-effectiveness, real or imagined, of Irish labor. As a result, local agents experimented with a recruiting system patterned after the older plan which had sent recruitment agents to Yankee farm women but which was now aimed at French-Canadians. They responded eagerly to offers of employment.[6] French-Canadians soon competed directly with the Irish for employment in Lowell's mills.

For those Irish who found work, the family, with its important kinship connections, became the primary avenue to mill employment. Word of an opening spread quickly through the family, whose members often worked together or lived nearby.[7] As A. Gibbs Mitchell has shown for Lowell, the family also offered essential services, such as babysitting, which were instrumental in strengthening family ties.[8] As for employment, Lowell's mills remained largely a woman's world. Because an Irish father provided only about 60 percent of family income in 1860, the role of Irish women was central to employment within the family. Irish women lived at home and remained largely outside the boardinghouse system, a tendency which increased to the Civil War. In 1836, for example, nearly 75 percent of the Hamilton's work force lived in company-owned boardinghouses, but by 1860, only about one-third of the mill workers lived there.[9] The predominance of Irish women among mill workers seriously undermined the sense of community among Yankee factory women, but their contribution to family income strengthened Irish family ties. These ties were reinforced by the immigration experience, the Irish neighborhood, the Catholic church, and nativism. While workers developed many of the same kind of emotional attachments as the Yankee women in their "community," the ties among the Irish were also much more economic.

The 1860 federal census illustrates the importance of Irish women to family wages. Of the 3,298 adult Irish living in the 1,050 households in the Dutton-Willie-Pawtucket-Merrimack streets neighborhood surrounding St. Patrick's Church in 1860, 1,581 individuals (47.9 percent) worked in the mills, the largest employer of Irish. Of these 1,581 Irish, 1,191 individuals (75.3 percent) were Irish women, indicating that three times as many women as men worked in the mills. As Irish women entered the mills, they became important contributors to family income. The median age of these women was twenty-one in 1860.[10] Irish daughters became an essential source of income, especially since most daughters married only in their mid-twenties.[11] Irish mothers did not join their daughters in the mills in significant numbers, with wives comprising only 3.5 percent of the Irish female mill workers. Among the 681 Irish wives in the 1,050 households, 133 women (19.5 percent) listed no occupation, while 500 Irish women (73.4 percent) identified themselves simply as "wives." Among Irish "mill wives," the median age was thirty, although wives without children or with only one child displayed a tendency to seek mill employment.[12] Apparently, those Irish wives who worked in the mills did so for a number of reasons, which varied with their perception of individual circumstances as well as with the willingness of mill agents to hire them.

The pattern of employment shifted considerably for Irish men in the 1850s. Of the seventy-seven male household heads identified in both censuses, sixty-seven indicated their occupations each time. Only three Irishmen felt that their situation had not improved or had remained static through the 1850s. Forty-two Irish men reported the same occupation in both censuses. The most interesting change was in the number of laborers who listed themselves as mill hands in 1860. Of the forty-eight who were laborers in 1850, thirteen had become mill hands by 1860, or over 25 percent of the 1850 laborers.[13] While every mill hand was not an operative, a significant percentage of those who reported their occupations in each year believed that they had changed the nature of their employment.

Those Irish men who remained in Lowell throughout the 1850s shared this same tendency among male household heads to find employment in the mills. The 1,050 households in the neighborhood which surrounded St. Patrick's Church in 1860 contained 1,215 adult Irish men, of whom 448 (36.8 percent) were laborers, representing a significant decrease from the 66 percent who were laborers in 1850. With a median age among Irish laborers of thirty-eight, it is clear that fewer young Irish men chose careers as laborers. The absence of steady employment for unskilled laborers combined with the opening of the mills to Irish men, particularly those exposed to public schools, to decrease the percentage of unskilled laborers among Irish men. Although laborers were still a large group, most young Irish men sought other employment. Whereas few Irish men had obtained mill employment in 1850, 390 men (32 percent) reported themselves as mill hands in 1860, almost as many as were laborers.[14] At the Hamilton Company, the proportion of men in the work force doubled between 1836 and 1860.[15]

Despite the shift to more steady employment in Lowell's mills, residential mobility among the Irish remained high. Only eighty-seven (13.3 percent) of the 1850 household heads could be located in the 1860 census.[16] Undoubtedly, many of these household heads had located in areas more distant from St. Patrick's Church but still within Lowell. Others had disappeared as the opportunities for unskilled laborers decreased. A few died in the unhealthy conditions which characterized the Irish neighborhoods. The shift in the pattern of employment also continued to have a major impact upon Irish children as mill owners made increasing use of them. Eventually, the Lowell school committee, with strong support from the mill agents, adopted a certificate statute to govern their employment. The Irish used the statute effectively, pulling their children out of school as the children found employment in the mills.[17] In 1847, for example, the schools committee noted: "more than ONE SEVENTH of the whole number of scholars connected with this school [Lowell Street's Grammar School Number 5] the past year, have received certificates for the mill from the Principal. This has fallen heavily upon the higher classes, taking away, in many instances, the best and most advanced scholars."[18] From 1852 to 1859, 2,370 certificates were issued allowing Irish children into the mills. In 1859, the largest concentration of Irish children working under the certificate statute were in the Lawrence, Hamilton, and Middlesex mills.[19]

In the late 1850s, most children entered the mills about their fifteenth birthday, after which, as the school committee reported, "they then work constantly."[20] While the mill agents believed that children educated in public schools were the most productive mill employees, the school committee also preached public education because of the republican values which were inculcated into each student. It warned in 1859 that "any one, who narrows the school time of these children by employing them contrary to law, not only does them a great wrong, but also inflicts a great injury upon the whole community."[21] In the early 1850s, the school committee had successfully implemented a plan which combined intermediate schools for older uneducated immigrant children, a truant officer, a House of Reformation, and the certificate statute to raise citywide attendance from 78 percent in 1836 to 87 percent in 1854.[22] Although the opening of the girls' school and Notre Dame Academy caused a drop in attendance at several nearby public schools, most Irish parents educated their children somewhere. Lowell's mill agents encouraged this development, and the school committee pressured Irish parents to conform to their dictates. There was no advantage for Irish parents in doing otherwise.

That education was a route to mill employment was not lost upon Lowell's Irish. Horatio Wood, the minister-at-large, had operated a "Free Evening School" for adults since the 1840s. By the 1850s, he ran several classes. Eventually, the school committee absorbed the entire system.[23] When he opened the Suffolk Street School near St. Patrick's Church in 1853, for example, Wood planned accommodations for seventy-five adult students but over three hundred registered for classes.[24] Imitating the school committee's approach on discipline, Wood moved quickly to control the rampant "spirit of insubordination and lawlessness":

> Mr. Wood always had a policemen at the outer door to keep roughs away from the entrance, but he never called the man inside to assist him in maintaining order, as he thought it would lessen his authority to do so. If a pupil was disorderly, he was quick to detect the offender and ordered him to leave the school for the evening. If a boy refused to go and clung to the chair Mr. Wood put him out at once. Although a small man, he had muscular strength and never feared that he should not accomplish what he undertook.[25]

By 1855, nearly four hundred Irish attended the Suffolk Street School, encouraged largely by Lowell's mill agents.[26] In one mill, Wood's program reduced illiteracy by almost 90 percent. Wood noted that some mill overseers testified publicly that illiterate mill workers were "the least profitable to their employers, received the lowest wages, and are the most turbulent and untractable."[27]

By the 1850s, several considerations, old and new, affected the school committee's actions and also served to illustrate the new relationship between Irish and Yankee Lowell. First, the school committee continued to uphold the relationship between public education and the good of the community. Second, the massive influx of thousands of destitute Famine Irish had turned Lowell's Irish neighborhoods, especially the Acre, into overcrowded tenement districts. This reinforced the need to impose order. The high percentage of children attending school throughout the influx indicated that the school committee was successful in its efforts to place children in public schools. Third, Catholic priests and their middle-class supporters, as well as the majority of the Irish community, had turned away from public education as "godless." At the same time, they raised no objection to educating Irish boys in public schools or to the attendance of adult Irish in the evening schools. The apparent paradox is even more striking in that Bishop Fitzpatrick, a staunch supporter of public education, praised the development of parochial schools in Lowell. The solution to this paradox rests in the perception of each group of the meaning of education in Lowell. For the O'Briens, the parochial system represented one stage of a much more complex local institutional development. The parochial school did not interfere with the subsequent employment of Irish girls in the mills, although the school committee periodically threatened such action and briefly implemented such a policy. For the Irish, a parochial school was part of a genuine commitment to Catholicism in America, which was strengthened under the O'Briens, around whom they had rallied during the Know-Nothing turmoil. This did not prevent Lowell's Irish from sending their sons to public schools or from attending schools themselves. In this respect, it was possible for the O'Briens to denounce public education as "godless" while still acknowledging the need to send Irish sons to public school. A boys' school would wait until 1882.[28]

The drive for public education in antebellum Lowell must be seen as a process in which many of the same motivations and much of the rhetoric justified school committee actions taken over forty years in an effort to adapt to the enormous internal changes within Lowell. Rev. Theodore Edson's goal of moral, responsible citizenship in 1830 still applied in 1855, but Lowell was a far larger and more complex city. It was overwhelmed by destitute Irish immigrants unaccustomed to the duties and responsibilities of good citizenship in America. Long gone were the days of the 1835 education agreement. Whereas local priests and the school committee had once worked together to bring the Irish into school, they were now adversaries battling for control of the minds and hearts (and souls) of Irish schoolchildren. Each side believed firmly in education and in the need to promote the good of the community, but they disagreed over what "community" should mean.

Still, some patterns in childrearing assumed forms which characterized assimilating immigrant communities in American industrial cities. The number of children in completed families dropped between 1850 and 1860. In 1850, the completed family, with the male household head between forty-one and fifty, contained an average of 4.86 children, but by 1860 the number of children had dropped to 3.92 per family. In addition, parents spaced their children closer together while limiting family size. In 1850, only 44 percent of the Irish parents spaced distance between the oldest and youngest child at less than ten years. By 1860, 50 percent of the

Irish parents did so. While Irish parents recognized the economic value of children in public schools, they adopted the nineteenth-century urban family pattern of smaller families. Since the average age at marriage varied little from 1850 to 1860, a number of other factors more directly affected family development.[29]

First, while the mills opened to Lowell's Irish, mill employment did not produce enough income to raise the quality of life for most Irish families. While 4.5 percent of the 1850 households in the Acre in 1850 reported real estate holdings, the figure rose to only 10 percent in 1860. Among those few households which persisted throughout the 1850s, the percentage of real estate owners increased to 24.1. The wealthiest Irish remained neighborhood merchants, tailors, and real estate speculators, although a few mill hands and laborers acquired a little property.[30] The mill produced enough income to meet basic needs among most Irish families but nothing more. Second, remittance to Ireland drained much of the savings which Irish families managed to acquire. In 1866, for example, one Lowell firm remitted $12,000 in passage money and an additional $32,000 to improve conditions among relatives who remained in Ireland. In a second example, "from another immigration agent in the same place . . . a striking instance of liberality is obtained. He says—'The most I received at any one time was 20£ or $140, from an industrious Irish girl in one of our mills.'"[31] Third, economic growth within Lowell slowed. While Irish replaced Yankee women when they withdrew from the mills, the real growth in Irish employment had come traditionally from a combination of replacement and the hiring of new workers as the mills expanded production. While mill output increased throughout the 1850s, the mills added few workers, particularly during the business depression in the late 1850s. The "pioneer Sister" noted that the Irish felt the effects of the 1850s business depression deeply: "not only individuals but whole families were kept by her [Mother Superior Desiree's] bounty. Food was prepared and dispensed at all hours at the convent door to men, women and children. The hard wooden bench of the schoolroom often served as a couch for the poor wanderers that had spent the day in search of employment while numbers of little ones were gathered together, fed and clothed until their parents were able to rent a room or two that they could call their own."[32]

Finally, Lowell remained an unhealthy place for the Irish. The number of female-headed households rose from 23 percent in 1850 to 31 percent in 1860 and the number of female households with boarders increased slightly from 37.6 percent to 41.8 percent.[33] While some female-headed households may have included husbands who worked in nearby mill cities or who searched the New England countryside for work, the congestion and deterioration in the quality of housing undoubtedly took its toll. After 1855, the city death rate hovered at about two per thousand. At the same time, the number of deaths from consumption in the Acre alone was about forty-five annually. If the Irish represented nearly half of Lowell's population about 1860, then the consumption rate among the Acre Irish was somewhere near 2.5 per thousand, or higher than the citywide rate. If other diseases and the Irish deaths which occurred outside the Acre are included, the Irish death rate per thousand perhaps was twice the general Lowell rate.[34]

While Irish family ties were strengthened in the 1850s by new employment patterns as well as by such factors as housing, nativism, and institutional Catholicism, the Irish family led a precarious existence. Declining opportunity for unskilled Irish laborers, recessions affecting mill employment, and overcrowded and unhealthy neighborhoods like the Acre influenced the direction taken by most Irish families. In such an environment, the Catholic church offered an especially attractive combination of philosophy and service. In 1854, the O'Briens had dedicated the new St. Patrick's Church amidst the Know-Nothing furor, emerging as the leaders of a new brand of local Irish whom they now nurtured as loyal Catholics. Irish Catholicism stressed the glory of the faith, symbolized in the massive new church arising among the Irish tenements in the Acre. Philosophically, however, the O'Briens counseled local Irish to accept persecution while working to better their lives under guidelines which the O'Briens established. Real reward awaited the Irish in heaven.[35]

Such was the formula for the O'Briens' success in Lowell. While the Irish had been promised equality and full citizenship under the terms dictated by Yankees in earlier days, the O'Briens argued that the Irish must now accept the limitations placed upon them by their existence in Lowell. When the Irish became the target of Know-Nothing hostility in response to local Yankee disappointment over the mill owners' decision to abandon Lowell's moral environment, any hope for a life based upon the old compromises vanished, even among the Irish middle class for whom Yankee promises held the most meaning. In its place, the O'Briens offered a philosophy which explained the persecution endured by Lowell's Irish as part of man's existence and, traditionally, a badge of Irish heritage. At the same time, they developed new standards for Irish Catholics which rejected accommodation to Yankee terms but which tied Lowell's Irish firmly to American Catholicism stamped in the mold of Irish immigrants.

The O'Briens also based much of their success on the services which made their philosophy on the position of Lowell's Irish particularly attractive. First, they displayed genuine fatherly concern for their parishioners who were either embittered or indifferent from their years with Father McDermott. Next, they provided a visible symbol of their philosophy by constructing the new St. Patrick's Church. When Horatio Wood complained in 1858 that "the conviction is spreading wide, that they [Lowell's Catholic priests] do not now care and provide for their poor as they are able," he criticized a phase in the O'Briens' plans without understanding their strategy.[36] Even before the new St. Patrick's had been dedicated, the O'Briens operated a girls' school, extending their influence in education in a manner similar to the school committee's approach twenty years earlier. After the school, they opened Notre Dame Academy and organized devotional societies as well as poor relief. In 1862, the O'Briens founded a fledgling hospital when they rented a room in a boardinghouse owned by Hugh Cummiskey.[37] In the same period, they also reinforced early institutions such as the Mathew Institute, which held a popular "Erina Ball" annually. Additionally, they supported the Young Men's Catholic Library Association.[38] When the Know-Nothing agitation died down, the O'Briens encouraged the resurgence of the Lowell Irish Benevolent Society which had once figured so prominently in early parish disputes.

With the astonishing variety of religious, social, educational, fraternal, and cultural associations, St. Patrick's parishioners found that their needs outside the mill were fulfilled. While there were always nonbelievers, the crowded Sunday Masses indicated that Catholicism influenced the lives of most Irish. It reinforced family ties and provided an important social outlet for Irish Catholic women. With the O'Briens as vigorous defenders of the new order, there was almost no intrusion by Yankee Lowell into the private lives of Lowell's Irish Catholics beyond the mill and institutions such as public schools. When Yankee Lowell intruded, the O'Briens met them at the convent door and when "rum-fired bigots" attacked, the O'Briens were ready. If the Yankees had been permitted entry unmolested, the O'Briens would have lost much more than church property. At the same time, they were patriotic Americans and, in their own way, es-

St. Patrick's in the late nineteenth century. Courtesy of Arthur L. Eno, Jr.

poused the old republican virtues of the earlier compromises. The call to rally to the Union cause in 1861, for example, emanated from the Catholic as well as the Protestant pulpits of Lowell.[39]

The philosophy which governed the Irish presence in Lowell following the Know-Nothing debacle also had its drawbacks. The world over which the O'Briens presided was narrow and provincial and, at times, pessimistic. While Catholicism gave the Acre Irish vitality, purpose, and fraternity, Catholic philosophy, which accepted persecution and advocated separatism beyond the workplace, was harshly pragmatic and, at times, bleak and barren. In this sense, it is no surprise that Thernstrom found that Newburyport's Irish were interested in home ownership and displayed a lack of social mobility in the late nineteenth century. As nineteenth-century American Catholicism was developing a particularly Irish stamp in the Northeast, it encouraged what for its leaders had been part of their upbringing—conformity and security. It was hard to climb above this level and American Catholicism discouraged immigrants from reaching beyond it.[40] In short, Irish Catholic leaders won in part because they promised less than the old Yankee compromises. In a world rapidly industrializing and bitterly antagonistic to immigrant workers, less was all one could expect. Thus Catholicism worked because it served its immigrant parishioners. In the process, nineteenth-century American Catholicism became anti-intellectual, traditional, and blue-collar—a religion of the working class which posed no threat to Lowell's mill owners. Catholicism preached obedience, good citizenship, and tradition, urging its followers to turn inward to find comfort and fulfillment.

By the Civil War, the pattern of development which would govern Lowell's Irish community until the 1940s had been established. In the 1880s, enough naturalized Irish voters joined with native-born American Irish to dominate local politics, but the Irish family and the Catholic church remained the cornerstones of Irish community development.[41] After the Civil War, the mill owners sold the boardinghouses to speculators. Older Irish neighborhoods lost some of their cohesiveness as electrified trolleys opened new areas to settlement in Centralville and South Lowell. In addition, thousands of French Canadians, Greeks, Poles, Portuguese, and Jews, among others, joined Lowell's Irish. The Irish became an ethnic minority as the total number of French Canadians in Lowell surpassed them in the early twentieth century.[42] Despite political opportunity and residential mobility, however, the allegiances which had been formed in the 1850s still held. By 1900, St. Patrick's had become the most highly institutionalized parish in Lowell.[43]

The strength of the new ties forged among the Irish in the 1850s says a great deal about the nature of community in nineteenth-century America. John Higham suggested that research into American ethnic history has encouraged a division of historians into "hard" and "soft" pluralists. The first view history in terms of class analysis, while the others look more to family, neighborhood, and institutional development.[44] The growth of community among Lowell's Irish indicates that there is a need to bridge the gap between the two groups. If there is any value to the study of ethnicity within the "new urban history," it lies in the ability of those examining it to take a more intensive look at the process of urbanization. As John McClymer suggested, community history is an attractive approach in part because it permits historians to freeze the process of change in small increments.[45]

The story of the development of community among Lowell's Irish is an excellent illustration of urban process. Lowell was part of a much larger "system of cities," many of them established on the Lowell model. All exhibited a high degree of economic and demographic interdependence.[46] The mill owners throughout New England shared, and often determined, the values held in those communities which they established.[47] Sometimes they acted, as in the 1840s, to change these values. Their decision placed Lowell's Irish in the midst of a community in transition. In that sense, the growth of Lowell, influenced initially by a strong humanitarian impulse among mill owners, a transient native female labor force, and resident Yankee middle-class reformers, was different from that of such cities as Holyoke and Lawrence, which were always heavily immigrant.[48] As Frisch demonstrated, modernization in cities like Lowell did not bring an end to community, but the structure of community within them changed.[49] Lowell is an excellent example of a city in which the paternal capitalism of the Yankee factory village gave way to the more formal relationships of an immigrant industrial city.

At the same time, the specific conditions affecting Lowell's growth also contributed directly to the experiences shared by immigrants there. The growth of an Irish community demonstrated the importance of neighborhood subsystems in which the direction of community development is multilayered rather than linear.[50] As Mirel and Angus noted, families made decisions about what was best for them not on the basis of economic constraints but more on values never subject to quantification.[51] Put another way, immigrants themselves ultimately had the most direct impact upon their own lives. Much of the weakness in recent research in American social history has come from the failure of historians to see power as broadly conceived. It need not be a term applied exclusively to class analysis. Power can be measured much more subtly in terms of the goals held by immigrants and their ability to achieve them. No matter how insignificant the goals, the smaller the distance between ambition and achievement—at least from an immigrant's perspective—the greater the power held by an immigrant over his own life. In a very basic way, power is a "quality of life" issue.

Stuart Blumin recently suggested that the most critical question concerning the process of community development is whether the various dimensions of experience converge in such a way that they contribute to a distinct way of life for a distinct subgroup of the population.[52] For Lowell's Irish, the process of community development indicates that these dimensions did converge in a unique way. Although the "Irishness" of Lowell's immigrants made a neat and easy accommodation impossible, the pattern of community development suggests what McClymer called a mixture of primary and secondary relations.[53] Lowell's Irish, above all else, were Irish. At the same time, they used those institutions which helped them. Some, such as the family, remained important throughout the process of community development; indeed, the family's position was enhanced by factors such as the economic conditions in Lowell. Others, like the Catholic church, rose in importance in response to changing needs. As the Irish were slowly incorporated into Lowell's economy, these relations became more formal. Still, the pattern of Irish community development allows us to see the parameters of human choice.[54]

In this sense, the Irish made their choices because they were Irish and in response to internal dynamics within the paddy camps as well as to external changes in the world beyond them. The process of community development, however, was one of constant change. As relations became more formal, Irish identity became less foreign and more American, Catholic, and working class. Drawing strength from matriarchal families with whom it maintained close ties, the Catholic church created an Irish Catholic subculture. In time, a new mixture of primary and secondary relations altered the process of community development.[55] The Catholic "ghetto" mentality broke down. Until then, the sense of community, nurtured in the volatile first years of the Irish presence in Lowell, served the Irish well.

TABLES AND FIGURES

Table 1
Population of Lowell

1826 (est.)	2,500	1840	20,981
1828	3,532	1850	33,383
1830	6,477	1860	36,827
1833	12,363	1870	40,928
1837	18,010	1880	59,485

Source: "Appendix A," in *Cotton Was King*, ed. Arthur L. Eno, Jr. (Lowell: Lowell Historical Society, 1976), p. 255.

Table 2
Statistics of Lowell Manufactures

Year	1835	1843	1847	1855	1868	1878	1888
No. of Mills	22	33	47	52	50	100	175
No. of Spindles	116,804	201,076	301,297	392,234	457,512	745,048	932,600
No. of Looms	3,933	6,194	8,749	11,773	12,188	18,261	28,139
Females Employed	5,051	6,295	8,635	8,820	8,980	11,660	13,358
Males Employed	1,512	2,345	3,995	4,367	4,737	7,625	7,691
Pounds (or Bales of Cotton Consumed per Wk.	670 (bales)	1,120 (bales)	637,000	690,000	677,000	1,000,000	1,452,700
Yards of Cotton Produced per Wk.	753,270	1,425,800	1,920,900	2,246,000	2,328,000	3,444,500	4,676,000

Source: "Appendix B" in *Cotton Was King*, ed. Arthur L. Eno, Jr. (Lowell: Lowell Historical Society, 1976), p. 256. Eno uses Annual Statistics of Manufacturing in Lowell; Statistics of Lowell Manufactures.

Table 3
Baptisms and Marriages, St. Patrick's and St. Peter's Parishes, 1837–46

	St. Patrick's		St. Peter's	
Year	Baptisms	Marriages	Baptisms	Marriages
1837	178	45	—	—
1838	163	35	—	—
1839	165	39	—	—
1840	183	43	—	—
1841	179	42	—	—
1842	145	50	70	10
1843	151	36	97	18
1844	133	37	95	23
1845	164	51	—	—
1846	222	71	131	38

Source: Year-end reports: Fenwick and Fitzpatrick Memoranda, Archives, Archdiocese of Boston, Brighton, Mass.

Table 4
Representative Diseases, the Acre and Lowell, 1842–49

Disease: The Acre	Year							
	1842	'43	'44	'45	'46	'47	'48	'49
Consumption	11	14	10	12	28	39	51	56
Typhoid Fever	2	3	—	3	23	52	18	13
Measles	1	—	2	—	6	—	6	—
Dysentery	16	4	1	—	3	65	60	31
Dropsy	1	3	5	1	9	7	12	7
Croup	—	—	3	—	3	4	15	7
Cholera Inf.	—	1	5	4	8	5	2	—
Disease: Lowell	Year							
	1842	'43	'44	'45	'46	'47	'48	'49
Consumption	70	73	77	71	103	128	124	139
Typhoid Fever	43	38	26	40	101	95	58	37
Measles	12	—	10	4	17	2	27	1
Dysentery	17	11	2	—	23	206	152	80
Dropsy	23	20	31	21	46	29	30	27
Croup	12	6	11	11	19	26	41	19
Cholera Inf.	34	27	31	26	48	51	22	20

Source: Acre: *Vital Records of Lowell, Massachusetts, to the End of the Year 1849* and *Vital Records,* 1826–61; Lowell: *Daily Journal and Courier,* 1 Feb. 1850, p. 2.

Table 5
Number of Cases of Drunkenness,
Recorded Feb. – Aug., 1847
and Feb. – Aug., 1848

	1847	1848
February	92	177
March	68	200
April	91	168
May	94	160
June	83	176
July	147	228
August	134	234
Total	709[a]	1,343

[a] Wood's *Report* says 509.

Source: Horatio Wood, *Fourth Annual Report* (1848), p. 23.

Table 6
Whole Number of Prosecutions for
Drunkenness before Lowell Police
Court, 1850–60

Year	Number	Year	Number
1850	273	1856	606
1851	329	1857	476
1852	304	1858	594
1853	414	1859	562
1854	419	1860	225
1855	517		

Source: *Address of Benjamin G. Sargent
to the City of Lowell, at the Organization
of the Government*, 7 Jan. 1861, p. 5.

Table 7
Number of Cases Handled by the Ministry-at-Large, 1859–60

1859				1860			
Applications		Relief Given[a]		Applications		Relief Given	
American	193	American	134	American	185	American	149
English	43	English	36	English	71	English	59
Scotch	21	Scotch	21	Scotch	27	Scotch	24
Irish	111	Irish		Irish		Irish	
		Catholic	44	Catholic	78	Catholic	40
		Protestant		Protestant		Protestant	
		Irish	40	Irish	25	Irish	23
French	20	French	2	Welsh	12	Welsh	8
German	1	German	1	Italian	1	Italian	0
Colored	1	Colored	1	Portuguese	2	Portuguese	2
				German	2	German	2
				Colored	7	Colored	5

[a] Specific assistance included food, fuel, clothing, and lodging, depending upon need.

Sources: Horatio Wood, *Fifteenth Annual Report* (1859), p. 5; Wood, *Sixteenth Annual Report* (1860), p. 4.

Table 8

Average Number Belonging and Percent Attendance, Lowell Public Schools, 1836–54

Year	Average No. Belonging	Percent Attendance	Year	Average No. Belonging	Percent Attendance
1836	1,083	78	1846	3,991	82
1837	2,505	73	1847	4,092	85
1838	2,673	72	1848	4,736	80
1839	2,695	72	1849	5,168	76
1840	3,229	74	1850	5,261	81
1841	3,449	81	1851	5,692	76
1842	3,547	81	1852	5,410	82
1843	3,657	82	1853	5,155	84
1844	3,856	84	1854	5,197	87
1845	3,770	83			

Source: *Annual Lowell School Committee Report* (1854), p. 25.

Table 9

Number of Certificates Issued, 1838–59

Year	Total	Year	Total
1838	225	1849	206
1839	267	1850	168
1840	311	1851	186
1841	343	1852	271
1842	145	1853	247
1843	58	1854	341
1844	42	1855	311
1845	132	1856	375
1846	185	1857	240
1847	236	1858	227
1848	225	1859	358

Source: 1838–51: *Annual Lowell School Committee Report* (1851), p. 18; 1852–59: *Annual Lowell School Committee Report* (1859), p. 58.

Table 10
Number of Children Employed in Lowell in Compliance with Certificate
Statute, 1859

Corporation	Number	Corporation	Number
Lawrence	38	Lowell Bleachery	4
Merrimack	13	Cowley's Mills	8
Lowell	15	Mather's Mills	12
Appleton	18	Tremont	1
Belvedere	13	Massachusetts	13
Suffolk	13	Hamilton	43
Boott	34	Prescott	4
Middlesex	28	American Bolt Co.	6
		Total	263

Source: *Annual School Committee Report* (1859), p. 59.

Table 11
Household Structure: The Acre, 1850 and 1860

Households	1850 Number	Percent of Total	Households	1860 Number	Percent of Total
Households with One or More Children at Home	542	83.3	Households with One or More Children at Home	951	90.5
Households with Boarders	190	35.0	Households with Boarders	667	29.9
Households without Boarders	352	64.9	Households without Boarders	284	70.1
Living Alone	7	1.0	Living Alone	27	2.5
Female-headed	125	23.0	Female-headed	325	31.0
Female with Boarders	47	37.6	Female with Boarders	136	41.8
Female without Boarders	78	62.4	Female without Boarders	189	58.2
Total Number of Households	650		Total Number of Households	1,050	

Source: Federal Manuscript Census (1850), M432, Rolls 326, 327, and (1860), M653,
Roll 507.

Table 12
Occupations of Male Household Heads in 1850

Male Household Heads (Total Number)		499
Occupation	Number	Percent of Total
Laborer	318	63.7
"Other" Including	104	20.9
Construction Support	Service Trades	In Mills
Carpenter 8	Manufacturer 9	Blacksmith 8
Mason 6	Shoe Maker 9	Dyer 7
Iron Founder 4	Peddler 5	Machinist 7
Moulder 2	Tailor 5	Operative 2
Stone Mason 2	Clerk 3	Calico Painter 1
Cabinet Maker 1	Brewer 2	Engineer 1
Contractor 1	Clergyman 2	Mechanic 1
Cooper 1	Harness Maker 2	Weaver 1
Painter 1	Trader 2	Woolcarter 1
Slater 1	Boot Maker 1	
Stonecutter 1	Butcher 1	
Teamster 1	Grocer 1	
	Gunsmith 1	
	Tanner 1	
	Watchman 1	
	Woodturner 1	
Unspecified	77	15.4
Total	499	100.0

Source: Federal Manuscript Census (1850)

Table 13
Mill Employment among Acre Irish, 1860

Households	Number	Percent of Total
Adult Irish within Household	3,298	—
Adult Irish Working in Mills	1,581	47.9
Male Irish Mill Workers	390	24.7
Female Irish Mill Workers	1,191	75.3

Source: Federal Manuscript Census (1860)

Table 14
Mill Employment among Acre Irish Wives, 1860

Households	Number	Percent of Total
Irish Wives within Households	681	—
Wives Listed as "Wives"	500	73.4
Wives Listed as "Mill Hands"	42	6.1
Wives Listed with No Occupation	133	19.5
Wives Listed in Other Occupations	6	1.0

Source: Federal Manuscript Census (1860).

Table 15
Occupations of Adult Irish Men in 1860

	Number	Percent of Total
Adult Irish Men in 1860	1,215	—
Laborers	448	36.8
Mill Hands	390	32.0
Other Occupations	377	31.2

Source: Federal Manuscript Census (1860).

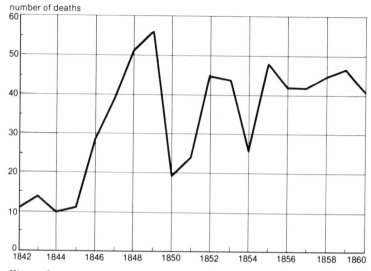

Figure 1
Tuberculosis: The Acre, 1842–60

Source: Vital Records, 1821–61.

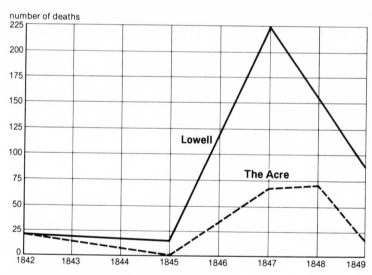

Figure 2
Dysentery: The Acre and Lowell, 1842–49

Source: Vital Records, 1821–61.

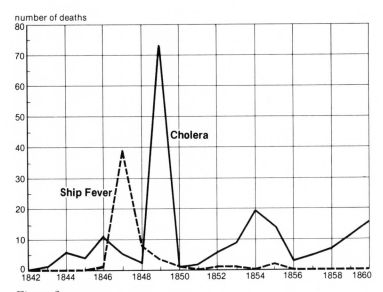

number of deaths

Figure 3
Cholera and Ship Fever: The Acre, 1842–60

Source: Vital Records to 1849; Vital Records, 1821–61.

NOTES

1. INTRODUCTION

1. Caroline F. Ware, *The Early New England Cotton Manufacture: A Study in Industrial Beginnings* (Boston: Houghton Mifflin Co., 1931; reprint, New York: Johnson Reprint Corporation, 1966); Hannah Josephson, *The Golden Threads: New England's Mill Girls and Magnates* (New York: Duell, 1949; reprint, New York: Russell & Russell, 1967).

2. Leo Marx, *The Machine in the Garden: Technology and the Pastoral Ideal in America* (London: Oxford University Press, 1964); John F. Kasson, *Civilizing the Machine: Technology and Republican Values in America, 1778–1900* (New York: Grossman, 1976); Thomas Bender, *Toward an Urban Vision: Ideas and Institutions in Nineteenth Century America* (Lexington: University Press of Kentucky, 1975); and Jonathan Prude, *The Coming of the Industrial Order: Town and Factory Life in Rural Massachusetts, 1810–1860* (New York: Cambridge University Press, 1983).

3. George S. Gibb, *The Saco-Lowell Shops: Textile Machinery Building in New England, 1813–1949* (Cambridge: Harvard University Press, 1950); Robert G. Layer, *Earnings of Cotton Mill Operatives, 1825–1914* (Cambridge: Harvard University Press, 1955); Alexander James Field, "Educational Expansion in Mid-Nineteenth Century Massachusetts: Human-Capital Formation or Structural Reinforcement?" *Harvard Education Review* 46 (1976): 521–52. Other related studies include Paul D. McGouldrick, *New England Textiles in the Nineteenth Century* (Cambridge: Harvard University Press, 1968); Pamela J. Nickless, "A New Look at Productivity in the New England Cotton Textile Industry, 1830–1860," *Journal of Economic History* 34 (1979): 889–910; as well as more general national studies, especially Douglas C. North, *The Economic Growth of the United States, 1790–1860* (Englewood Cliffs, N.J.: Prentice-Hall, 1961) and Douglas T. Miller, *The Birth of Modern America, 1820–1850* (Indianapolis: Bobbs-Merrill Co., 1970).

4. Josephson, p. 207; Kasson, p. 85.

5. Cf. Donald B. Cole, *Immigrant City, Lawrence, Massachusetts, 1845–1921* (Chapel Hill: University of North Carolina Press, 1963); Tamara Hareven and Randolph Langenbach, *Amoskeag: Life and Work in an American Factory City* (New York: Pantheon Books, 1978); Stephan Thernstrom, *Poverty and Progress: Social Mobility in a Nineteenth Century City* (Cambridge: Harvard University Press,

1964); and Howard P. Gitelman, *Workingmen of Waltham* (Baltimore: Johns Hopkins University Press, 1974).

6. Thomas Dublin, *Women at Work: The Transformation of Work and Community in Lowell, Massachusetts, 1826–1860* (New York: Columbia University Press, 1979).

7. Dublin's research reflected his deliberate effort to restrict his writing to the transformation of work and community among Yankee mill women. While the Irish left no diaries and few eyewitness accounts, the impact of the shifting pattern of employment upon the Irish and upon Lowell generally was described in a number of sources, including nineteenth-century newspapers, Lowell school committee reports, and the reports of the Ministry at-Large.

8. William Forbes Adams, *Ireland and Irish Emigration from 1815 to the Famine* (New Haven: Yale University Press, 1932; reprint, New York: Russell & Russell, 1967); Carl Wittke, *We Who Built America: The Saga of the Immigrant* (New York: Prentice Hall, 1939; reprint, Cleveland: Press of Case Western Reserve, 1964); Marcus Lee Hansen, *The Immigrant in American History* (Cambridge: Harvard University Press, 1942).

9. Oscar Handlin, *Boston's Immigrants: A Study in Acculturation* (New York: Atheneum, 1977).

10. Robert Ernst, *Immigrant Life in New York City, 1825–1863* (Port Washington, N.Y: Ira J. Freeman, 1965); Dennis Clark, *The Irish in Philadelphia: Ten Generations of Urban Experience* (Philadelphia: Temple University Press, 1973); Lynn Lees, *Exiles of Erin: Irish Migrants in Victorian London* (Ithaca: Cornell University Press, 1979). Other sources include Oscar Handlin, *The Uprooted* (Boston: Little, Brown & Co., 1973); George Potter, *To the Golden Door: The Study of the Irish in Ireland and America* (Westport, Conn.: Greenwood Press, 1960); Joseph P. O'Grady, *How the Irish Became Americans* (New York: Twayne Publishers, 1973); and, of course, Daniel P. Moynihan's classic argument on Irish assimilation in Nathan Glazer and Daniel Patrick Moynihan, *Beyond the Melting Pot* (Cambridge: M.I.T. Press, 1963). For an excellent discussion of the problems of nineteenth-century assimilation, see John Higham, "Integrating America: The Problem of Assimilation in the 19th Century," *Journal of American Ethnic History* 1 (1981): 7–25, and, on the state of research, his "Current Trends in the Study of Ethnicity in the United States," *Journal of American Ethnic History* 2 (1982): 5–15.

11. Thomas N. Brown, *Irish-American Nationalism*, (Philadeliphia: J. B. Lippincott Company, 1966). Cf. James P. Shannon, *Catholic Colonization of the Western Frontier* (New Haven: Yale University Press, 1957) for colonization schemes; Thomas F. Moriarty, "The Irish American Response to Catholic Emancipation," *Catholic Historical Review* 66 (1980): 353–73; Vincent Lannie, *Public Money and Parochial Education: Bishop Hughes, Governor Seward, and the New York School Controversy* (Cleveland: Press of Case Western Reserve, 1968) on Irish immigrants and public schools; Eward J. O'Day, "Constructing the Western Railroad: The Irish Dimension," *Historical Journal of Massachusetts* 11 (1983): 7–21, on work experiences outside New England's urban centers; Martin G. Towey and Margaret Sullivan Lopicculo, "The Knights of Father Mathew: Parallel Ethnic Re-

form," *Missouri Historical Review* 75 (1981): 168–83, on Irish American reform movements; Edward M. Levine, *The Irish and Irish Politicians* (Notre Dame, Ind.: University of Notre Dame Press, 1966), on Chicago politics; and any material on the Fenians, especially C. C. Tansill, *America and the Fight for Irish Freedom, 1886–1922* (New York: Devin-Adair Company, 1957).

12. William Shannon, *The American Irish* (New York: Macmillan Company, 1974); Lawrence J. McCaffrey, *The Irish Diaspora in America* (Bloomington: Indiana University Press, 1976); Andrew M. Greeley, *That Most Distressful Nation: The Taming of the American Irish* (Chicago: Quadrangle Books, 1972); John B. Duff, *The Irish in America* (Belmont, Calif.: Wadsworth Publishing Company, 1971); Kerby Miller, *Emigrants and Exiles: Ireland and the Irish Exodus to North America* (New York: Oxford University Press, 1985); and Timothy J. Meagher, ed., *From Paddy to Studs: Irish-American Communities in the Turn of the Century Era, 1880 to 1920* (Westport, Conn.: Greenwood Press, 1986).

13. John Tracy Ellis, *American Catholicism* (Chicago: University of Chicago Press, 1956); Thomas T. McAvoy, *A History of the Catholic Church in the United States* (Notre Dame, Ind.: University of Notre Dame Press, 1969) and with Thomas N. Brown, *The United States of America: The Irish Clergyman, the Irish Layman* (Dublin: Gill and Macmillian, 1970); Jay Dolan's impressive *American Catholic Experience: A History from Colonial Times to the Present* (New York: Doubleday & Co., 1985), as well as the massive four-volume original study by John Gilmary Shea, *A History of the Catholic Church within the Limits of the United States, from the First Attempted Colonization to the Present Time* (New York, 1890).

14. Thernstrom used such resources as bank accounts, the census, and church records to show that, for Newburyport's Irish, social mobility was limited and measured by such standards as home ownership.

15. Herbert Gutman, *Work, Culture, and Society in Industrializing America: Essays in American Working Class History* (New York: Alfred A. Knopf, 1976).

16. Stephan Thernstrom and Richard Sennett, *Nineteenth Century Cities: Essays in the New Urban History* (New Haven: Yale University Press, 1974); Howard P. Chudacoff, "A New Look at Ethnic Neighborhoods," *Journal of American History* 60 (1973): 76–93; as well as a number of studies arising from the Harvard Urban History series including Kathleen Neils Conzen, *Immigrant Milwaukee, 1836–1860: Accommodation and Community in a Frontier City* (1976); Michael Frisch, *Town into City: Springfield, Massachusetts and the Meaning of Community, 1840–1880* (1972); Clyde Griffen and Sally Griffen, *Natives and Newcomers: The Ordering of Opportunity in Mid-Nineteenth Century Poughkeepsie* (1978); and Alan Dawley, *Class and Community: The Industrial Revolution in Lynn* (1976).

17. Stephan Thernstrom, *The Other Bostonians* (Cambridge: Harvard University Press, 1974); Peter Knights, *The Plain People of Boston, 1830–1860* (New York: Oxford University Press, 1971); Daniel J. Walkowitz, *Worker City, Company Town: Iron and Cotton Worker Protest in Troy and Cohoes, New York, 1855–1884* (Urbana: University of Illinois Press, 1978); Susan E. Hirsch, *Roots of the American Working Class: The Industrialization of Crafts in Newark, 1800–1860* (Philadelphia: University of Pennsylvania Press, 1978); Bruce Laurie, *The Working*

People of Philadelphia, 1800–1850 (Philadelphia: Temple University Press, 1980); Michael Katz, *The People of Hamilton, Canada West: Family and Class in a Mid-Nineteenth Century City* (Cambridge: Harvard University Press, 1975); Josef Barton, *Peasants and Strangers: Italians, Rumanians, and Slovaks in an American City, 1890–1950* (Cambridge: Harvard University Press, 1975).

18. Jay P. Dolan, *The Immigrant Church: New York's Irish and German Catholics, 1815–1865* (Baltimore: Johns Hopkins University Press, 1975); Donna Merwick, *Boston's Priests, 1848–1910: A Study of Social and Intellectual Change* (Cambridge: Harvard University Press, 1973); and James Hennessey, *American Catholics: A History of the Roman Catholic Community in the United States* (New York: Oxford University Press, 1981).

19. Lynn Lees and John Modell, "The Irish Countryman Urbanized: A Comparative Perspective on the Famine Migration," *Journal of Urban History* 3 (1977): 391–408; Michael Katz, *The Irony of Early School Reform: Educational Innovation in Mid-Nineteenth Century Massachusetts* (Cambridge: Harvard University Press, 1968); and Michael Holt, "The Politics of Impatience: The Origins of Know-Nothingism," *Journal of American History* 60 (1973): 309–31.

20. The tendency to focus upon one aspect of immigrant experience, for example, labor protest, has real merit in that it allows careful examination of important phases of that experience. A discussion of the growth of community has the added value of integrating these experiences while developing the concept of community building as a process subject to a variety of factors.

21. Bernard Bailyn, "The Challenge of Modern Historiography," *American Historical Review* 87 (1982): 1–24.

22. George Hedrick, "Reminiscences and Recollections of Lowell, since 1831," *Old Residents Historical Association* (hereafter ORHA) 1 (1879): 367.

23. In the late 1840s, construction picked up briefly with the development of the Northern Canal.

24. Although the Famine Irish delivered the final blow to the pattern of employment making use of Yankee farm women, the Irish had obtained entry on a growing scale several years prior to the arrival of Famine Irish.

25. Merwick, pp. 1–11.

26. "Irish Girls in Lowell," Boston *Pilot*, 16 Aug. 1851, p. 7.

27. To this end, Boston's capitalists acted as catalysts in the growth of nativist bigotry because they made the Irish convenient local targets for nativist aggression.

2. THE EARLY IMMIGRANTS, 1821–30

1. Nathan Appleton, *Introduction to the Power Loom and Origin of Lowell* (Lowell, 1858), p. 19.

2. Harry C. Dinmore, "Proprietors of Locks and Canals: The Founding of Lowell," in Arthur L. Eno, Jr., ed., *Cotton Was King* (Lowell: Lowell Historical Society, 1976), pp. 69–73.

3. Patrick Malone, *The Lowell Canal System* (Lowell: Lowell Museum, 1976), pp. 4–6.

4. Josephson, pp. 62–66.

5. Ibid., p. 67.

6. The social and moral environment of Lowell was emulated widely throughout New England.

7. Amos Lawrence and Kirk Boott, as cited in Josephson, pp. 58–59.

8. Frederika Bremer, *The Homes of the New World: Impressions of America*, 2 vols.(New York: Harper and Bros., 1868; reprint, New York: Negro Universities Press, 1968); Anthony Trollope, *North America*, 2 vols. (New York: Harper and Bros., 1862; reprint, New York: Kelley, 1970); Michel Chevalier, *Society, Manners, and Politics in the United States: Letters on North America* (Boston: Weeks, Jordan & Co., 1839; reprint, New York: Kelley, 1966); Charles Dickens, *American Notes for General Circulation* (New York: Harper and Bros., 1842; reprint, New York: AMS, 1972).

9. Dickens, p. 65.

10. Elizabeth Coon Hawley, ed., *The American Diaries of Richard Cobden* (Princeton: Princeton University Press, 1952; reprint, New York: Greenwood Press, 1969), p. 117. Cobden returned to England and became involved in the effort to institute national elementary education. He also worked on behalf of the incorporation of Manchester and the Manchester Atheneum and he turned the Anti-Corn Law League into the Repeal movement.

11. No formal record survives in any newspaper advertisments for laborers in the early 1820s among newspapers in the Boston area. It is likely that word spread more informally among Boston's Irish.

12. My thanks to Martha Mayo, Special Collections, University of Lowell, for this information.

13. Robert H. Lord, John E. Sexton, and Edward P. Harrington, *History of the Archdiocese of Boston*, 3 vols. (New York: Sheed and Ward, 1944), 2:53–55; Ephraim Brown, "Glass-Making in the Merrimack Basin," *ORHA* 2 (1882): 180-200.

14. George O'Dwyer, *Irish Catholic Genesis of Lowell* (Lowell: Sullivan Brothers Printers, 1920), p. 7; John F. McEvoy, "Letter," 22 Feb. 1876, in *Proceedings in the City of Lowell at the Semi-Centennial Celebration of the Incorporation of the Town of Lowell*, Lowell Historical Society, 1876: 132–36.

15. "Another Old Citizen Gone," *Lowell Daily Courier*, 14 Dec. 1871, p. 4.

16. Statement of Expenses for the Town of Lowell in the Year 1831, Special Collections, University of Lowell.

17. "Celebration of St. Patrick's Day in Lowell, by the Lowell Irish Benevolent Society," *Lowell Courier*, 21 Mar. 1843, p. 2.

18. "Progress of Repeal in the U. States, Lowell," Boston *Pilot*, 29 May 1841, p. 171.

19. By then Bishop Fenwick had established either small churches or missions in the larger Catholic centers of New England including Salem, New Haven, Providence, and New Bedford.

20. Handlin, *Boston's Immigrants*, p. 49.

21. Thernstrom, *Poverty and Progress*, pp. 158–59.

22. McCaffrey, *Irish Diaspora*, pp. 59–60.

23. Potter, pp. 134–35.

24. Employment elsewhere, particularly in farming, fishing, commerce, and shipbuilding, induced many Irish to remain in northern New England and small colonies of Irish appeared along emigration routes.

25. Potter, p. 137.

26. Ibid.

27. Ibid.

28. Federal Manuscript Census (1850), M 432, Roll 326 and M 434, Roll 327. A breakdown shows the following: Atlantic Provinces (25), Canada (14), Maine (10), New Hampshire (5), Vermont (2), New York (9), Connecticut (2), and Rhode Island (6).

29. Lees, pp. 22–41; Barbara Kerr, "Irish Seasonal Migration to Great Britain, 1800–1838," *Irish Historical Studies* 3 (1943): 38–62; Edith Abbott, ed., *Immigration: Historical Aspects of the Immigration Problem* (Chicago: University of Chicago Press, 1926); Michael Anderson, *Family Structure in Nineteenth Century Lancashire* (Cambridge: Cambridge University Press, 1971); Frederick Engels, *The Condition of the Working Class in England in 1844* (London, 1892; reprint, London: George Allen & Unwin, 1952); Oliver McDonough, "Irish Overseas Emigration during the Famine," in *The Great Famine: Studies in Irish History*, eds. R. Dudley Edwards and T. Desmond Williams (New York: New York University Press, 1957), pp. 319–88; T. W. Freeman, *Ireland: A General and Regional Geography* (London: Methuen & Co., 1969); Robert Kennedy, Jr., *The Irish: Emigration, Marriage, and Fertility* (Berkeley: University of California Press, 1973); Raymond L. Cohn, "Mortality on Immigrant Voyages to New York, 1836–1853," *Journal of Economic History* 44 (1984): 289–300; S. H. Cousens, "The Regional Variations in Emigration between 1821 and 1841," *Transactions and Papers of the Institute of British Geographers* 37 (1965): 22–29.

30. The end of Lowell's building boom occurred at approximately the same time as the initial development of the first cities based on the Lowell plan. Within a decade of the founding of Lowell, towns like Chicopee were also developed. The construction of additional textile towns on the Lowell model increased employment opportunities for unskilled Irish laborers but it also increased their transiency within New England.

31. Despite this tendency, the largest migration "by county" was from Cork.

32. The pattern also supported the development of large camps of Corkonians and Connaught men within Lowell.

33. Handlin, *Boston's Immigrants*, pp. 25–53.

34. This wait is hardly surprising in that unskilled Irish laborers, who made up most of Lowell's male Irish population, seldom remained long enough to meet residency requirements and to obtain naturalized or native American character witnesses. In addition, not all Irishmen actively sought American citizenship.

35. According to the 1830 census, Lowell had 6,477 people. At the St. Patrick's Church dedication in 1831, Bishop Fenwick estimated that 500 Irish worshipped regularly. The 500 parishioners represent 7.7 of Lowell's 1830 population. See Table 1.

36. Anderson's work is one of a number of revisions, either direct or implied, of the Handlin position.

37. Dublin, *Women at Work*, pp. 155–56. Dublin's discussion of segregation in the boardinghouses based upon nativity of operatives confirms that the pattern of segregation between Irish and Yankees in Lowell went well beyond the workplace.

38. Malone, *Lowell Canal System*, p. 6.

39. *Lowell Daily Courier*, 14 Dec. 1871, p. 4.

40. Boott's most valuable land, obviously, was along river and power canals, creating, in effect, a compact factory village well within the boundaries of the land acquired for industrial development.

41. Although the total population of Irish increased to several hundred, the figure masks a high rate of transiency among them.

42. Paul Hill, "Reminiscences of Lowell, Fifty Years Ago," *ORHA* 5 (1894): 280.

43. The land on which the Irish settled was useful to Locks and Canal officials only in that it was necessary to the construction of the Western Canal; it was unsuitable for mill construction.

44. For a discussion of the nineteenth-century Irish faction, see Patrick O'Donnell, *The Irish Faction Fighters of the 19th Century* (Dublin: Anvil Books, 1975). A more scholarly treatment of the general history of Irish factionalism awaits further research, although several good studies of specific types of factions exist.

45. McEvoy, p. 132. For a discussion of the location of individual paddy camps and the ancestry of their inhabitants, see "Riot among the Irish," *Lowell Advertiser*, 11 Sept. 1849, p. 2; "Row and Fight among the Irish," *Daily Journal and Courier*, 10 Sept. 1849, p. 2; and "The Irish Riot," *Vox Populi*, 14 Sept. 1849, p. 2.

46. A. B Wright, "Lowell in 1826," *ORHA* 3 (1887): 405.

47. With the exception of the 1849 Irish riot, most of the battles were more individualized in nature.

48. "New Dublin" referred to the settlement along Dublin Street—a main thoroughfare in the Corkonian camp.

49. McEvoy, p. 132.

50. Hedrick, p. 367.

51. *Niles Register* as quoted in O'Dwyer, p. 8.

52. A. B. Wright, p. 405.

53. "Plan from Record Book 373," 18 May 1832, 373 (Cambridge, Mass.: Middlesex County Registry of Deeds, South District, 1898), 403; and "Plan of Land Being in Part the Paddy Camps Lands, So-Called," 20 Feb. 1839, 380 (Cambridge, Mass.: Middlesex County Registry of Deeds, South District, 1898), n.p.

54. Hedrick, p. 367.

55. Charles Cowley, "The Foreign Colonies of Lowell," *ORHA* 2 (1983): 2.

56. McEvoy, p. 173.

57. Paul Hill, pp. 277–79.

58. Ibid., pp. 277–79; J. B. French, "Early Recollections of an Old Resident," *ORHA* 1 (1879): 257. There were a few other potential employers. Thomas Carroll of Fenwick Street, for example, was a baggage master on the Merrimack River steamboat which plied the river above the Middlesex Canal. See Atkinson C. Varnum, "Navigation on the Merrimack River," *ORHA* 1 (1877): 321–22.

59. *Sketch of Lowell* (Lowell, 1842), p. 38.

60. Workers labored intensively on one or two projects at a time. Boott did de-

tach some workers for small projects such as street-grading. While Boott's principal goal was to place the mills in operation quickly, he also provided important city services such as streets, schools, and even a bank.

61. "Celebration of St. Patrick's Day in Lowell," *Lowell Courier*, 21 Mar. 1843, p. 2.

62. It is likely that other Irish work teams were employed at projects not connected directly with Locks and Canals construction but, apparently, Locks and Canals initially channeled most of the work in which they employed Irish through Cummiskey.

63. "Agent's Journals, August, 1826–February, 1832," Aug., Sept., and Nov., 1828, GC-1, Locks and Canals Collection, Baker Library, Harvard Graduate School of Business Administration, Boston (hereafter L & C).

64. "Receipts for Labor, August, 1826–December, 1828," RA-2, L & C. As examples of minimum wage scales, James Casey: $17.71 for 21¼ days; Edward O'Neil: 83¢ for 1 day; Morris Fielding: $25 for 30 days; and Timothy Raggen: $11.87 for 14½ days.

65. The L & C records show with remarkable consistency that in off-season months such as January the company employed Yankees almost exclusively. This pattern continued well into the 1850s. As one example, see "Pay Roll, Mechanics and Laborers," RF-2, L & C.

66. William Austin to Lowell *Mercury*, Lowell *Mercury*, 20 Feb. 1835, p. 1. The Fuel Society maintained an account in the Lowell Institution for Savings which paid $113.04 when closed in March, 1835. Lowell Fuel Society, Account No. 1786, 12 Apr. 1834–14 Mar. 1835, *Records of the Lowell Institution for Savings, Lowell Massachusetts*. In a second example, the Howard Benevolent Society, organized in the late 1830s, obtained funding from "all parties and sects." *Ladies Pearl*, Apr., 1842, p. 218.

67. "Work by Teams, Moses Shattuck," Dec., 1826, RG-1, L & C.

68. Dublin, *Women at Work*, pp. 153–64.

69. Indigent Yankee work teams and young agricultural workers comprised much of the unskilled labor force.

70. "Out-Door Hands," RB-1, L & C.

71. Constance Rourke, *American Humor: A Study of the National Character* (New York: Harcourt, Brace & Co., 1931; reprint, New York: Anchor Books, 1953), p. 116.

72. *Lowell Courier*, 14 Sept. 1839, p. 2.

73. *Lowell Weekly Compendium*, 6 Sept. 1832, p. 2; "Riot," Lowell *Mercury*, 21 May 1831, p. 3; "The Yankee and Paddy Quarrel," Lowell *Mercury*, 28 May 1831, p. 3.; Lowell *Evangelist*, 21 May 1831, p. 19.

74. "Riot," Lowell *Mercury*, 21 May 1831, p. 3.

75. Memoranda of Bishop Benedict Fenwick, 8 Oct. 1827, Archives, Archdiocese of Boston, Brighton, Mass., 1:63.

76. As one example: "An Irish maid, boasting of her in industrious habits, said she rose at four, made a fire, put on the tea-kettle, prepared breakfast, and made all the beds before anyone in the house was up." *Voice of Industry*, 8 May 1846, p. 2.

3. THE FIRST YEARS, 1830–35

1. Lord, Sexton, and Harrington, 2:56. On 13 July 1830 Fenwick identified about four hundred Catholics living in Lowell, although he wrote to Rome in his report of 24 Apr. 1831 that Lowell contained 800 to 900 Catholics (Arch. Con. Prop., F., Guilday Transcripts, no. 2330) as quoted in Lord et al. n. 10, 2:56.

2. Ibid., p. 314. The first Catholic school opened as early as 1824 or 1825. "An Irishman approved by the priest" ran the first school, which closed quickly. Patrick Collins opened another Catholic school in 1829.

3. Patrick Malone, *Canals and Industry: Engineering in Lowell, 1821–1880* (Lowell: Lowell Museum, 1983), p. 6.

4. Joseph W. Lipchitz, "The Golden Age," in Eno, p. 99. In 1839, the Boston Associates bought Kirk Boott's home as a corporation hospital for sick operatives. It eventually became St. Joseph's Hospital.

5. That policy changed somewhat by the late 1830s when town officials began to extend town services, especially streets and sewers, into the Irish district.

6. Merwick, pp. 3–5.

7. Ibid., p. 4. Charles Bullfinch, the famous early American architect, designed Holy Cross. One-fifth of the total cost was pledged by Boston's Protestants; John Adams headed the subscription list with a pledge of $100.

8. Ibid., p. 5.

9. Patrick Carey, "The Laity's Understanding of the Trustee System, 1785–1855," *Catholic Historical Review* 44 (1978): 357–76; Peter Guilday, "Trusteeism," *Historical Records and Studies* 18 (1928): 14–73; G. C. Treacy, "The Evils of Trusteeism," *Historical Records and Studies* 8 (1915): 136–56; David A. Gerber, "Modernity in the Service of Tradition: Catholic Lay Trustees at Buffalo's St. Louis Church and the Transformation of European Communal Traditions, 1829–1865," *Journal of Social History* 15 (1982): 655–84; and Patrick S. Dignan, *A History of the Legal Incorporation of Catholic Church Property in the United States (1784–1932)*, Studies in American Church History (Washington, D.C.: Catholic University Press, 1933) all deal with trusteeism.

10. Fenwick clearly recognized the importance of Lowell's Catholic community to his diocese if he was willing to assign one of his small staff to it.

11. Fenwick Memoranda, 5 Oct. 1827, 1:62.

12. O'Dwyer, p. 59.

13. Fenwick Memoranda, 8 Oct. 1827, 1:63.

14. Ibid., 26 Oct. 1828, 1:94.

15. Ibid., 1:94; Merwick, pp. 5–6. Although Fenwick continued the policies of Cheverus on accommodation, he faced violent nativist outbreaks such as the Ursuline convent burning at Charlestown in 1834. Still, the accommodationist spirit prevailed.

16. Fenwick Memoranda, 5 Oct. 1827, 1:62.

17. Ibid., 26 Oct. 1828, 1:94.

18. Ibid., 13–14 July 1830, 1:139.

19. O'Dwyer, p. 15.

20. *United States Catholic Miscellany*, 23 July 1831, as quoted in O'Dwyer, p. 19.

21. Ibid., p. 19.

22. "Proprietors of Locks and Canals on Merrimack River to Benedict Fenwick," 6 June 1835 (Cambridge: Middlesex County Registry of Deeds, South District), 45:346.

23. Fenwick Memoranda, 13 July 1830, 1:139.

24. O'Dwyer, p. 13.

25. Fenwick Memoranda, 3 July 1831, 1:158.

26. O'Dwyer, p. 59.

27. Ibid., p. 20.

28. Fenwick found about fifty Catholic children in Lowell in 1830, when Catholics regionally numbered about four hundred. About a year later, he confirmed thirty-nine children. While precise estimates are impossible, the numbers suggest that a few dozen families had formed a small resident "middle class," especially in that the first land sales and the construction of St. Patrick's Church also occurred during these years. Fenwick Memoranda, 13 July 1830, 1:139; 14 July 1830, 1:139; 3 July 1831, 1:158.

29. This figure is based upon the number of Irishmen attending the 1833 organization meeting of the men's fraternal association which became the forerunner to the Lowell Irish Benevolent Society.

30. "Locks and Canals to Hugh Cummiskey et al.," 1830–31 (Cambridge: Middlesex County Registry of Deeds, South District), 9:183.

31. While a ten-year lease was not the same as owning a home, the length of the lease indicates the commitment of some Irish to their life in the booming factory village.

32. O'Dwyer, p. 51.

33. The Corkonian camp was attractive in part because it was an especially convenient location, adjacent to the Lowell Machine Shop and Swamp Locks.

34. "A Resident in Lowell Street," *Bulletin*, 24 Sept. 1834, p. 1. See: "The Melvin Suits" and *Flagg* v. *Mann*. For the Melvin Suits, refer to John P. Robinson, "The Melvin Suits," *ORHA* 2 (Lowell, 1883): 201–5. Court cases include: 16 Pick 137, 16 Pick 161, 17 Pick 246, 17 Pick 255, 5 Metc 15. Also "The Melvin Cases," Lowell *Patriot*, 6 May 1836, p. 3 and 3 June 1836, p. 3. For *Flagg* v. *Mann*, see, for example, O'Dwyer, p. 50 and 9 Fed Cas 202, among others.

35. The dispute reached federal court because one of the parties lived in Michigan.

36. O'Dwyer, p. 50. Between 1833 and 1840, the land was tied up in court disputes.

37. Cowley, "The Foreign Colonies of Lowell," *ORHA* 2 (1883): 1:167.

38. "Plan from Record Book 373," 18 May 1832.

39. "Plan of the Town of Lowell and Belvedere Village by Benjamin Mather, 1832," Lowell Historical Society, Special Collections, University of Lowell.

40. "Plan of the City of Lowell, Massachusetts, 1850," Lowell Historical Society, Special Collections, University of Lowell.

41. *Vox Populi*, 10 Aug. 1849, p. 1; "Cit." to the Editor, *Daily Journal and Courier*, 27 Dec. 1850, p. 2.

42. By the 1850s a few Irishmen such as Hugh McEvoy, a tailor, had purchased land in rural sections of Lowell such as Christian Hill but these were exceptions to the rule.

43. *Lowell Advertiser*, 10 May 1839, p. 2. Cummiskey petitioned the mayor and the Board of Aldermen for someone to "preserve the peace, and maintain order and quiet in the neighborhood of the Catholic Church, on Sunday."

44. "Celebration of St. Patrick's Day in Lowell, by the Lowell Irish Benevolent Society," *Lowell Courier*, 21 Mar. 1843, p. 2. In this example, the speaker at a St. Patrick's Day dinner praised America, "where the exiled son of unhappy Erin can breathe the air of freedom."

45. Actual support for Repeal was lukewarm, especially when measured by contributions. Throughout 1841–42, however, Yankee Lowell was fascinated with the idea and Lowell's newspapers were full of reports and editorials on Repeal.

46. O'Dwyer, p. 40. Dues were 25 cents a month and were placed in a general fund "so that any of its members being taken sick knows where to call for it." *Lowell Courier*, 28 Mar. 1837, p. 2.

47. Status in the Benevolent Society was determined through the volunteer toasts made at annual St. Patrick's Day dinners in the 1830s and early 1840s. A comparison of these lists with city directories established the preeminence of the Benevolent Society as a haven for an emerging Irish middle class.

48. *Lowell Compendium*, 21 Mar. 1833, p. 3.

49. "Celebration of St. Patrick's Day," *U.S. Catholic Intelligencer*, 3 Mar. 1832, p. 215.

50. "The Fifth Anniversary of the Lowell Irish Benevolent Society," Boston *Pilot*, 23 Mar. 1839, p. 67.

51. "St. Patrick's Day Celebration," *Lowell Advertiser*, 26 Mar. 1838, p. 2.

52. This tendency is not surprising in that Lowell's Irish shopkeepers, foremen, and schoolteachers were the most likely to remain in Lowell, had the most invested in it, and had sufficient disposable income to afford membership fees.

53. O'Dwyer, pp. 43–44.

54. Schouler participated prominently at St. Patrick's Day celebrations just before his election to the state legislature in the early 1840s.

55. Unlike Handlin, who saw the Irish as settling in the Northeast because they lacked the resources to move elsewhere, the Irish in Lowell viewed Lowell as "the home of our choice—may its prosperity be as durable as the hills and mountains and as progressive as the waters of her rivers and fountains." For at least some, Lowell represented the realization of their dreams in a land of opportunity. *Lowell Advertiser*, 25 Mar. 1842, p. 3. On New England's pool of unskilled laborers, see Thernstrom, *Poverty and Progress*, p. 31.

56. Martha Zimiles and Murray Zimiles, *Early American Mills* (New York: Bramhall House, 1978), offer a brief but effective overview on the development of New England's textile centers.

57. "Gone," *Lowell Daily Courier*, 14 Dec. 1871. p. 4.

58. O'Dwyer, p. 46.

59. As late as August, 1854, only eleven Irishmen were listed as resident tax-payers who paid "$50 and upwards of taxes on property." They typically paid around $60 annually. Only one Irishman, real estate speculator Stephen Castles, paid more than $80 ($397.50). "List of Taxpayers," *Lowell Daily Journal and Courier*, 12 Aug. 1854, p. 2.

60. Fenwick Memoranda, 6 May 1833, 1:237–38.

61. "Celebration of St. Patrick's Day," *U.S. Catholic Intelligencer*, 3 Mar. 1832, p. 215.

62. Mary H. Blewett, "The Mills and the Multitudes: A Political History," in Eno, pp. 174–75.

63. Butler has been the subject of a number of biographies. The best among them include: Robert J. Holzman, *Stormy Ben Butler* (New York: Macmillan, 1954); Howard P. Nash, Jr., *Stormy Petrel: The Life and Times of Con. Benjamin F. Butler, 1818–1893* (Rutherford, N.J.: Fairleigh Dickinson University Press, 1969); Hans Louis Trefousse, *Ben Butler: The South Called Him Beast* (New York: Twayne Publishers, 1957); Robert S. West, *Lincoln's Scapegoat General: A Life of Benjamin F. Butler, 1818–1893* (Boston: Houghton Mifflin Co., 1965); and Margaret S. Thompson, "Ben Butler versus the Brahmins: Patronage and and Politics in Early Gilded Age Massachusetts," *New England Quarterly* 55 (1982): 163–86.

64. "Election of Maguire—Its Object and Its Influence," *Daily American Citizen*, 29 Jan. 1856, p. 2. Maguire was elected clerk of the Common Council and Lowell's auditor.

65. "The Whig Party in Lowell," *Lowell Advertiser*, 16 Nov. 1854, p. 2.

66. Josephson, p. 284.

67. In the mid 1840s, Charles M. Short and Stephen Castles were appointed "inspectors of elections" in wards One and Five. Another Irishman named O'Neil was defeated in a Common Council battle in Ward Three. *Lowell Courier*, 11 Mar. 1843, p. 2.

68. "Constable Election, Ward Five, November 1844," Election Commission Office, Lowell City Hall, Lowell, Mass. Those election records which have survived are remarkable both for the lack of Irish candidates, even at the ward level, and for the failure of almost any candidate to build a ward base.

69. Boston *Pilot* , 7 Mar. 1840, p. 501.

70. Elwood P. Cubberly, *Public Education in the United States: A Study and Interpretation of American Educational History* (Boston: Houghton Mifflin Co., 1934).

71. Bernard Bailyn, *Education in the Forming of American Society: Needs and Opportunities for Study* (Chapel Hill: University of North Carolina Press, 1960); Lawrence Cremin, *The American Common School: An Historical Conception* (New York: Columbia University Press, 1961). More recent revisionists include Michael B. Katz, *Irony of Early School Reform*, and *Class, Bureaucracy, and Schools: The Illusion of Educational Change in America* (New York: Praeger, 1971); Colin Greer, *The Great School Legend: A Revisionist Interpretation of American Public Education* (New York, Basic Books, 1972); Samuel Bowles and Herbert Gintis, *Schooling in Capitalist America* (New York: Basic Books, 1976);

and R. Freeman Butts, *Public Education in the United States: From Revolution to Reform* (New York: Holt, Rinehart, and Winston, 1978).

72. John W. Meyer et al., "Public Education as Nation-Building in America," *American Journal of Sociology* 85 (1979): 591–613.

73. Alfred Gilman, "History of the Lowell Grammar Schools," *ORHA* 4 (1891): 87–91. In 1825, Chelmsford appropriated only $113.50 for upkeep of its schools.

74. Ibid., p. 93.

75. Harriet Hanson Robinson, *Loom and Spindle: or Life among the Early Mill Girls* (New York, 1898; reprint, Kailua, Hawaii: Press Pacifica, 1976), pp. 13–14, which is especially good on the Protestant sects in Lowell.

76. Gilman, p. 93. Edson called for a $20,000 appropriation. The disagreement grew intensely personal and Boott withdrew from St. Anne's. The Merrimack Manufacturing Company evicted Edson from St. Anne's parsonage in a protracted legal battle which lasted until 1866, when Edson returned to the parsonage after his congregration purchased it for him.

77. Edson served on the Lowell school committee throughout the period, with terms in 1826–27, 1831–35, 1837–39, 1846–47, and 1852.

78. Gilman, pp. 93–94.

79. Ibid., pp. 93–95.

80. Boott's concern was to represent the interests of the Boston Associates, whose labor force was primarily transient Yankee farm women.

81. Meyer et al., p. 599.

82. Lord, Sexton, and Harrington, 2:314.

83. *Eighteenth Annual Report of the Lowell School Committee* (Lowell, 1844), p. 6.

84. Ibid., p. 6; Lord, Sexton, and Harrington, 2:314–15.

85. *Eighteenth Annual Report*, pp. 6–7; Lord, Sexton, and Harrington, 2:315.

86. *Eighteenth Annual Report*, p. 7.

87. *Twelfth Annual Report of the Lowell School Committee* (Lowell, 1846), pp. 8–14; *Eighteenth Annual Report*, p. 7.

88. Boston *Pilot*, 28 Mar. 1840, p. 79.

89. "St. Patrick's Day," *Lowell Courier*, 21 Mar. 1843, p. 2.

90. "Annual Report of the School Committee for 1836," manuscript, Lowell School Department, Lowell, Mass.

91. Boston *Pilot*, 28 Mar. 1840, p. 79.

92. Merwick, pp. 4–7.

93. *Eighteenth Annual Report*, pp. 7–8.

94. Ibid., pp. 7–8; Gilman, p. 99.

95. Just as the exhortations of local priests kept Irish children out of public schools before the 1835 education agreement, their support undoubtedly encouraged many Irish parents to send their children to public school after 1835.

96. Boston *Pilot*, 28 Mar. 1840, p. 79.

4. GROWING PAINS, 1836–48

1. Josephson, pp. 46–47.

2. Desmond J. Keenan, *The Catholic Church in Nineteenth Century Ireland: A Sociological Study* (Dublin: Gill & Macmillan, 1983), as well as James O'Shea, *Priest, Politics, and Society in Post-Famine Ireland: A Study of County Tipperary, 1850–1891* (Dublin: Wolfhound Press, 1983); S. J. Connolly, *Priest and People in Pre-Famine Ireland, 1780–1845* (Dublin: Gill & Macmillan, 1982) and his "Catholicism in Ulster, 1800–1850," in *Plantation to Partition: Essays in Ulster History in Honour of J. L. McCracken*, ed. Peter Roebuck (Belfast: Blackstaff Press, 1981), pp. 151–71. An older interpretation, focusing primarily upon post-Famine institutionalization, is Emmet Larkin, "The Devotional Revolution in Ireland, 1850–1875," *American Historical Review* 77 (1972): 625–52. Cf. David W. Miller, "Irish Catholicism and the Great Famine," *Journal of Social History* 9 (1975): 81–98.

3. Kevin Whelan, "The Catholic Parish, the Catholic Chapel, and Village Development in Ireland," *Irish Geography* 16 (1983): 1–15.

4. Fenwick Memoranda, 27 July 1841, 2:227.

5. Ibid., 23 June 1833, 1:243; 10 Aug. 1835, 1:346–47.

6. Ibid., 9 Aug. 1835, 1:346.

7. Ibid., 20 Dec. 1837, 2:107–9.

8. Carey, "Laity's Understanding of the Trustee System," offers the most succinct account of the importance of these battles in American Catholic history.

9. Fenwick Memoranda, 5 Dec. 1832, 1:219.

10. Ibid., 6 May 1833, 1:237–38; John Mahoney to Bishop Benedict Fenwick, 5 Mar. 1834, Fenwick Papers, Archives, Archidocese of Boston, Brighton, Mass.

11. Mahoney to Fenwick, 5 Mar. 1834.

12. Fenwick Memoranda, 20 Jan. 1836, 2:18. As early as 5 Sept. 1835, Fenwick relieved Mahoney and Connolly of some parish responsibilities, "leaving the spiritual matters of the Church with the Clergymen."

13. Lord, Sexton, and Harrington, 2:145.

14. Fenwick Memoranda, 13 July 1836, 2:38–39; 25 Aug. 1837, 2:91.

15. Ibid., 29 Aug. 1837, 2:91.

16. Ibid., 31 Aug. 1837,.2:93.

17. Ibid., 5 Sept. 1837, 2:93.

18. Ibid., 2 Sept. 1831, 1:172.

19. At the close of each year, Fenwick usually indicated where each priest under his jurisdiction was stationed.

20. Mahoney, Curtin, Connolly, and McCool. At the height of the McCool schism, Fenwick appointed one priest, Father O'Bierne, who returned three days later "extremely ill" but "was much better by the next day" after Fenwick had relieved him of his Lowell duties. Fenwick Memoranda, 11 July 1836, 2:38.

21. Although Connolly was only an assistant to Mahoney when he negotiated the education agreement, McDermott initially served alone; hence, McDermott held direct control over appointment power.

22. Fenwick Memoranda, 6 Sept. 1835, 1:351–52; 4 Oct. 1835, 2:5.

23. Ibid., 8 Feb. 1840, 2:175.

24. Ibid., 5 Sept. 1835, 1:351; 23 Sept. 1835, 2:4.

25. Ibid., 8 Feb. 1840, 2:205–6.

26. Ibid., 2:205–6.

27. Ibid., 2:206. His personal salary was not excessive for his position. McDermott made about twice the weekly wage of an unskilled laborer, although his upkeep was partially defrayed by other parish accounts.

28. Fenwick Memoranda, 5 Jan. 1841, 2:246.

29. Ibid.; Annual Statement, St. Patrick's Parish, Lowell, 1838, in Fenwick Memoranda, 2:161; and for 1839, 2:201.

30. Ibid., 29 May 1838, 2:130.

31. *Juventus* to Boston *Pilot*, Boston *Pilot*, 27 Apr. 1839, p. 117.

32. Juventus (Daniel McEvoy) and his opponents sparred further. Cf. Boston *Pilot*, 18 May 1839, pp. 133–34; 25 May 1839, p. 143. Cummiskey's request at about the same time for constables to patrol the neighborhood around St. Patrick's Church indicated that Cummiskey supported the McElroy-McDermott faction.

33. Fenwick Memoranda, 25 July 1841, 2:271–72; 30 July 1841, 2:274. Fenwick requested that Conway purchase a lot from the Hamilton Manufacturing Company. Conway secured one hundred feet of frontage at 40 cents a square foot. Fenwick ordered his architect to design a church ninety feet long and sixty feet wide. Plans included a basement and a belfry tower.

34. "Dedication of St. Peter's," Boston *Pilot*, 22 Oct. 1842, p. 352.

35. On the Benevolent Society, see *Freemen's Journal*, 29 July 1843, p. 43; *Courier*, 15 Aug. 1843, p. 2.

36. Fenwick Memoranda, 25 Oct. 1841, 2:292–93. Fenwick dismissed a delegation of McDermott's supporters "quite unsatisfied," indicating that he was rather certain that his plan to construct St. Peter's had a broad base of support.

37. *Freemen's Journal*, 29 July 1843, p. 43.

38. "Tempest in a Teapot," Boston *Bee*, 2 Aug. 1843, p. 2.

39. Lord, Sexton, and Harrington, 2:318.

40. Fenwick Memoranda, 6 Mar. 1847, 3:264.

41. "St. Patrick's Day in Lowell," *Lowell Courier*, 21 Mar. 1844, p. 2.

42. "Lowell City Schools," Boston *Pilot*, 6 July 1844, p. 214.

43. Lord, Sexton, and Harrington, 2:318.

44. Ibid., 2:145.

45. Kerby A. Miller, Bruce Boling, and David N. Doyle, "Emigrants and Exiles: Irish Cultures and Irish Emigration to North America, 1790–1922," *Irish Historical Studies* 40 (1980): 116–34.

46. "Temperance in Lowell," Lowell *Mercury*, 23 May 1834, p. 2.

47. Lowell *Mercury*, 10 July 1830, p. 3.

48. Richard Hofstadter, *The Age of Reform: From Bryan to FDR* (New York: Random House, 1955), p. 282.

49. William J. Rorabaugh, *The Alcoholic Republic: An American Tradition* (New York: Oxford University Press, 1981). For a similar perspective, see Ian R. Tyrell, *Sobering Up: From Temperance to Prohibition in Antebellum America, 1800–1860* (Westport, Conn.: Greenwood Press, 1979).

50. Lowell *Patriot*, 15 July 1836, p. 2.

51. McDermott recounted the pattern of development among Catholic temperance societies in a temperance sermon. See "Rev. Mr. McDermott's Temperance Sermon," *Lowell Courier*, 22 May 1841, p. 2.

52. Maurice Dineen, *The Catholic Total Abstinence Movement in the Archdiocese of Boston* (Boston: E. L. Grimes, 1908), is quite good on Mathew's visit to New England.

53. "McDermott's Sermon," *Lowell Courier*, 22 May 1841, p. 2.

54. Ibid., p. 2; *Lowell Morning Courier*, 11 Nov. 1840, p. 2, in which the editor, William Schouler, argued that "the Irish but lately perverbial for intemperance, bid fair become the most temperate people on the globe."

55. O'Dwyer, pp. 42–43. O'Dwyer noted that "in the early forties, Father McDermott waged an unending war against the ravages of the small saloons which dotted the city, and the men of the Society, in recognition of his efforts, gave the fighting pastor a purse of $200."

56. "McDermott's Sermon," *Lowell Courier*, 22 May 1841, p. 2.

57. Donohoe was the local link with events occurring in Ireland, providing an Irish slant to international events gleaned from European newspapers.

58. "Father Mathew to the Mayor of Lowell," *Daily Journal and Courier*, 14 Sept. 1849, p. 2.

59. Ibid.

60. Ibid.

61. Ibid. Obviously, a number of Irish who lived in rural districts near Lowell also came to the city to see Fr. Mathew.

62. Dineen, p. 203.

63. Sean O'Faolain, *King of the Beggars: A Life of Daniel O'Connell, the Irish Liberator, in a Study in the Rise of Modern Irish Democracy* (New York: Viking Press, 1938), p. 302.

64. "Attending Mass," *Daily Morning Herald*, 22 Feb. 1844, p. 2.

65. "Celebration of St. Patrick's Day in Lowell, by the Lowell Irish Benevolent Society," *Lowell Courier*, 21 Mar. 1843, p. 2.

66. O'Faolain, p. 302.

67. The Irish middle class were the most prominent contributors, and headed the subscription lists but the majority of contributors, judging from a check with the listing of occupations in city directories from 1840 to 1843, were unskilled Irish laborers.

68. *Lowell Courier*, 21 Mar. 1843, p. 2.

69. Ibid.

70. Ibid.

71. "Repeal in Lowell," Boston *Pilot*, 28 Feb. 1841, p. 70.

72. Ibid.

73. Ibid.

74. "Progress of Repeal in the United States: Lowell," Boston *Pilot*, 29 May 1841, p. 171.

75. "The Boston *Pilot* on Repeal," *Lowell Courier*, 18 July 1843, p. 2.

76. Cecil Woodham-Smith, *The Great Hunger* (New York: Harper & Row, 1962), p. 29; R. B. McDowell, "Ireland on the Eve of the Famine," in *The Great*

Famine: Studies in Irish History, ed. R. Dudley Edwards and T. Desmond Williams (New York: New York University Press, 1957), p. 4. For a discussion of population increase prior to the Famine, see Kenneth H. Connell, *The Population of Ireland, 1750–1845* (Oxford: Clarendon Press, 1950) and subsequent revisionists of Connell, especially Michael Drake, "Marriage and Population Growth in Ireland, 1750–1845," *Economic History Review* 16 (1963): 301–13; and Joseph Lee, "Marriage and Population in Pre-Famine Ireland," *Economic History Review* 21 (1968): 283–95.

77. Landlord-assisted schemes ended because of unfavorable publicity generated by scandals caused by the deaths of Irish emigrants on Canadian timber ships which had been engaged as transports by Irish landlords to ferry tenant-emigrants to Canada.

78. *Voice of Industry*, 12 Feb. 1847, p. 3.

79. "Eloisa," *Voice of Industry*, 26 Mar. 1847, p. 1.

80. "Irish Relief Meeting," *Lowell Advertiser*, 20 Feb. 1847, p. 2.

81. "Christian Citizen to Friend Drew," *Voice of Industry*, 30 Apr. 1847, p. 2; "Relief for Scotch and Irish," *Lowell Advertiser*, 18 Mar. 1847, p. 2.

82. *Daily Journal and Courier*, 5 Aug. 1848, p. 2; 28 Aug. 1848, p. 2.

5. THE PATTERN OF EMPLOYMENT, 1838–50

1. Annual Statement, St. Patrick's parish, Lowell (1838), 2:161; (1841) 2:301.

2. See Table 1.

3. "An Irish Way of Putting a Horse into a Wagon," *Lowell Daily Courier*, 14 Aug. 1847, p. 2; "Irishmen's Blunders," *Daily Journal and Courier*, 22 Nov. 1842, p. 2.

4. In 1851, for example, Lowell's officials annexed Centralville from Dracut, expanding the city's boundaries, for the first time, to the north bank of the Merrimack River.

5. *Lowell Daily Courier*, 27 Sept. 1847, p. 2.

6. "McEvoy and Connelly," *Lowell Advertiser*, 18 Nov. 1842, p. 4. The firm was located at No. 6, Mechanics Building, Dutton Street, Lowell. McEvoy would later move to Central Street where he opened his own shop.

7. Cawley, p. 117.

8. "List of Hands in the Lowell Machine Shop, 1838- 1844," RF-1, L & C.

9. "Lowell Coonery," *Lowell Advertiser*, 30 Nov. 1842, p. 2.

10. Zimiles and Zimiles, pp. 170ff.; Hareven and Langenbach, pp. 13–14.

11. Zimiles and Zimiles, p. 181.

12. "Pay-Rolls, July, 1845–May, 1847," January, 1846, R-1, L & C.

13. Samuel Wood and Joseph Tapley operated one of the most successful teamster companies in Lowell, using nearly 150 horses in their operations before the Boston and Lowell Railroad cut into their trade. See French, p. 257.

14. *Daily Journal and Courier*, 12 Sept. 1849, p. 2.

15. Dublin, *Women at Work*, pp. 108–31.

16. Nathan Appleton, *Labor, Its Relations in Europe and the United States Compared* (Boston, 1844), pp. 9–10.

17. Josephson, pp. 255ff.

18. Among male household heads living in the paddy camps at the time of the 1850 federal census, only two were operatives. Federal Manuscript Census (1850).

19. "The Last Card of Lowell Coonery," *Lowell Advertiser*, 30 Nov. 1842, p. 2.

20. Potter, p. 137.

21. Edward C. Kirkland, *Men, Cities, and Transportation: A Case Study in New England History, 1820–1900* (Cambridge: Harvard University Press, 1948; reprint, New York: Russell & Russell, 1968); George Rogers Taylor, *The Transportation Revolution, 1815–1860* (New York: Holt, Rinehart, 1951).

22. *Lowell Advertiser*, 23 Dec. 1845, p. 4. Andrew Barr and Son, 47 Merrimack Street, represented Byrne and Co. Emigrant Passage Office in Lowell.

23. *Daily Morning Herald*, 17 Feb. 1844, p. 4.

24. Lord, Sexton, and Harrington, 2:145. The original church, which was doubled in size in 1836, could accommodate about nine hundred parishioners, but only if two Masses were held. Typically "the hours of divine service are, in the summer at 10:00 A.M. and 3:00 P.M.; in the winter at 10:00 A.M. and 2:00 P.M. Sermon morning and evening." *The Catholic Almanac; or, Laity's Directory, for the Year 1833* (Baltimore, 1833), p. 47.

25. Annual Statement, St. Patrick's parish, Lowell, 1837, in which the priest recorded performing 178 baptisms and 45 marriages, 2:107–9; and 1838: 163 (b), 35 (m), 2:161; 1839: 165 (b), 39 (m), 2:201; 1840: 183 (b), 43 (m), 2:245.

26. Ibid., 3:13. See Table 3, 1842.

27. Richard Walsh to "Friend Donohoe," Boston *Pilot*, 13 May 1843, p. 149.

28. Annual Statement, St. Patrick's parish (1844), 2:138; (1846), 2:254. See Table 3.

29. The 1855 Massachusetts state census listed 10,369 native-born Irish out of a total population of 37,553, or 27.6 percent of Lowell's general population. State Manuscript Census (1855), Commonwealth of Massachusetts, Lowell, vol. 16, Massachusetts State Archives, State House, Boston.

30. In time, Fall River, Massachusetts, and Manchester, New Hampshire, would outstrip Lowell in total output of goods produced.

31. Malone, pp. 15–24. Cf. James B. Francis to Boody, Stone & Co., Springfield, Mass., 26 Mar. 1846, in "Letter Books, Locks and Canals Agent James B. Francis, 1827–1850," James B. Francis Index, DA-2C, L & C.

32. Previous construction projects of equal magnitude had been completed before the Panic of 1837.

33. "Pay-Rolls, July, 1845–May, 1847," January, 1846, R-1, L & C.

34. Ibid., Aug. 1847.

35. *Lowell Daily Courier*, 9 July 1847, p. 2. Thomas Cox and Mathew Moriarty died on the same day. Cox worked for Boody and Ross, while Moriarty worked for Locks and Canals. Apparently the cold water induced a stroke.

36. *Lowell Daily Courier*, 27 Oct. 1847, p. 2. Ducy left a wife and fourteen children.

37. Ibid., p. 2.

38. A comparison of payroll records for Moses Shattuck's work teams, Locks and

Canals employees during Northern Canal construction, and the Lowell Gas Company indicated that a uniform payment per diem prevailed.

39. Nathaniel Hill: $36 for 24 days; 18 Jan.–23 Feb. 1850, R-2, L & C. One year later, Hill had increased his pay to $2 a day for 25 days or $50; 27 Jan.–22 Feb. 1851, R-2, L & C.

40. It is uncertain as to whether the cold, the dangerous work, or the availability of labor influenced the upward trend in wages.

41. Dublin, *Women at Work*, pp. 145–64.

42. Ibid., pp. 165–68.

43. *Lowell Offering and Magazine* (1843), p. 148.

44. Federal Manuscript Census (1860) M 653, Roll 507. Of the 681 Irish wives in the 1860 households bounded by Dutton, Willie, Pawtucket, and Merrimack streets, 500, or 73.4 percent, identified themselves as "wives." Of those remaining, 133 Irish women, or 19.5 percent, listed no occupation. Six women, or 1 percent, were in "other" occupations and 6.1 percent were mill women.

45. Marriage Register, May, 1844–May, 1846, St. Patrick's parish, Lowell, Archives, Archdiocese of Boston.

46. Boston: 15.3 percent of working Irish population in 1850, Handlin, *Boston's Immigrants*, p. 253; Poughkeepsie: 84 percent of Irish working women in 1860, Griffen and Griffen, *Natives and Newcomers*, p. 233; Milwaukee: 47 percent in 1850, Conzen, *Immigrant Milwaukee*, p. 93; London: 42.7 percent in 1851, Lees, *Exiles of Erin*, p. 93.

47. The percentage of those living with their employers was small principally because the small physical size of Lowell made "living-in" unnecessary and because of the tendency of Irish to live in proximity to one another.

48. See Table 2. Among Lowell's work force in the mills, there was a total of 8,635 female workers in 1847. It is safe to assume a female work force of about 7,000, up from 6,295 workers in 1843. If the Irish were 8 percent of the female work force througout Lowell—the percentage Dublin found at the Hamilton—then about 600 Irish women were employed in Lowell's mills as early as 1845. The *total* population of Lowell's Irish was 5,000 in 1844; hence, a large percentage of Irish women had found employment in Lowell's mills before the Famine emigrants arrived.

49. Stephen Dubnoff, "Gender, the Family and the Problem of Work Motivation in a Transition to Industrial Capitalism," *Journal of Family History* 4 (1979): 121–36; Dublin, *Women at Work*, Table 10.2, p. 168, showing that three-fourths of all immigrant women living at home were daughters in 1860.

50. The 1850 federal census demonstrates that of the 499 male household heads living in the paddy camps, 318 Irishmen (63.7 percent) identified themselves as laborers, while an additional 15.4 percent listed no occupation. If most of this latter group were laborers, then nearly three-fourths of the male household heads were laborers. Among adult men, including adult sons living within a household, 66.4 percent identified themselves as laborers. Federal Manuscript Census (1850).

51. Harriet Hanson Robinson, p. 12.

52. Ibid.

53. Ibid.

54. "Appendix B," Eno.

55. "Irish Girls in Lowell," Boston *Pilot*, 16 Aug. 1851, p. 7.

56. "The Irish in Lowell," *Lowell Advertiser*, 19 Aug. 1851, p. 2.

57. Dublin, *Women at Work*, pp. 145–64.

58. Ibid., 2:46. Annual Statements, 1844 and 1850, St. Patrick's parish (1844), 2:138; (1850) 3:36.

59. In 1843, five thousand Irish lived in Lowell. By 1855, over ten thousand native-born Irish resided in Lowell.

60. There were small ethnic enclaves of other immigrants, indicated by names such as John Bull's Row and Scotch Block.

61. Henry A. Miles, *Lowell As It Was and As It Is* (Lowell, 1846; reprint, New York: Arno Press, 1972), p. 215.

62. Emit Duncan Grizzell, *Origin and Development of the High School in New England before 1865* (Philadelphia: J. B. Lippincott, 1923), pp. 76–78; Rev. Lincoln Varnum, "My Schools and Teachers in Lowell, Sixty Years Ago," ORHA 3 (1887): 128–29; C. C. Chase, "Reminiscences of the High School," ORHA 3 (1887): 117, on the development of Lowell High School. *One Hundredth Anniversary Celebration of St. Joseph's Hospital* (Lowell, 1940), p. 4, and Nancy Zaroulis, "Daughters of Freemen: The Female Operatives and the Beginning of the Labor Movement," in Eno, p. 117, on the history of the Corporation Hospital.

63. Lowell *Patriot*, 8 July 1836, p. 2.

64. Since McDermott favored assimilation on Yankee terms, he undoubtedly saw no special need to establish separate Catholic societies in a parish already heavily indebted.

65. Lowell National Historical Park and Preservation District, Cultural Resources Inventory; Prepared for division, North Atlantic Regional Office, National Park Service, Lowell (Centralville), Special Collections, University of Lowell.

66. "Locks and Canals to James T. McDermott," 1839, Bk. 11, Lot 17.

67. Cultural Resources Inventory, the Acre through Broadway Street, scattered references.

68. Valuation Books, 1855 and 1865, Office of the City Assessor, Lowell City Hall, Lowell, Mass.; Federal Manuscript Census (1850) and (1860); "Property and Insurance," Catalogue of 113 Lots of Land in Lowell, 1845, OA-1, L & C.

69. Albert Gibbs Mitchell, Jr., "Irish Family Patterns in Nineteenth Century Ireland and Lowell, Mass." (Ph.D. dissertation, Boston University, 1976), pp. 201–11.

70. *Vox Populi*, 15 Aug. 1851, p. 2.

71. Elisha Bartlett, *Address of the Mayor of the City Lowell, to the City Council, Monday, April 3, 1837* (Lowell, 1837), p. 4, as a representative discussion on the development of Lowell's sewer system.

72. Blewett, "Mills and the Multitudes," in Eno, p. 167.

73. Director's Report, Lowell Gas Light Company, 21 Dec. 1849, on fire protection. Lowell's officials constructed a separate gravity-flow system, placing large water tanks on mill roofs to alleviate the danger of fire.

74. Horatio Wood, *The Fourth Annual Report of the Ministry-at-Large in Lowell, to the Lowell Missionary Society* (Lowell, 1848), pp. 15–18.

75. "The Irish in Lowell," *Lowell Advertiser*, 19 Aug. 1851, p. 2.

76. Letter, Horatio Wood to Josiah Curtis, M.D., cited in Josiah Curtis, "Brief Remarks on the Hygiene of Massachusetts but More Particularly on the Cities of Boston and Lowell," in *Transactions of the American Medical Association* 2 (Philadelphia, 1849), p. 38.

77. Curtis to Wood, in Curtis, pp. 35, 40.

78. Wood, *Fifth Annual Report*, pp. 11–12.

79. "Irish Labor," *Vox Populi*, 22 Aug. 1851, p. 2.

80. *Vox Populi*, 8 Aug. 1851, p. 2.

81. "The Irish in Lowell," *Lowell Advertiser*, 10 Aug. 1851, p. 2.

82. *Vox Populi*, 8 Aug. 1851, p. 2.

83. "Irish Labor—Catholic Lowell," *American Citizen*, 25 Nov. 1854, p. 3.

6. THE IMPACT OF FAMINE EMIGRANTS, 1845–55

1. "Irish Girls in Lowell," Boston *Pilot*, 16 Aug. 1851, p. 7.

2. Federal Manuscript Census (1850) and (1860); Valuation Books (1855) and (1865).

3. Federal Manuscript Census (1850) and (1860).

4. Federal Manuscript Census (1850) and (1860). Only 87 of the 650 households in the 1850 census (13.3 percent) could be found in the 1,050 households of the 1860 census.

5. By the late 1850s, unskilled laborers earned $1.00 a day, most likely after construction at the Northern Canal had raised rates slightly in Lowell.

6. Fidelia O. Brown, "Decline and Fall," in Eno, p. 145.

7. Federal Manuscript Census (1850). See Table 11 (includes one- and two-parent households). For Milwaukee, London, and Hamilton, see Table 12, Conzen, *Immigrant Milwaukee*, p. 56; Table A.7, Lees, *Exiles of Erin*, p. 260; and Table 5.4, Katz, *People of Hamilton*, p. 228, respectively.

8. John Francis Maguire, *Father Mathew: A Biography* (London, 1863), pp. 322–23.

9. Dublin, *Women at Work*, Table 10.1, p. 167; Albert Gibbs Mitchell, pp. 280–83.

10. Albert Gibbs Mitchell, pp. 320–25, on widows, where he notes that work was often connected with the age of children; and pp. 349ff. on Irish children leaving their parents' home upon marriage.

11. Thomas D'Arcy McGee, *A History of the Irish Settlers in North America*, 6th ed. (Boston, 1855), p. 236.

12. Hasia R. Diner, *Erin's Daughters in America: Irish Immigrant Women in the Nineteenth Century* (Baltimore: Johns Hopkins University Press, 1983); pp. 68–69. O'Connell as quoted in Diner, p. 68.

13. See Table 12.

14. Marriage Register, St. Patrick's parish, 1844–46. The median age at mar-

riage was twenty-four. Conzen, *Immigrant Milwaukee*, p. 35, on marriage and employment. See her Table 13.

15. Dublin, *Women at Work*, pp. 155–56.

16. Albert Gibbs Mitchell, pp. 274–85, 351–61.

17. Harriet Hanson Robinson, p. 12. Cf. "Foreign Populations of Lowell," *American Citizen*, 7 Oct. 1854, p. 2.

18. The Prescott Corporation led the way in 1848 and other mills such as the Hamilton soon followed.

19. Bartlett, *Mayor's Report* (1837), p. 4; Handlin, *Boston's Immigrants*, p. 114.

20. James B. Francis to Charles S. Storrow, Treasurer, Essex Company, 22 Nov. 1851, "Notes on Land and Property," OA-3, L & C.

21. Blewett, "Mills and the Multitudes," in Eno, p. 167. The first Merrimack River water ran untreated through a waterworks system after 1855.

22. *Vital Records of Lowell, Massachusetts, to the End of the Year 1849*, 4 vols. (Salem, Mass.: Essex Institute, 1930); *Vital Records, 1826–61*, City Clerk, Lowell, Mass. Consumption killed 644 Irish, while dysentery claimed 365 lives.

23. See Table 4.

24. See Figure 1.

25. See Table 4 and Figure 2.

26. *Report of the Bill of Mortality in the City of Lowell for the Year 1859*, Special Collections, University of Lowell, p. 3. The report identified "ship fever" as typhus and the term "ship fever" was applied commonly throughout the 1840s. See Figure 3.

27. *Address of Josiah B. French, Mayor of the City of Lowell, in the Organization of the Government, January 7, 1850* (Lowell, 1850), p. 17.

28. Handlin, *Boston's Immigrants*, pp. 114–15, on Boston; Figure 3 on Lowell.

29. See Table 4. In 1843, Lowell had almost 5,000 Irish; in 1849, almost 10,000.

30. Elisha Bartlett, *A Vindication of the Character and Condition of the Females Employed in the Lowell Mills against the Charges Contained in the Boston Times and the Boston Quarterly Review* (Lowell, 1841; reprint, New York: Arno Press, 1975).

31. "Lowell Dispensary," *Lowell Advertiser*, 21 Sept. 1842, p. 3; "Lowell Dispensary—1846," *Lowell Advertiser*, 31 Jan. 1846, p. 2; *Ladies Pearl*, Apr. 1842, p. 218; "Lowell Dispensary," *Lowell Morning Courier*, 9 Jan. 1840, p. 2.; "Constitution and By-Laws of the Lowell Dispensary," Lowell *Patriot*, 2 May 1836, pp. 2 and 3. The dispensary furnished medicine and medical advice to the worthy poor in Lowell.

32. The transiency among the Irish undoubtedly exacerbated this problem as Lowell's officials grappled with offering relief to applicants for whom Lowell was a temporary stop.

33. Handlin's findings were similar for Boston's Irish, for whom he found an association with criminality as a result of minor misdemeanors committed under the influence of alcohol. *Boston's Immigrants*, p. 121.

34. "The Irish Riot," *Vox Populi*, 14 Sept. 1849, p. 2; "Riot on Lowell Street," Lowell *Tri-Weekly American*, 10 Sept. 1849, p. 2; "Riot among the Irish," *Lowell*

Advertiser, 11 Sept. 1849, p. 2; "Row and Fight among the Irish," *Daily Journal and Courier*, 10 Sept. 1849, p. 2, and 12 Sept. 1849, p. 2.

35. *Vox Populi*, 14 Sept. 1849, p. 2. "The Companies here are turning out of their employ every man known to have been engaged in this riot. This is right, and will have a most salutary influence. No man who was engaged in that affair can get work here again." *Daily Journal and Courier*, 12 Sept. 1849, p. 2, on dismissals.

36. *Lowell Tri-Weekly American*, 10 Sept. 1849, p. 2.

37. Brian Harrison, *Drink and the Victorians: The Temperance Question in England, 1835–1872* (London: Faber and Faber, 1971).

38. The moral environment of Lowell also limited the number of licensed establishments.

39. *Lowell Daily Courier*, 10 Oct. 1846, p. 2.

40. Wood, *Sixth Annual Report*, p. 24.

41. Wood, *Fifth Annual Report*, p. 24.

42. Tyrell, p. 9.

43. Wood, *Sixth Annual Report*, p. 24.

44. Wood, *Fourth Annual Report*, pp. 22–23. See Tables 5 and 6.

45. *Address of Benjamin C. Sargent, Mayor of the City of Lowell, at the Organization of the Government, January 7, 1861* (Lowell, 1861), p. 5. Representative crimes were chosen from those charged to the inmates of the Lowell city jail at the time of the 1850 federal census.

46. *Vox Populi*, 14 Sept. 1849, p. 2.

47. *Semi-Centennial Report of the Overseers of the Poor of the City of Lowell* (Lowell, 1876), p. 4.

48. Ibid., pp. 4, 8, and 9.

49. Ibid., p. 5.

50. "A Visit to the Poor Farm," *Daily Journal and Courier*, 19 Sept. 1849, p. 2.

51. Handlin, *Boston's Immigrants*, p. 118. The percentage of Irish in the Lowell Almshouse corresponded to the figure for Boston, where almost all incarcerated were also Irish.

52. Blewett, "Mills and the Multitudes," in Eno, p. 170.

53. In 1842, for example, the Lowell school committee noted that the Irish primaries were "quite too full" and recommended the acquisition of additional space. *Annual School Committee Report* (1842), p. 4.

54. *Annual School Committee Report* (1853), pp. 25, 36, 73, on intermediate schools. The public schoolteachers kept the certificate attendance records. Between 1838 and 1851, 2,739 certificates were issued. *Twenty-Sixth Annual School Committee Report* (1852), p. 18. Between 1852 and 1859, an additional 2,370 certificates were granted. *Thirty-Fourth Annual School Committee Report* (1860), p. 58. See Table 9.

55. *Annual Report of the School Committee of the City of Lowell, for the Municipal Year, 1853*, pp. 42–43.

56. *Eighteenth Annual School Committee Report*, p. 7. Within six months, 459 children had enrolled, with 208 students attending on averge daily.

57. *Twenty-Second Annual School Committee Report* (1847), p. 18, on No. 12

Primary School, Lewis Street; *Twenty-Fifth Annual School Committee Report* (1850), p. 16, on Mann School.

58. *Thirty-First Annual School Committee Report* (1856), p. 38.

59. O'Dwyer, pp. 36–37.

60. *Twenty-Fifth Annual School Committee Report* (1850), p. 15.

61. Katz, *People of Hamilton*, p. 38; Lees, *Exiles of Erin*, p. 201, on school attendance. Katz, *People of Hamilton*, p. 38; Lees, *Exiles of Erin*, p. 201; Conzen, *Immigrant Milwaukee*, pp. 90–92, and "Summary of Lowell Public Schools," *Eighteenth Annual School Committee Report* (1844) on the percentage of boys and girls attending school. Conzen, *Immigrant Milwaukee*, pp. 90–92, and Walkowitz, p. 115, on the percentage of older children attending school and on Irish attendance versus that of other immigrant groups.

62. O'Dwyer, p. 37.

63. *Thirty-Fourth Annual School Committee Report* (1860), pp. 58–59. See Table 10.

64. *Twenty-Fifth Annual School Committee Report*, p. 18.

65. Griffen and Griffen, p. 81; Conzen, *Immigrant Milwaukee*, pp. 90–92; and Walkowitz, p. 115.

66. *Thirtieth Annual School Committee Report*, p. 10.

67. Homer Bartlett to Horace Mann, in the "Fifth Annual Report of the Secretary of the Board of Education," *Annual Reports on Education* (Boston, 1868), pp. 103–7.

68. William Cardinal O'Connell, *Recollections of Seventy Years* (Boston: Houghton Mifflin Co., 1934).

69. Vincent P. Lannie, "Alienation in America: The Immigrant Catholic and Public Education in Pre–Civil War America," *Review of Politics* 32 (1970): 503–21. On the O'Briens' commitment, Fitzpatrick Memoranda, 20 Sept. 1852, 3:91, and Annals of St. Patrick's Convent (Sept. 1852) are illustrative.

70. While local officials still exercised considerable control over development, they reacted to situations rather than creating them.

71. Their detractors also chastised them for their absentee ownership, calling them "capitalists in Boston."

72. Abbott Lawrence to Daniel Webster, in Hamilton Andrews Hill, ed., *Memoir of Abbott Lawrence* (Boston, 1883). Lawrence noted that emigration from Ireland at the end of the Famine was "composed of a much better class than has usually gone to America," p. 2.

73. "The Irish in Lowell," *Lowell Advertiser*, 19 Aug. 1851, p. 2.

74. *Vox Populi*, 25 July 1851, p. 2; 15 Aug. 1851, p. 2.

75. Ibid., 15 Aug. 1851, p. 2.

76. The Whig-backed *Courier* reported only correspondence generated by the *Vox Populi* attack.

77. "Irish Labor—Catholic Lowell," *American Citizen*, 25 Nov. 1854, p. 3.

7. THE KNOW-NOTHING CRISIS, 1847–55

1. Fitzpatrick Memoranda, 6 Mar. 1847, 2:264.

2. Ibid., 15 Mar. 1847, 2:264–65.

3. Ibid., 22 Mar. 1848, 2:303. The retreat was "filled with great fruits."

4. John Fitzpatrick to Hilary Tucker, 24 Apr. 1850, Fitzpatrick Papers, Archives, Archdiocese of Boston.

5. Lord, Sexton, and Harrington, 2:518, 520.

6. Ibid., 2:536.

7. John and Timothy O'Brien were succeeded by their nephew, Michael, who served until 1900. Michael's cousin, Msgr. William O'Brien, became pastor and remained until his death in 1922.

8. Lord, Sexton, and Harrington, 2:526.

9. *Pioneer History of the Sisters of Notre Dame de Namur, at St. Patrick's, Lowell*, pp. 13–14, on the Sisters' view of Fr. Timothy O'Brien. Sister Miriam of the Infant Jesus, S.N.D., *The Finger of God: History of the Massachusetts Province of Notre Dame de Namur, 1849–1963* (Boston: Mission Church Press, 1963), p. 62; Fitzpatrick Memoranda, 20 Sept. 1852, 3:92; *Annals of St. Patrick's Convent* (Sept. 1852); *American Foundations of the Sisters of Notre Dame, Compiled from the Annals of Their Convents by a Member of the Congregation* (Philadelphia: Dolphin Press, 1928), p. 234.

10. Kevin Whelan argued that the predominant features of the pre-Famine Irish church were carried to North America in "County Wexford Priests in Newfoundland," *Journal of Wexford Historical Society* 10 (1985): 55–68. Whelan suggested that the ease of mobility created the equivalent of an "Irish" diocese in Newfoundland.

11. All had served briefly at the ward level—typically as inspectors of elections.

12. Butler's enthusiasm for his Irish supporters diminished after his reform coalition failed. The *Lowell Courier* reported that at one meeting "after Mr. Adams, came B. F. Butler, who felt indignant toward the Irish-Americans because they had aided to defeat the new constitution." *Daily Journal and Courier* 28 Nov. 1853, p. 2; Handlin, *Boston's Immigrants*, pp. 194–97, on the Irish impact upon the constitution vote.

13. *Souvenir History of St. John's Hospital Written for the Quarter-Centennial Celebration of the Founding of the Institution* (Lowell, 1892), on citywide Catholic support for the development of St. John's Hospital.

14. By the late nineteenth century, Lowell was also home to two other large patent medicine companies: C. I. Hood and Company and J. C. Ayer and Company, which had national reputations. Cf. James H. Young, *The Toadstool Millionaires: A Social History of Patent Medicines in America before Federal Regulation* (Princeton: Princeton University Press, 1961), pp. 135ff.

15. *A Century in Lowell, 1852–1952: Courtesy of the Sisters of Notre Dame de Namur, May 30, 1952* (Lowell, 1952), p. 9.

16. Fitzpatrick Memoranda, 3:36.

17. Ibid., 3:41. St. Patrick's: 94 marriages, 196 baptisms; St. Peter's: 138 marriages, 207 baptisms; St. Mary's: 48 marriages, 80 baptisms.

18. *Report, St. Patrick's Parish to the Boston Diocese* (Jan. 1856), Archives, Archdiocese of Boston. The Appleton Bank, Lowell, granted the $15,000 mortgage. In 1855, Lowell's Irish population, including native-born Irish, American Irish, and their children, was probably about 17,000. If St. Patrick's priests performed about 40 percent of the baptisms and marriages, as was the case in the mid-1850s, then somewhere around 6,000 to 7,000 Irish owed at least nominal allegiance to St. Patrick's.

19. Lord, Sexton, Harrington, 3:307. "By the end of the century St. Patrick's with its stately church edifice, its schools, its Academy, its Home for Working Girls, its convent for the Sisters of Notre Dame, and its residence for the Xaverian Brothers, its numerous sodalities and societies, its Lyceum, its cadet corps and band, etc., was probably the most highly organized parish in Lowell and certainly one of the most prosperous."

20. Dennis Clark, p. 99.

21. Sister Miriam, *Finger of God*, p. 62. Fr. Timothy O'Brien "with every passing day became more keenly aware that something was lacking in St. Patrick's" where the Sisters, upon arrival, "thanked God for the blessing of a new spot in the vast harvest field in which to labor for His glory." On Protestant charity in the 1850s, see Table 7.

22. Ibid., p. 62.

23. Fitzpatrick Memoranda, 20 Sept. 1852, 3:92; *Annals of St. Patrick's Convent* (Sept. 1852).

24. *American Foundations*, p. 234.

25. Ibid., p. 231; *Century in Lowell*, p. 9.

26. *Century in Lowell*, p. 9; Sister Miriam, *Finger of God*, p. 62.

27. *Century in Lowell*, p. 9.

28. *American Foundations*, p. 232.

29. *Annual Report of the Lowell School Committee* (1853), pp. 43–47.

30. *American Foundations*, p. 232.

31. Ibid. By then, the Sisters had opened four classrooms.

32. Ibid.

33. *Century in Lowell*, p. 9; Sister Miriam, *Finger of God*, p. 64.

34. Boston *Pilot*, 19 Nov. 1859, p. 6.

35. *Pioneer History*, pp. 9–10.

36. Boston *Pilot*, 19 Nov. 1859, p. 6.

37. "St. Patrick's Church," *Daily Journal and Courier*, 12 Oct. 1854, p. 2. In 1855, St. Patrick's Church was among the grandest buildings in the Boston diocese.

38. "Dedication of the New Catholic Church," *Lowell Advertiser*, 31 Oct. 1854, p. 2; "Dedication—St. Patrick's," *Daily Journal and Courier*, 12 Oct. 1854, p. 2.

39. In addition to Ray Allen Billington, *The Protestant Crusade, 1800–1860: A Study in the Origins of Nativism* (Chicago: Quadrangle Books, 1964), see George H. Haynes, "A Know-Nothing Legislature," *American Historical Association Report* (1896): 177–87 and "The Causes of Know-Nothing Success in Massachusetts," *American Historical Review* 3 (1897): 67–82, for some early interpretations.

40. "Naturalized American Candidates," *Daily Journal and Courier*, 13 Dec. 1853, p. 2.

41. "The Election," Boston *Pilot*, 25 Nov. 1854, p. 2.

42. From 1827 to 1859, only one Democrat, Gayton F. Osgood (1833–35), had served in Congress from the Lowell district.

43. Blewett, "Mills and the Multitudes," in Eno, p. 170.

44. Handlin, *Boston's Immigrants*, pp. 194–97.

45. Dale Baum, "Know-Nothingism and the Republican Majority in Massachusetts: The Political Realignment of the 1850s," *Journal of American History* 64 (1978): 959–86.

46. Michael F. Holt, "Politics of Impatience: The Origins of Know-Nothingism," *Journal of American History* 60 (1973): 309–33.

47. "The Whig Party in Lowell," *Lowell Advertiser*, 16 Nov. 1854, p. 2.

48. Holt, "Politics of Impatience," pp. 332–33.

49. *Annual Report of the Lowell School Committee* (1853), p. 48.

50. *American Citizen*, 3 June 1854, p. 2; "'Gabriel' in Lowell," *American Citizen*, 24 June 1854, p. 2; "Orr's Visit to Lowell," ibid.

51. "'Gabriel,'" *American Citizen*, 24 June 1854, p. 2.

52. Ibid. The *Citizen* blamed the other Lowell newspapers, "all breathing the same spirit, saying hard things of the stranger and intimating that trouble was brooding." "Orr's Visit," *American Citizen*, 24 June 1854, p. 2.

53. *Pioneer History*, p. 3.

54. Ibid., pp. 4–6; *Annals of St. Patrick's Convent* (June, 1854).

55. "Unnecessary Alarm among the Irish," *Daily Journal and Courier*, 24 June 1854, p. 2.

56. "The Irish Alarmed," *American Citizen*, 1 July 1854, p. 2.

57. "Unnecessary Alarm," *Daily Journal and Courier*, 24 June 1854, p. 2.

58. *Pioneer History*, pp. 6–7.

59. Ibid., pp. 7–8, 12–14.

60. "The Nunnery Investigation," *Daily Evening Advertiser*, 13 Apr. 1855, p. 2. Ben Butler defended Hiss against the charges raised over the Lowell visit. Later, Butler claimed somewhat lamely that he wished "to expose Know-Nothing hypocrisy." Trefousse, p. 43. For proceedings, 3 Gray 468.

61. "Nunnery Report," Boston *Pilot*, 5 May 1855, p. 2.

62. Nash, pp. 29–30. Cf. Benjamin F. Butler, *Butler's Book* (Boston, 1892), p. 126, in which Butler noted that "matters were so fixed that my residence came in the territory of the Sixth Regiment, and the Fifth Regiment was put somewhere else where I could not be colonel."

63. "Colonel Butler and the Jackson Musketeers," *American Citizen*, 27 Jan. 1855, p. 2.

64. "The Disbanded Irish Companies," *Daily Evening Advertiser*, 23 Feb. 1855, p. 2. The editor applauded the actions of the Irish militiamen, noting that "it requires a great deal more philosophy and patience than most Yankees are supposed to possess, quietly and unresistantly to submit to an act calculated to reproach their honor and their pedigrees."

65. Holt, p. 330.

8. AFTERMATH: THE MEANING OF COMMUNITY, 1855–61

1. Massachusetts State Census (1855); see Table 1.

2. Horatio Wood, Jr., "Memoir of Horatio Wood, by his Son, for Twenty-Four Years Minister-at-Large in Lowell," *ORHA* 4 (1891): 387.

3. See Table 2. In 1855, there were 13,187 employees; thirteen years later, the figure had risen to 13,717. A figure of 13,500 employees in 1860 seems accurate.

4. See Table 2.

5. Dublin, *Women at Work*, p. 153.

6. Francis H. Early, "The French Canadian Family Economy and Standard-of-Living in Lowell, Massachusetts, 1870," *Journal of Family History* 7 (1982): 181–82.

7. "Foreign Populations of Lowell," *American Citizen*, 7 Oct. 1854, p. 2.

8. Albert Gibbs Mitchell, pp. 351–61.

9. Dublin, *Women at Work*, p. 165.

10. Federal Manuscript Census (1860). See Table 13.

11. Marriage Register, St. Patrick's parish.

12. Federal Manuscript Census (1850) and (1860). There was no indication among Lowell's mill agents as to whether they discriminated actively against married women in favor of the unmarried. See Table 14.

13. Ibid. There were exceptions. Owen Farrell, for instance, left weaving and became a peddler; William Connelly, once an operative, became a laborer; Dennis Sweeney, who had been a machinist, was a laborer in 1860.

14. Ibid. Laborers and mill hands accounted for almost all employed Irishmen in 1860. See Table 15.

15. Dublin, *Women at Work*, pp. 141–42.

16. Federal Manuscript Census (1850) and (1860).

17. *Twenty-Sixth Annual School Committee Report*, p. 17. Horatio Wood also discussed the process by which Irish parents placed their children in the mills. He reported that the Irish "have come, because they have heard of the mills, have thought they could get employment for themselves and *little ones*, as soon as they arrived." Wood, *Fourth Annual Report*, p. 15.

18. *Twenty-Second Annual School Committee Report*, p. 20.

19. *Thirty-Fourth Annual School Committee Report*, pp. 58–59. See Table 10.

20. Ibid., p. 57.

21. Ibid., pp. 57–58.

22. *Annual School Committee Report* (1855), p. 25. The "percent attendance" figure represented a proportion taken from the "average number belonging." See Table 8.

23. Wood, *Fifteenth Annual Report*, pp. 17–18. Wood educated over 10,000 students before the school committee assumed control of his evening schools.

24. Wood, *Ninth Annual Report*, pp. 20–21.

25. Horatio Wood, Jr., p. 18.

26. Wood, *Eleventh Annual Report*, p. 21.

27. Ibid., p. 24.

28. "Terms of Agreement, St. Patrick's School, 8 Aug. 1882," Xaverian Brothers Provincial Archives, Kensington, Md.

29. Federal Manuscript Census (1850) and (1860); Susan E. Hirsch, *Roots of the American Working Class: The Industrialization of Crafts in Newark, 1800–1860* (Philadelphia: University of Pennsylvania Press, 1978) pp. 57–60. Completed families are determined by taking the range in ages between the youngest and the oldest child producing a figure comparable to the duration of childbearing. The range increased as the father aged for all Irishmen but it decreased for Irish over fifty as their children left home. Married Irish males between forty-one and fifty can be used, therefore, as a means to measure completed families.

30. Federal Manuscript Census (1850) and (1860).

31. Maguire, *Irish in America*, pp. 322–23.

32. *Pioneer History*, p. 17.

33. Federal Manuscript Census (1850) and (1860). See Table 11.

34. Vital Records, 1826–61; *Daily Journal and Courier*, 17 Sept. 1860, p. 2.

35. The O'Briens could not affect the economic life of their parishioners but could influence most other areas.

36. Wood, *Thirteenth Annual Report*, p. 29.

37. *Souvenir History of St. John's Hospital* pp. 10–16.

38. "Young Men's C. L. Association," *Daily Evening Advertiser*, 16 Feb. 1861, p. 2; "Ball," *Daily Evening Advertiser*, 11 Apr. 1857, p. 2, on the Mathew Institute's Erina Balls.

39. "The Lowell Pulpit on the War," *Lowell Daily Courier*, 29 Apr. 1861, p. 2.

40. Thernstrom, *Poverty and Progress*, pp. 184–85; and McCaffrey's discussion of the applicability of Thernstrom's conclusions to the general experience of the Irish in America, *Irish Diaspora*, pp. 77–79.

41. Questionnaires regarding the parameters of parish life were distributed to St. Patrick's parishioners in 1977 and to St. Michael's parishioners in 1983. (St. Michael's was a territorial parish carved from within the old boundaries of St. Patrick's in 1883). Both groups of parishioners, including a large number with Irish ancestry, stressed traditional church and family ties.

42. George F. Kenngott, *The Record of a City: A Social Survey of Lowell, Massachusetts* (New York: Macmillan, 1912), pp. 28ff.

43. St. Patrick's parish flourished until after World War II. The parish suffered from urban renewal just before the war and from the loss of parishioners to other sections of Lowell and to the suburbs or nearby New Hampshire.

44. John Higham, "Current Trends in the Study of Ethnicity in the United States," *Journal of American Ethnic History* 2 (1982): 5–15.

45. John F. McClymer in his multiple review of the most recent writings of Bender, Bodner, Hareven and Langenbach, Proctor and Maturzeski, and Wrobel titled, "The Study of Community and the 'New' Social History," *Journal of Urban History* 7 (1980): 103–18.

46. Cf. Allen Pred, *Urban Growth and City Systems in the United States, 1849–1860* (Cambridge: Harvard University Press, 1980); Francis X. Blouin, Jr., *The Boston Region, 1810–1850: A Study in Urbanization* (Ann Arbor, Mich.: UMI

Research Press, 1978); Burton W. Folsom, Jr., *Urban Capitalists: Entrepreneurs and City Growth in Pennsylvania's Lackawanna and Lehigh Regions 1800–1920* (Baltimore: John Hopkins University Press, 1981); and David R. Goldfield, "The New Regionalism," *Journal of Urban History* 10 (1984): 171–86.

47. Cf. Philip Scranton, "Varieties of Paternalism: Industrial Structures and the Social Relations of Production in American Textiles," *American Quarterly* 36 (1984): 235–57; Michael B. Katz, Michael J. Doucet, and Mark J. Stern, *The Social Organization of Early Industrial Capitalism* (Cambridge: Harvard University Press, 1982); Jane H. Pease and William H. Pease, "Social Structure and the Potential for Urban Change: Boston and Charleston in the 1830s," *Journal of Urban History* 8 (1982): 171–95; and Geoffrey Blodgett, "Yankee Leadership in a Divided City: Boston, 1860–1910," *Journal of Urban History* 8 (1982): 371–96.

48. Marianne Pedulla, "Labor in a City of Immigrants: Holyoke, 1882–1888," *Historical Journal of Massachusetts* 13 (1985): 147–61.

49. Michael Frisch, *Town into City: Springfield, Massachusetts and the Meaning of Community, 1840–1880* (Cambridge: Harvard University Press, 1972).

50. Philip Scranton, "Milling About: Family Firms and Urban Manufacturing in Textile Philadelphia, 1840–1865," *Journal of Urban History* 10 (1984): 259–94.

51. Jeffrey E. Mirel and David L. Angus, "From Spellers to Spindles: Work-Force Entry by the Children of Textile Workers, 1888–1890," *Social Science History* 9 (1985): 123–43.

52. Stuart M. Blumin, "The Hypothesis of Middle Class Formation in Nineteenth Century America: A Critique and Some Proposals," *American Historical Review* 90 (1985): 337. Although Blumin considered the process by which the middle class formed in nineteenth-century America, his notion of class formation has applicability to the development of an Irish Catholic consciousness in antebellum Lowell.

53. Miller, Boling, and Doyle, p. 124, on Irish accommodation; McClymer, pp. 114–15, on changing relations between primary and secondary institutions.

54. McClymer, p. 117.

55. The decline of St. Patrick's parish after World War II, the growth of regional electronics and, later, high technology, at the expense of traditional industries, and the emergence of suburban Lowell as attractive residential towns, among other factors, contributed to the decline of Lowell's Irish Catholic subculture.

BIBLIOGRAPHY

Manuscript Materials in Depositories or Privately Owned
Includes corporation records, annals, church records, diaries, and letters.

Archdiocese of Boston, Archives, Brighton, Mass.
  Fenwick Papers, 1825–46
    Letter, Rev. John Mahoney to Bishop Benedict Fenwick, 5 Mar. 1834.
    Memoranda, 1825–46.
  Fitzpatrick Papers, 1846–61
    Letter, Bishop John Fitzpatrick to Rev. Hilary Tucker, 24 Apr. 1850.
    Memoranda, 1846–61.
Baker Library, Harvard Graduate School of Business Administration, Boston, Mass.
  Locks and Canals Collection
    James B. Francis Index, to 1850, DA-2C
    Agent's Journals, Aug., 1826–Feb., 1832, GC-1.
    Catalogue of 113 Lots of Land for Sale in Lowell,1845, OA-1.
    Notes on Land and Property, 1838–52, OA-3.
    Pay-Rolls, R-1, 2, and 3.
    Receipts for Labor, Aug., 1825–July, 1826, RA-1; Aug., 1826–Dec., 1828, RA-2.
    List of Hands in Lowell Machine Shop, 1838–44, RF-1.
    Pay-Roll, Mechanics and Laborers, RF-2.
    Work by Teams, Moses Shattuck, RG-1.
    Boston and Lowell Railroad, Time Book, 1834, No. 395.
Bapst Library, Irish Special Collections, Boston College, Chestnut Hill, Mass.
  George O'Dwyer notes in preparation of *Irish Catholic Genesis of Lowell.*
Gas Light Company, The Lowell
  Director's Records, 1850–61.
  Pay-Roll Records, 1850–61.
Lowell Historical Society Collection, Special Collections, University of Lowell, Lowell, Mass.
  Maps and City Atlas, 1850 and 1879.
  Plan of the Town of Lowell and Belvedere Village, by Benjamin Mather, 1832.

Theodore Edson Diary, to 1861.
Rosarian Confraternity Notice, 1856.
Lowell Institution for Savings, Lowell, Mass.
Savings Account Ledgers, to 1861.
Lowell National Historical Park, Lowell, Mass.
Letter, Kirk Boott to Isaac Biddle & Sons, 24 Dec. 1821; Letter, 9 Jan. 1822.
Notre Dame de Namur, Sisters of, Provincial Archives, Ipswich, Mass.
Annals of St. Patrick's Convent.
History of the Sisters of Notre Dame by the Pioneer Sister, St. Patrick's Convent, Lowell, Mass.
St. Patrick's Parish, Lowell, Mass.
Annual Statement, 1856.
Vital Records; Births, Marriages, 1832–61, including Marriage Register, 1844–46.
University of Lowell, Special Collections, Lowell, Mass.
Locks and Canals Collection.
Xaverian Brothers, Provincial Archives, Kensington, Md.
Terms of Agreement, St. Patrick's School, 8 Aug. 1882.

Government Records and Publications

LOCAL RECORDS

Addresses of the Mayor of the City of Lowell at the Incorporation of the City Government, 1835–61.
Bills of Mortality for the City of Lowell, scattered references.
Reports of the Election Commission on Voting, Lowell, scattered references.
Lowell School Committee Reports, 1827–61. Lowell School Committee Manuscript, 1827–35; printed, 1836–60.
Statement of Expenses for the Town of Lowell in theYear 1831.
Valuations of Property in Lowell, 1826–61. Assessor's Office.
Vital Records, 1826–61. City Clerk's Office.
Vital Records of Lowell, Massachusetts, to the End of the Year 1849. 4 vols. Salem, Mass.: Essex Institute, 1930.

STATE RECORDS

Middlesex, County of, Superior Court, Cambridge and Lowell, Mass.
Declaration of Intentions to Become United States Citizens, Lowell, to 1850.
Hiss Case, The. 3 Gray 468.
Land Transactions, Lowell, 1826–61, vols. 1–21.
Letters
Proprietors of Locks and Canals on Merrimack River to Hugh Cummiskey et al., 1830–31, 9:183.
——— to Benedict Fenwick, 6 Jun. 1835, 45:346.
——— to James T. McDermott, 1835, Bk. 11, Lot 17.

Melvin Suits, The. 16 Pick 137, 16 Pick 161, 17 Pick 246, 17 Pick 255, 5 Metc 15.

Plan from Record Book 373, 18 May 1832, 373.

Plan of Land Being in Part the Paddy Camp Lands, so-called, 20 Feb. 1839, 280.

State House, Archives, Boston, Mass.

State Manuscript Census (1855), Commonwealth of Massachusetts, Lowell, vol. 16.

FEDERAL RECORDS

Federal Manuscript Census (1850), Microcopy 432, Rolls 326, 327.

Federal Manuscript Census (1860), Microcopy 653, Roll 507.

Flagg versus *Mann*, 9 Fed. Cas. 202.

Lowell National Historical Park and Preservation District, Cultural Resources Inventory; Prepared for Division of Cultural Resources, North Atlantic Regional Office, National Park Service, by Shepley, Bullfinch, Richardson, and Abbott, including "The Acre through Broadway Street," "Centralville," and scattered references.

Contemporary Published Works

Address from the Irish Temperance Society of Boston, to their Countrymen in America. Boston, 1836.

American Citizen. 1854–56.

Appleton, Nathan. *Introduction to the Power Loom and Origin of Lowell*. Lowell, 1858.

———. *Labor, Its Relations in Europe and the United States Compared*. Boston, 1844.

———. *Memoir of Hon. Abbott Lawrence*. Boston, 1856.

Ayer, James C. *Some of the Uses and Abuses in the Management of Our Manufacturing Corporations*. Lowell, 1863.

Bartlett, Elisha. *A Vindication of the Character and Condition of the Females Employed in the Lowell Mills against the Charges Contained in the Boston Times and the Boston Quarterly Review*. Lowell, 1841; reprint, New York: Arno Press, 1975.

Bland, T. A. *Life of Benjamin F. Butler*. Boston, 1879.

Boston *Bee*. 1843.

Boston *Pilot*. 1830–61.

Bremer, Frederika. *The Homes of the New World: Impressions of America*. 2 vols. New York: Harper and Bros., 1868; reprint, New York: Negro Universities Press, 1968.

Brown, Ephraim. "Glass-Making in the Merrimack Basin." *Old Residents Historical Association Collection* 2 (1882): 180–200.

The Bulletin. 1834.

Butler, Benjamin F. *Butler's Book*. Boston, 1892.

The Catholic Almanac, or, Laity's Directory, for the Year 1833. Baltimore, 1833.

Cawley, Elizabeth Hoon, ed. *The American Diaries of Richard Cobden*. Princeton: Princeton University Press, 1952; reprint, New York: Greenwood Press, 1969.

Chase, C. C. "Reminiscences of the High School." *Old Residents Historical Association Collection* 3 (1887): 113–44.

Chevalier, Michel. *Society, Manners, and Politics in the United States: Letters on North America*. Boston, 1839; reprint, New York: Kelley, 1966.

Courier-Citizen Company. *Illustrated History of Lowell*. Boston, 1868.

Cowley, Charles. *Illustrated History of Lowell*. Boston, 1868.

———. "The Foreign Colonies of Lowell." *Old Residents Historical Association Collections* 2 (1883): 165–79.

Crockett, David. *The Life of David Crockett*. New York: A. L. Burt Co., 1902.

Curtis, Josiah. "Brief Remarks on the Hygiene of Massachusetts But More Particularly of the Cities of Boston and Lowell, Being a Report to the American Medical Association." *Transactions of the American Medical Association* 2 (1849).

Daily American Citizen

Daily Evening Advertiser

Daily Journal and Courier

Daily Morning Herald. 1844.

Dickens, Charles. *American Notes for General Circulation*. New York: Harper and Bros., 1842; reprint, New York: AMS, 1966.

Dineen, Maurice. *The Catholic Total Abstinence Movement in the Archdiocese of Boston*. Boston: E. L. Grimes, 1908.

Engels, Frederick. *The Condition of the Working Class in England in 1844*. London, 1892; reprint, London: George Allen and Unwin, 1952.

Freemen's Journal, 1843.

French, J. B. "Early Recollections of an Old Resident." *Old Residents Historical Association Collections* 1 (1879): 252–64.

Gilman, Alfred. "History of the Lowell Grammar Schools." *Old Residents Historical Association Collections* 4 (1891): 87–109.

Hayes, George H. "A Know-Nothing Legislature." *American Historical Association Report* (1896): 177–87.

———. "The Causes of Know-Nothing Success in Massachusetts." *American Historical Review* 3 (1897): 67–82.

Hedrick, George. "Reminiscences and Recollections of Lowell since 1831." *Old Residents Historical Association Collections* 1 (1879): 353–72.

Hill, Hamilton Andrews, ed. *Memoir of Abbott Lawrence*. Boston, 1883.

Hill, Paul. "Personal Reminiscences of Lowell, Fifty Years Ago." *Old Residents Historical Association Collections* 5 (1894): 277–93.

Hurd, D. Hamilton. *History of Middlesex County, Massachusetts with Bibliographical Sketches of Many of Its Pioneers and Prominent Men*. 3 vols. Philadelphia, 1890.

The Ladies Pearl. 1842.

Lowell Advertiser, 1838–61.

Lowell *Compendium*, 1833.

Lowell Courier. 1840–61.

Lowell Daily Courier.

Lowell Directory, various titles and compliers. 1832–60.

Lowell *Evangelist.* 1831.

Lowell *Gazette.* 1861.

Lowell Historical Society. *Contributions.* 2 vols. Lowell: Butterfield, 1913 and 1926.

Lowell *Journal and Mercury.* 1830–35.

Lowell *Mercury.* 1830–35.

Lowell Morning Courier.

The Lowell Offering. 1840–45. Three single issues and five bound volumes.

Lowell *Patriot,* 1835–36.

Lowell *Tri-Weekly American.* 1849, 1851.

Lowell Weekly Compendium. 1832–33.

Lynch, P. "St. Patrick's Parish, Lowell." In *One Hundred Years of Progress: A Graphic and Pictorial Account of the Catholic Church of New England, Archdiocese of Boston.* Edited by James S. Sullivan. Boston, 1895.

McEvoy, John F. "Letter," 22 Feb. 1876. In *Proceedings in the City of Lowell at the Semi-Centennial Celebration of the Incorporation of the Town of Lowell,* Lowell Historical Society, 1876: 132–36.

McGee, Thomas D'Arcy. *A History of the Irish Settlers in North America, from the Earliest Period to the Census of 1850.* Boston, 1855.

Maguire, John Francis. *Father Mathew: A Biography.* London, 1863.

———. *The Irish in America.* London: Longman's & Green, 1868.

Mann, Horace. *Annual Reports on Education.* Boston, 1868.

Miles, Henry A. *Lowell As It Was and As It Is.* Lowell, 1846; reprint, New York: Arno Press, 1972.

New York Freemen's Journal and Catholic Reporter. 1843. Old Residents Historical Association. *Contributions.* Vols. 1–6. Lowell, 1874–1904.

One Hundredth Anniversary Celebration of St. Joseph's Hospital. Lowell, 1940.

Robinson, Harriet Hanson. *Loom and Spindle; or Life among the Early Mill Girls.* New York, 1898; reprint, Kailua, Hawaii: Press Pacifica, 1976.

Robinson, John P. "The Melvin Suits." *Old Residents Historical Association Collection* 2 (1813): 201–5.

Scoresby, William. *American Factories and Their Female Operatives.* Boston, 1845; reprint, New York: Russell & Russell, 1967.

Semi-Centennial Report of the Overseers of the Poor of the City of Lowell. Lowell, 1876.

Shea, John Gilmary. *A History of the Catholic Church within the Limits of the United States, from the First Attempted Colonization to the Present Time.* 5 vols. New York, 1890.

Sketch of Lowell. Lowell, 1842.

Souvenir History of St. John's Hospital: Written for the Quarter-Centennial Celebration of the Founding of the Institution. Lowell, 1892.

Trollope, Anthony. *North America.* 2 vols. New York: 1862; reprint, New York, Kelley, 1970.

U.S. Catholic Intelligencer. 1832.

Varnum, Atkinson C. "Navigation on the Merrimack River." *Old Residents Historical Association Collections* 1 (1877): 318–36.

Varnum, Rev. Lincoln. "My Schools and Teachers in Lowell, Sixty Years Ago," *Old Residents Historical Association Collections* 5 (1894): 125–46.

Voice of Industry. 1846–47.

Vox Populi. 1849, 1851.

Whittier, John Greenleaf. *The Stranger in Lowell.* Boston, 1845.

Wood, Horatio. *Report of the Minister-at-Large in Lowell, to the Lowell Missionary Society.* 1844–61.

Wood, Horatio, Jr. "Memoir of Horatio Wood, by his Son, for Twenty-Four Years Minister-at-Large in Lowell." *Old Residents Historical Association Collections* 3 (1887): 379–405.

Wright, A. B. "Lowell in 1826." *Old Residents Historical Association Collections* 3 (1887): 402–34.

Zion's Banner. 1841.

Secondary Sources

Abbott, Edith, ed. *Immigration: Historical Aspects of the Immigration Problem.* Chicago: University of Chicago Press, 1926.

Adams, Russell B., Jr. *The Boston Money Tree.* New York: Thomas Y. Crowell Co., 1977.

Adams, William Forbes. *Ireland and Irish Immigration from 1815 to the Famine.* New Haven: Yale University Press, 1932; reprint, New York: Russell & Russell, 1967.

Aldrich, Mark. "Determinants of Mortality among New England Cotton Mill Workers during the Progressive Era." *Journal of Economic History* 42 (1982): 845–62.

American Foundations of the Sisters of Notre Dame, Compiled from the Annals of Their Convents by a Member of the Congregation. Philadelphia: Dolphin Press, 1928.

Anderson, Michael. *Family Structure in Nineteenth Century Lancashire.* Cambridge: Cambridge University Press, 1971.

Arensburg, Conrad, and Kimball, Solon T. *Family and Community in Ireland.* Cambridge: Harvard University Press, 1968.

Armstrong, John Borden. *Factory under the Elms: A History of Harrisville, New Hampshire, 1774–1969.* Cambridge: MIT Press, 1969.

Bailyn, Bernard. *Education in the Forming of American Society: Needs and Opportunities for Study.* Chapel Hill: University of North Carolina Press, 1960.

———. "The Challenge of Modern Historiography." *American Historical Review* 87 (1982): 1–24.

Barton, Josef. *Peasants and Strangers: Italians, Rumanians, and Slovaks in an American City, 1890–1950.* Cambridge: Harvard University Press, 1975.

Baum, Dale. *The Civil War Party System: The Case of Massachusetts.* Chapel Hill: University of North Carolina Press, 1984.

—————. "Know-Nothingism and the Republican Majority in Massachusetts: The Political Realignment of the 1850s." *Journal of American History* 64 (1978): 959–86.

Bean, William G. "Puritan *vs.* Celt, 1850–1860." *New England Quarterly* 23 (1924): 319–24.

Beckett, J. C. *The Making of Modern Ireland, 1603–1923.* New York: Alfred A. Knopf, Inc., 1966.

—————. *A Short History of Ireland.* New York: Hutchinson's University Library, 1966.

Bender, Thomas. *Toward an Urban Vision: Ideas and Institutions in Nineteenth Century America.* Lexington: University Press of Kentucky, 1975.

Berkner, Lutz. "The Stem Family and the Developmental Cycle of the Peasant Household: An 18th Century Austrian Example." *American Historical Review* 77 (1972): 398–418.

Berlin, Ira, and Gutman, Herbert G. "Natives and Immigrants, Free Men and Slaves: Urban Workingmen in the Antebellum South." *American Historical Review* 88 (1983): 1175–1200.

Berrol, Selma C. "Urban Schools: The Historian as Critic." *Journal of Urban History* 8 (1982): 206–16.

Bidwell, Charles E. "The Moral Significance of the Common School." *History of Education Quarterly* 6 (1966): 50-91.

Billington, Ray Allen. *The Protestant Crusade, 1800–1860: A Study in the Origins of Nativism.* Chicago: Quadrangle Books, 1964.

Bils, Mark. "Tariff Protection and Production in the Early U.S. Cotton Textile Industry." *Journal of Economic History* 44 (1984): 1033–45.

Binder, Frederick M. *The Age of the Common School, 1830–1865.* Studies in the History of American Education. New York: John Wiley & Sons, 1974.

Blewett, Mary H., ed. *Surviving Hard Times: The Working People of Lowell.* Lowell: Lowell Museum, 1982.

—————. "The Mills and the Multitudes: A Political History." In *Cotton Was King: A History of Lowell, Massachusetts*, pp. 161–89. Edited by Arthur L. Eno, Jr. Lowell: Lowell Historical Society, 1976.

Blodgett, Geoffrey. "Yankee Leadership in a Divided City: Boston, 1860–1910." *Journal of Urban History* 8 (1982): 371–96.

Blouin, Francis X., Jr. *The Boston Region, 1810–1850: A Study of Urbanization.* Ann Arbor, Mich.: UMI Research Press, 1978.

Blumin, Stuart. "The Hypothesis of Middle Class Formation in Nineteenth Century America: A Critique and Some Proposals." *American Historical Review* 90 (1985): 299–338.

Bodnar, John; Weber, Michael; and Simon, Roger. "Migration, Kinship, and Urban Adjustment: Blacks and Poles in Pittsburg, 1910–1930." *Journal of American History* 66 (1979): 548–65.

Bolton, G. C. *The Passing of the English Act of Union: A Study in Parliamentary Politics.* Oxford: Oxford University Press, 1966.

Boskin, Joseph, and Dorinson, Joseph. "Ethnic Humor: Subversion and Survival." *American Quarterly* 37 (1985): 81–97.

Bowles, Samuel, and Gintis, Herbert. *Schooling in Capitalist America.* New York: Basic Books, 1976.

Breitenbach, William. "Sons of the Fathers: Temperance Reformers and the Legacy of the American Revolution." *Journal of the Early Republic* 3 (1983): 69–82.

Brown, Fidelia O. "Decline and Fall." In *Cotton Was King: A History of Lowell, Massachusetts*, pp. 141–58. Edited by Arthur L. Eno, Jr. Lowell: Lowell Historical Society, 1976.

Brown, Thomas N. *Irish-American Nationalism.* Philadelphia: J. B. Lippincott Co., 1966.

Brown, Thomas N., and McAvoy, Thomas. *The United States of America: The Irish Clergyman, the Irish Layman.* Dublin: Gill and Macmillan, 1970.

Bruck, David J. "The Schools of Lowell, 1824–1861: A Case Study in the Origins of Modern Public Education in America." Senior B.A. thesis, Harvard University, 1971.

Bukowczyk, John J. "Immigrants and Their Communities." *International Labor and Working Class History* 25 (1984): 47–57.

————. "The Transformation of Working Class Ethnicity: Corporate Control, Americanization, and the Polish Immigrant Middle Class in Bayonne, New Jersey, 1915-1925." *Labor History* 25 (1984): 53–82.

Burchill, R. A. *The San Francisco Irish, 1848–1880.* Manchester: Manchester University Press, 1979.

Burton, William L. "Irish Regiments in the Union Army: The Massachusetts Experience." *Historical Journal of Massachusetts* 11 (1983): 104–19.

Bushman, Richard L. "Family Security in the Transition from Farm to City, 1750–1850." *Journal of Family History* 6 (1981): 238–56.

Butts, R. Freeman. *Public Education in the United States: From Revolution to Reform.* New York: Holt, Rinehart, and Winston, 1978.

Carey, Patrick. "Republicanism within American Catholicism, 1785–1860." *Journal of the Early Republic* 3 (1983): 413–37.

————. "The Laity's Understanding of the Trustee System, 1785–1855." *Catholic Historical Review* 44 (1978): 357–76.

A Century in Lowell, 1852–1952: Courtesy of the Sisters of Notre Dame de Namur, May 30, 1952. Lowell, 1952.

A Chronicle of Textile Machinery, 1824–1924, Issued to Commemorate the One Hundredth Anniversary of the Saco-Lowell Shops. Boston: By the Company, 1924.

Chudacoff, Howard P. "A New Look at Ethnic Neighborhoods." *Journal of American History* 60 (1973): 76–93.

Clark, Dennis. *The Irish in Philadelphia: Ten Generations of Urban Experience.* Philadelphia: Temple University Press, 1973.

Clark, Samuel. *Social Origins of the Irish Land War.* Princeton: Princeton University Press, 1979.

Clarke, Mary Stetson. *The Old Middlesex Canal.* Melrose, Mass.: Hilltop Press, 1974.

Coburn, Frederick W. *History of Lowell and Its People*. 3 vols. New York: Lewis Historical Publishing Co., 1920.

Cogley, John. *Catholic America*. New York: Dial Press, 1973.

Cohen, Isaac. "Worker's Control in the Cotton Industry: A Comparative Study of British and American Mule Spinning." *Labor History* 26 (1985): 53–85.

Cohen, Miriam. "Changing Education Strategies among Immigrant Generations: New York Italians in Comparative Perspective." *Journal of Social History* 15 (1982): 443–66.

Cohn, Raymond L. "Mortality on Immigrant Voyages to New York, 1836–1853." *Journal of Economic History* 44 (1984): 289–300.

Cole, Donald B. *Immigrant City, Lawrence, Massachusetts, 1845–1921*. Chapel Hill: University of North Carolina Press, 1963.

Coleman, Terry. *Going to America*. New York: Anchor Books, 1973.

Connell, Kenneth H. *The Population of Ireland, 1750–1845*. Oxford: Clarendon Press, 1950.

Connolly, S. J. *Priests and People in Pre-Famine Ireland, 1780–1845*. Dublin: Gill & Macmillan, 1982.

———. "Catholicism in Ulster, 1800–1850." In *Plantation to Partition: Essays in Ulster History in Honour of J. L. McCracken*, pp. 151–71. Edited by Peter Roebuck. Belfast: Blackstaff Press, 1981.

Conzen, Kathleen Neils. *Immigrant Milwaukee, 1836–1860: Accommodation and Community in a Frontier City*. Cambridge: Harvard University Press, 1976.

———. "Quantification and the New Urban History." *Journal of Urban History* 13 (1983): 653–77.

———. "Immigrants, Ethnic Neighborhoods, and Ethnic Identity: Historical Issues." *Journal of American History* 66 (1979): 602–15.

Coolidge, John. *Mill and Mansion*. New York: Columbia University Press, 1942.

Costigan, Giovanni. *A History of Modern Ireland*. New York: Pegasus, 1969.

Cousens, S. H. "The Regional Variations in Emigration between 1821 and 1841." *Transactions and Papers of Institute of British Geographers* 37 (1965): 22–29.

Crawford, William H. "Economy and Society in South Ulster in the Eighteenth Century." *Clogher Record* 8 (1975): 241–58.

Cremin, Lawrence. *American Education: The National Experience, 1783–1896*. New York: Harper & Row, 1980.

———. *The American Common School: An Historical Conception*. New York: Columbia University Press, 1961.

Cubberly, Elwood P. *Public Education in the United States: A Study and Interpretation of American Educational History*. Boston: Houghton Mifflin Co., 1934.

Cullen, L. M., and Furet, F. *Ireland and France—17th–20th Centuries: Towards a Comparative Study of Rural History*. Proceedings of the First Franco-Irish Symposium on Social and Economic History. Ann Arbor, Mich.: UMI Press, 1980.

Cullen, L. M., and Smout, T. C., eds. *Comparative Aspects of Scottish and Irish Economic and Social History, 1600–1900.* Edinburgh: John Donald Publishers, 1977.

Cumbler, John T. "The Politics of Charity: Gender and Class in Late 19th Century Charity Policy." *Journal of Social History* 14 (1980): 99–111.

———. "The City and the Community: The Impact of Urban Forces on Working Class Behavior." *Journal of Urban History* 3 (1977): 427–42.

Curtis, Edmund. *A History of Ireland.* New York: Barnes & Noble, 1968.

Dalzell, Robert F. "The Rise of the Waltham-Lowell System and Some Thoughts on the Political Economy of Modernization in Antebellum Massachusetts." *Perspectives in American History* 9 (1975): 229–68.

Dannenbaum, Jed. *Drink and Disorder: Temperance Reform in Cincinnati from the Washingtonian Revival to the Women's Christian Temperance Union.* Urbana: University of Illinois Press, 1984.

———. "The Origins of Temperance Activism and Militancy among American Women." *Journal of Social History* 15 (1981): 235–52.

Darroch, A. Gordon, and Ornstein, Michael. "Family and Household in Nineteenth Century Canada: Regional Patterns and Regional Economies." *Journal of Family History* 9 (1984): 158–77.

Dawley, Alan. *Class and Community: The Industrial Revolution in Lynn.* Cambridge: Harvard University Press, 1976.

Dignan, Patrick S. *A History of the Legal Incorporation of Catholic Church Property in the United States (1784–1932).* Studies in American Church History. Washington, D.C.: Catholic University Press, 1933.

Diner, Hasia R. *Erin's Daughters in America: Irish Immigrant Women in the Nineteenth Century.* Baltimore: Johns Hopkins University Press, 1983.

Dinmore, Harry C. "Proprietors of Locks and Canals: The Founding of Lowell." In *Cotton Was King: A History of Lowell, Massachusetts,* pp. 69–79. Edited by Arthur L. Eno, Jr. Lowell: Lowell Historical Society, 1976.

Dolan, Jay P. *The American Catholic Experience: A History from Colonial Times to the Present.* New York: Doubleday & Co., 1985.

———. *The Immigrant Church: New York's Irish and German Catholics, 1815–1865.* Baltimore: Johns Hopkins University Press, 1975.

Donnelly, James S., Jr. *The Land and People of Nineteenth Century Cork: The Rural Economy and the Land Question.* London: Routledge & Kegan Paul, 1975.

Doucet, Michael J. "Urban Land Development in Nineteenth Century North America: Themes in the Literature." *Journal of Urban History* 8 (1982): 299–342.

Doyle, David N. *Ireland, Irishmen, and Revolutionary America, 1760–1820.* Dublin: Mercier, 1981.

Drake, Michael. "Marriage and Population Growth in Ireland, 1750–1845." *Economic History Review* 16 (1963): 301–13.

Dublin, Thomas. *Women at Work: The Transformation of Work and Community in Lowell, Massachusetts, 1826–1860.* New York: Columbia University Press, 1979.

Dublin, Thomas, ed. *Farm to Factory: The Mill Experience and Women's Lives in New England, 1830–1860.* New York: Columbia University Press, 1981.

Dubnoff, Stephen. "Gender, the Family, and the Problem of Work Motivation in a Transition to Industrial Capitalism." *Journal of Family History* 4 (1979): 121–36.

————. "The Family and Absence from Work: Irish Workers in a Lowell, Massachusetts Cotton Mill, 1860." Ph. D. dissertation, Brandeis University, 1976.

Dudden, Faye E. *Serving Women: Household Services in Nineteenth Century America.* Middletown, Conn.: Wesleyan University Press, 1983.

Duff, John B. *The Irish in America.* Belmont, Calif.: Wadsworth Publishing Co., 1971.

Early, Francis H. "The French Canadian Family Economy and Standard-of-Living in Lowell, Massachusetts, 1870." *Journal of Family History* 7 (1982): 180–99.

Eisler, Benita, ed. *The Lowell Offering: Writings by New England Mill Women.* New York: Harper & Row, 1977.

Ellis, John Tracy. *American Catholicism.* Chicago: University of Chicago Press, 1956.

Eltis, David. "Free and Coerced Transatlantic Migrations: Some Comparisons." *American Historical Review* 88 (1983): 251–80.

Engerman, Stanley. "Up or Out: Social and Geographical Mobility in the United States." *Journal of Interdisciplinary History* 5 (1975): 469–90.

Eno, Arthur L., Jr., ed. *Cotton Was King.* Lowell: Lowell Historical Society, 1976.

Ernst, Robert. *Immigrant Life in New York City, 1825–1863.* Port Washington, N.Y.: Ira J. Freeman, 1965.

Fahler, Paul, and Dawley, Alan. "Working Class Culture and Politics in the Industrial Revolution: Sources of Loyalism and Rebellion." *Journal of Social History* 9 (1975): 466–80.

Field, Alexander James. "Educational Expansion in Mid-Nineteenth Century Massachusetts: Human-Capital Formation or Structural Reinforcement?" *Harvard Education Review* 46 (1976): 521–52.

Fitzpatrick, David. *Irish Emigration, 1801–1921.* Dublin: Dundalgan Press, 1984.

Folsom, Burton W., Jr. *Urban Capitalists: Entrepreneurs and City Growth in Pennsylvania's Lackawanna and Lehigh Regions, 1800–1920.* Baltimore: Johns Hopkins University Press, 1981.

Foner, Eric. *Free Soil, Free Labor, Free Men: The Ideology of the Republican Party before the Civil War.* New York: Oxford University Press, 1971.

Foner, Philip S., ed. *The Factory Girls: A Collection of Writings on Life and Struggles in the New England Factories of the 1840s.* Urbana: University of Illinois Press, 1977.

Formisano, Ronald P. *The Transformation of Political Culture: Massachusetts Parties, 1790s–1840s.* New York: Oxford University Press, 1983.

Freeman, T. W. *Ireland: A General and Regional Geography.* London: Methuen & Co., 1969.

Frisch, Michael. *Town into City: Springfield, Massachusetts and the Meaning of Community, 1840–1880.* Cambridge: Harvard University Press, 1972.

Frisch, Michael, and Walkowitz, Daniel J., eds. *Working-Class America: Essays on Labor, Community, and American Society.* Urbana: University of Illinois Press, 1983.

Gerber, David A. "Modernity in the Service of Tradition: Catholic Lay Trustees at Buffalo's St. Louis Church and the Transformation of European Communal Traditions, 1829–1865." *Journal of Social History* 15 (1982): 655–84.

Gibb, George S. *The Saco-Lowell Shops: Textile Machinery Building in New England, 1813–1949.* Cambridge: Harvard University Press, 1950.

Gibson, William. *A Mass for the Dead.* New York: Atheneum, 1968.

Gilman, Amy. "From Widowhood to Wickedness: The Politics of Class and Gender in New York City Private Charity, 1799–1860." *History of Education Quarterly* 24 (1984): 59–74.

Gilmore, William J. "Elementary Literacy on the Eve of the Industrial Revolution: Trends in Rural New England, 1760–1830." *Proceedings of the American Antiquarian Society* 92, pt. 1 (1982): 87–171.

Gitelman, Howard P. *Workingmen of Waltham.* Baltimore: Johns Hopkins University Press, 1974.

Glasco, Lawrence. "The Life Cycles and Household Structure of American Ethnic Groups: Irish, Germans, and Native-Born Whites in Buffalo, New York, 1855." *Journal of Urban History* 1 (1975): 338–64.

Glazer, Nathan, and Moynihan, Daniel Patrick. *Beyond the Melting Pot.* Cambridge: MIT Press, 1963.

Glenn, Myra C. "School Discipline and Punishment in Antebellum America." *Journal of the Early Republic* 1 (1981): 395–408.

Goldfield, David R. "The New Regionalism." *Journal of Urban History* 10 (1984): 171–86.

Greeley, Andrew M. *That Most Distressful Nation: The Taming of the American Irish.* Chicago: Quadrangle Books, 1972.

Green, Constance McLaughlin. *Holyoke, Massachusetts: A Case History of the Industrial Revolution in America.* New Haven: Yale University Press, 1939.

Greenslet, Ferris. *The Lowells and Their Seven Worlds.* Boston: Houghton Mifflin Co., 1946.

Greer, Colin. *The Great School Legend: A Revisionist Interpretation of American Public Education.* New York: Basic Books, 1972.

Gregory, Francis W. *Nathan Appleton, Merchant and Entrepreneur, 1779–1861.* Charlottesville: University of Virginia Press, 1976.

Griffen, Clyde, and Griffen, Sally. *Natives and Newcomers: The Ordering of Opportunity in Mid-Nineteenth Century Poughkeepsie.* Cambridge: Harvard University Press, 1978.

Griffin, Sara Swan. *Quaint Bits of Lowell History: A Few Interesting Stories about Earlier Days.* Lowell: Butterfield Printing Company, 1928.

Grizzell, Emit Duncan. *Origin and Development of the High School in New England before 1865.* Philadelphia: J. B. Lippincott, 1923.

Grob, Gerald. "The Social History of Medicine and Disease in America: Problems and Possibilities." *Journal of Social History* 10 (1977): 391–409.

Groneman, Carol. "Working Class Immigrant Women in Mid-Nineteenth Century New York: The Irishwoman's Experience." *Journal of Urban History* 4 (1978): 255–74.

Guilday, Peter. "Trusteeism." *Historical Records and Studies* 18 (1928): 14–73.

Gutman, Herbert. *Work, Culture, and Society in Industrializing America: Essays in American Working Class History*. New York: Alfred A. Knopf, 1976.

Gwyn, Denis. *Young Ireland and 1848*. Oxford: B. H. Blackwell, 1949.

Hamill, Pete. *The Gift*. New York: Ballantine, 1974.

Hammett, Theodore M. "Two Mobs of Jacksonian Boston: Ideology and Interest." *Journal of American History* 62 (1976): 845–68.

Handlin, Oscar. *Boston's Immigrants: A Study in Acculturation*. New York: Atheneum, 1977.

———. *The Uprooted*. Boston: Little, Brown & Co., 1973.

Handlin, Oscar, and Crouch, Barry A. "Amos A. Lawrence and the Formation of the Constitutional Union Party: The Conservative Failure in 1860." *Historical Journal of Massachusetts* 8 (1980): 46–58.

Hanlan, James P. *The Working Population of Manchester, New Hampshire, 1840–1866*. Ann Arbor, Mich.: UMI Press 1981.

Hannon, Joan Underhill. "Poverty in the Northeast: The View from New York State's Poor Relief Rolls." *Journal of Economic History* 44 (1984): 1001–32.

Hansen, Marcus Lee. *The Immigrant in American History*. Cambridge: Harvard University Press, 1942.

Hareven, Tamara. "Cycles, Courses and Cohorts: Reflections on the Theoretical and Methodological Approaches to the History of Family Development." *Journal of Social History* 12 (1978): 97–109.

———. "The Laborers of Manchester, New Hampshire, 1912–1922: The Role of Family and Ethnicity in Adjustment to Industrial Life." *Labor History* 16 (1975): 249–65.

———. "The Family Process: The Historical Study of the Cycle." *Journal of Social History* 7 (1974): 322–27.

Hareven, Tamara, and Chudacoff, Howard. "From Empty Nest to Family Dissolution: Life Course Transitions into Old Age." *Journal of Family History* 4 (1979): 69–83.

Hareven, Tamara, and Langenbach, Randolph. *Amoskeag: Life and Work in an American Factory City*. New York: Pantheon Books, 1978.

Harris, Barbara J. "Recent Work on the History of the Family: A Review Article." *Feminist Studies* 3 (1976): 159–72.

Harrison, Brian. *Drink and the Victorians: The Temperance Question in England, 1825–1872*. London: Faber & Faber, 1971.

Hennessey, James S., S.J. *American Catholics: A History of the Roman Catholic Community in the United States*. New York: Oxford University Press, 1981.

Hershberg, Theodore, and Alter, George. "Immigrants and Industry: The Philadelphia Experience, 1850–1880." *Journal of Social History* 9 (1975): 219–48.

Higham, John. *Strangers in the Land: Patterns of American Nativism, 1860–1925*. New York: Atheneum, 1963.

———. "Current Trends in the Study of Ethnicity in the United States." *Journal of American Ethnic History* 2 (1982): 5–15.

————. "Integrating America: The Problem of Assimilation in the 19th Century." *Journal of American Ethnic History* 1 (1981): 7–25.

Hirsch, Susan E. *Roots of the American Working Class: The Industrialization of Crafts in Newark, 1800–1860.* Philadelphia: University of Pennsylvania Press, 1978.

Hofstadter, Richard. *The Age of Reform: From Bryan to F.D.R.* New York: Random House, 1955.

Holt, Michael F. "The Politics of Impatience: The Origins of Know-Nothingism." *Journal of American History* 60 (1973): 309–31.

Holzman, Robert J. *Stormy Ben Butler.* New York: Macmillan, 1954.

Immaculata, Sister Agnes. *Profile History of the Ohio Province of the Sisters of Notre Dame de Namur, 1901–1970.* Cincinnati: M. Rosenthal Company, 1974.

Ingham, John N. "Rags to Riches Revisited: The Effect of City Size and Related Factors in the Recruitment of Business Leaders." *Journal of American History* 63 (1976): 615–37.

Jackson, John Archer. *The Irish in Britain.* London: Routledge & Kegan Paul, 1963.

Jackson, Sidney L. *America's Struggle for Free Schools: Social Tension and Education in New England and New York, 1827–1842.* New York: Russell & Russell, 1965.

Johnson, David R. *Policing the Urban Underworld: The Impact of Crime on the Development of the American Police, 1800–1887.* Philadelphia: Temple University Press, 1979.

Josephson, Hannah. *The Golden Threads: New England's Mill Girls and Magnates.* New York: Duell, 1949; reprint, New York: Russell & Russell, 1967.

Julie de la Sainte Famille, Sister. *History of the Rules and Constitutions of the Sisters of Notre Dame de Namur.* N.d.

Kaestle, Carl F. "Social Change, Discipline, and the Common School in Early 19th Century America." *Journal of Interdisciplinary History* 9 (1978): 1–17.

Kasson, John F. *Civilizing the Machine: Technology and Republican Values in America, 1778–1900.* New York: Grossman, 1976.

Katz, Michael. *The People of Hamilton, Canada West: Family and Class in a Mid-Nineteenth Century City.* Cambridge: Harvard University Press, 1975.

————. *Class, Bureaucracy, and Schools: The Illusion of Educational Change in America.* New York: Praeger, 1971.

————. *The Irony of Early School Reform: Educational Innovation in Mid-Nineteenth Century Massachusetts.* Cambridge: Harvard University Press, 1968.

Katz, Michael B.; Doucet, Michael J.; and Stern, Mark J. *The Social Organization of Early Industrial Capitalism.* Cambridge: Harvard University Press, 1982.

————. "Migration and the Social Order in Erie County, New York, 1865." *Journal of Interdisciplinary History* 8 (1978): 669–702.

Katzman, David M. *Seven Days a Week: Women and Domestic Service in Industrializing America.* Urbana: University of Illinios Press, 1981.

Kearney, H. F. "Fr. Mathew: Apostle of Modernization." In *Studies in Irish His-*

tory: Presented to R. Dudley Edwards, pp. 164–75. Edited by Art Cosgrove and Donal McCartney. Dublin: University College, 1979.

Keenan, Desmond J. *The Catholic Church in Nineteenth Century Ireland: A Sociological Study*. Dublin: Gill & Macmillan, 1983.

Kennedy, Liam, and Ollerenshaw, Philip. *Economic History of Ulster*. Manchester: University of Manchester Press, 1985.

Kennedy, Robert, Jr. *The Irish: Emigration, Marriage and Fertility*. Berkeley: University of California Press, 1973.

Kenngott, George F. *The Record of a City: A Social Survey of Lowell, Massachusetts*. New York: Macmillan, 1912.

Kenny, Donna S. "Women at Work: Views and Visions from the Pioneer Valley, 1870–1945." *Historical Journal of Massachusetts* 13 (1985): 30–41.

Kerr, Barbara. "Irish Seasonal Migration to Great Britain, 1800–1838." *Irish Historical Studies* 3 (1943): 38–62.

Kirkland, Edward C. *Men, Cities, and Transportation: A Case Study in New England History, 1820–1900*. Cambridge: Harvard University Press, 1948; reprint, New York: Russell & Russell, 1968.

Knights, Peter. *Plain People of Boston, 1830–1860*. New York: Oxford University Press, 1971.

Knobel, Dale T. "A Vocabulary of Ethnic Perception: Content Analysis of the American Stage Irishman, 1820–1860." *Journal of American Studies* 15 (1981): 45–71.

Knowles, Malcolm S. *The Adult Education Movement in the United States*. New York: Holt, Rinehart, and Winston, 1962.

Kocolowksi, Gary P. "Alternative to Record Linkage in the Study of Labor Migration: The Uses of Naturalization Records." *Historical Methods Newsletter* 14 (1981): 139–42.

Kohl, Lawrence Frederick. "The Concept of Social Control and the History of Jacksonian America." *Journal of the Early Republic* 5 (1985): 21–34.

Koppes, Clayton R., and Norris, William P. "Ethnicity, Class and Mortality in the Industrial City: A Case Study of Typhoid Fever in Pittsburg, 1890–1910." *Journal of Urban History* 11 (1985): 259–79.

Kremm, Thomas W. "Cleveland and the First Lincoln Election: The Ethnic Response to Nativism." *Journal of Interdisciplinary History* 8 (1977): 69–86.

Lane, Roger. *Policing the City, Boston, 1822–1885*. Cambridge: Harvard University Press, 1967.

Lannie, Vincent. *Public Money and Parochial Education: Bishop Hughes, Governor Seward, and the New York School Controversy*. Cleveland: Press of Case Western Reserve, 1968.

———. "Alienation in America: The Immigrant Catholic and Public Education in Pre-Civil War America." *Review of Politics* 32 (1970): 503–21.

Larkin, Emmet. "The Devotional Revolution in Ireland, 1850–1875." *American History Review* 77 (1972): 625–52.

Lasch, Christopher. "The Family and History." *New York Review of Books*, 13 Nov. 1975, pp. 30–33.

————. "The Emotions of Family Life." *New York Review of Books*, 27 Nov. 1975, pp. 37–42.

————. "What the Doctor Ordered." *New York Review of Books*, 11 Dec. 1975, pp. 50–54.

Laslett, Peter. *Household and Family in Past Time*. Cambridge: Cambridge University Press, 1972.

————. *The World We Have Lost*. New York: Charles Scribner's Sons, 1965.

Lasser, Carol. "A 'Pleasingly Oppressive' Burden: The Transformation of Domestic Service and Female Charity in Salem, 1800–1840." *Essex Institute Historical Collections* 116 (1980): 156–75.

Laurie, Bruce. *The Working People of Philadelphia, 1800–1850*. Philadelphia: Temple University Press, 1980.

Lawton, R. "Irish Emigration to England and Wales in the Mid-Nineteenth Century." *Irish Geography* 4 (1959): 35–54.

Layer, Robert G. *Earnings of Cotton Mill Operatives, 1825–1914*. Cambridge: Harvard University Press, 1955.

Lee, Joseph. *The Modernization of Irish Society*. London: Gill & Macmillan, 1973.

————. "Marriage and Population in Pre-Famine Ireland." *Economic History Review* 21 (1968): 283–95.

Lees, Lynn. *Exiles of Erin: Irish Migrants in Victorian London*. Ithaca: Cornell University Press, 1979.

Lees, Lynn, and Modell, John. "The Irish Countryman Urbanized: A Comparative Perspective on the Famine Migration. " *Journal of Urban History* 3 (1977): 391–408.

Levine, Edward M. *The Irish and Irish Politicians*. Notre Dame, Ind.: University of Notre Dame Press, 1966.

Leyburn, James G. *The Scotch-Irish: A Social History*. Chapel Hill: University of North Carolina Press, 1962.

Lipchitz, Joseph W. "The Golden Age." In *Cotton Was King: A History of Lowell, Massachusetts*, pp. 80–103. Edited by Arthur L. Eno, Jr. Lowell: Lowell Historical Society, 1976.

Lord, Robert H.; Sexton, John E.; and Harrington, Edward P. *History of the Archdiocese of Boston*. 3 vols. New York: Sheed and Ward, 1944.

McAvoy, Thomas T. *History of the Catholic Church in the United States*. Notre Dame, Ind.: University of Notre Dame Press, 1969.

McCaffrey, Lawrence J. *The Irish Diaspora in America*. Bloomington: Indiana University Press, 1976.

————. *The Irish Question, 1800–1922*. Lexington: University Press of Kentucky, 1968.

McClymer, John. "The Study of Community and the 'New' Social History." *Journal of Urban History* 7 (1980): 103–18.

McDonald, Justile. *History of the Irish in Wisconsin in the 19th Century*. Washington, D.C.: Catholic University Press, 1954.

McDonough, Oliver. "Irish Overseas Emigration during the Famine." In *The*

Great Famine: Studies in Irish History, pp. 319–88. Edited by R. Dudley Edwards and T. Desmond Williams. New York: New York University Press, 1957.

―――. "The Irish Catholic Clergy and Emigration during the Great Famine." *Irish Historical Studies* 5 (1947): 287–302.

McDowell, R. B. "Ireland on the Eve of the Famine." In *The Great Famine: Studies in Irish History*, pp. 402–56. Edited by R. Dudley Edwards and T. Desmond Williams. New York: New York University Press, 1957.

―――. *Public Opinion and Government Policy in Ireland 1801–1846*. London: Faber & Faber, 1932.

McGouldrick, Paul D. *New England Textiles in the Nineteenth Century*. Cambridge: Harvard University Press, 1968.

McIntyre, Angus. *The Liberator: Daniel O'Connell and the Irish Party, 1830–1847*. London: Hamish Hamilton, 1965.

McLaughlin, Virginia Yans. *Family and Community: Italian Immigrants in Buffalo, 1880–1930*. Urbana: University of Illinois Press, 1981.

McSorley, Edward. *Our Own Kind*. New York: Harper & Row, 1946.

Maizlish, Stephen E., and Kushma, John J., eds. *Essays on American Antebellum Politics, 1840–1860*. College Station: Texas A & M University Press, 1982.

Malone, Patrick. *Canals and Industry: Engineering in Lowell, 1821–1880*. Lowell: Lowell Museum, 1983.

―――. *The Lowell Canal System*. Lowell: Lowell Museum, 1976.

Marty, Martin E. "The Catholic Ghetto and All Other Ghettos." *Catholic Historical Review* 68 (1982): 182-205.

Marx, Leo. *The Machine in the Garden: Technology and the Pastoral Ideal in America*. London: Oxford University Press, 1964.

Matthews, Glenna. "The Community Study: Ethnicity and Success in San Jose." *Journal of Interdisciplinary History* 7 (1976): 305–18.

Mazur, Stella M. *Roots and Heritage of Polish People in Lowell*. Lowell: Sullivan Brothers Printers, 1976.

Meagher, Timothy J., ed. *From Paddy to Studs: Irish-American Communities in the Turn of the Century Era, 1800 to 1920*. Westport, Conn.: Greenwood Press, 1986.

―――. "'Why Should We Care for a Little Trouble or a Walk through the Mud': St. Patrick's and Columbus Day Parades in Worcester, Massachusetts, 1845–1915." *New England Quarterly* 58 (1985): 5–26.

―――. "The Delayed Development of Parochial Education among Irish Catholics in Worcester." *Historical Journal of Massachusetts* 12 (1984): 44–59.

Meckel, Richard A. "Immigration, Mortality and Population Growth in Boston, 1840–1880." *Journal of Interdisciplinary History* 15 (1985): 393–417.

Mendels, Franklin F. "Social Mobility and Phases of Industrialization." *Journal of Interdisciplinary History* 7 (1976): 193–216.

Merwick, Donna. *Boston's Priests, 1848–1910: A Study of Social and Intellectual Change*. Cambridge: Harvard University Press, 1973.

Meyer, John W.; Tyack, David; Nagel, Joane; and Gordon, Audri. "Public Education as Nation-Building in America." *American Journal of Sociology* 85 (1979): 591–613.

Miller, David W. "Irish Catholicism and the Great Famine." *Journal of Social History* 9 (1975): 81–98.

Miller, Douglas T. *The Birth of Modern America, 1820–1850*. Indianapolis: Bobbs-Merrill Co., 1970.

Miller, Kerby. *Emigrants and Exiles: Ireland and the Irish Exodus to North America*. New York: Oxford University Press, 1985.

Miller, Kerby A.; Boling, Bruce; and Doyle, David N. "Emigrants and Exiles: Irish Cultures and Irish Emigration to North America, 1790–1922." *Irish Historical Studies* 40 (1980): 116–34.

Mirel, Jeffrey E., and Angus, David L. "From Spellers to Spindles: Work-Force Entry by the Children of Textile Workers, 1888–1890." *Social Science History* 9 (1985): 123–43.

Miriam of the Infant Jesus, S.N.D., Sister. *The Finger of God: History of the Massachusetts Province of Notre Dame de Namur, 1849–1963*. Boston: Mission Church Press, 1963.

Mitchell, Albert Gibbs, Jr. "Irish Family Patterns in Nineteenth Century Ireland and Lowell, Massachusetts." Ph.D. dissertation, Boston University, 1976.

Mitchell, Brian C. *On the North Bank: A Centennial History of the Parish of St. Michael, 1883–1983*. Lowell: Sullivan Brothers Printers, 1984.

———. "'They Do Not Differ Greatly': The Pattern of Community Development among the Irish in Late Nineteenth Century Lowell." In *From Paddy to Studs: Irish-American Communities in the Turn of the Century Era, 1880 to 1920*, pp. 53–73. Edited by Timothy J. Meagher. Westport, Conn.: Greenwood Press, 1986.

———. "Educating Irish Immigrants in Antebellum Lowell." *Historical Journal of Massachusetts* 11 (1983): 94–103.

———. "Teaching Local History: Lowell and the Adult Evening Experience." *Perspectives* 20 (1982): 16–17.

———. "Interpreting American Industrial History: The Lowell National Historical Park's *General Management Plan*: An Overview." *International Labor and Working Class History* 21 (1982): 69–72.

———. "Immigrants in Utopia: The Early Irish Community of Lowell, Massachusetts, 1821–1861." Ph D. dissertation, University of Rochester, 1981.

Modell, John, and Hareven, Tamara. "Urbanization and the Malleable Household: An Examination of Boarding and Lodging in American Families." *Journal of Marriage and the Family* 35 (1973): 467–79.

Mokyr, Joel. *Why Ireland Starved: A Quantitative and Analytical History of the Irish Economy, 1800–1850*. London: George Allen & Unwin, 1983.

Monkkoner, Eric H. "From Cop History to Social History: The Significance of the Police in American History." *Journal of Social History* 15 (1982): 575–91.

Montgomery, David. "The Shuttle and the Cross: Weavers and Artisans in the Kensington Riots of 1844." *Journal of Social History* 4 (1972): 411–46.

Moody, T. W., and Martin, F. X. *The Course of Irish History*. New York: Weybright & Talley, Inc., 1967.

Morgan, Myfanwy, and Golden, Hilda. "Immigrant Families in an Industrial City: A Study of Households in Holyoke, 1880." *Journal of Family History* 4 (1979): 59–68.

Moriarty, Thomas F. "The Irish American Response to Catholic Emancipation." *Catholic Historical Review* 66 (1980): 353–73.

Mormino, Gary Ross. *Immigrants on the Hill: Italian-Americans in St. Louis, 1882–1982.* Urbana: University of Illinois Press, 1986.

Mulkern, John R. "Scandal behind the Convent Walls: The Know-Nothing Nunnery Committee of 1855." *Historical Journal of Massachusetts* 11 (1983): 22–34.

Mulligan, William, Jr. "Mechanization and Work in the American Shoe Industry: Lynn, Massachusetts, 1852–1855." *Journal of Economic History* 41 (1981): 132–56.

Nasaw, David. *Schooled to Order: A Social History of Public Schooling in the United States.* New York: Oxford University Press, 1979.

Nash, Howard P., Jr. *Stormy Petrel: The Life and Times of Con. Benjamin F. Butler, 1818–1893.* Rutherford, N.J.: Farleigh Dickinson University Press, 1969.

Neufeld, Maurice. "The Persistence of Ideas in the American Labor Movement." *Industrial and Labor Relations Review* 35 (1982): 207–20.

———. "The Size of the Jacksonian Labor Movement: A Cautionary Account." *Labor History* 23 (1982): 599–607.

Nickless, Pamela J. "A New Look at Productivity in the New England Cotton Textile Industry, 1830–1860." *Journal of Economic History* 34 (1979): 889–910.

———. "Changing Labor Productivity and the Utilizing of Native American Workers in the American Cotton Textile Industry, 1825–1860." Ph. D. dissertation, Purdue University, 1976.

Niehaus, Earl F. *The Irish in New Orleans, 1800–1860.* Baton Rouge: Louisiana State University Press, 1965.

Nisonoff, Laurie. "Bread and Roses: The Proletarianization of Woman Workers in New England Textile Mills, 1827–1848." *Historical Journal of Massachusetts* 9 (1981): 3–14.

North, Douglas C. *The Economic Growth of the United States, 1790–1860.* Englewood Cliffs, N.J.: Prentice-Hall, 1961.

Nowlan, Kevin B. *The Politics of Repeal: A Study in the Relations between Great Britain and Ireland, 1841–1860.* London: Routledge & Kegan Paul, 1965.

O'Brien, Michael J. *Pioneer Irish in New England.* New York: P. J. Kennedy & Sons, 1937.

O'Connell, William. *Recollections of Seventy Years.* Boston: Houghton Mifflin Co., 1934.

O'Connor, Thomas H. *Fitzpatrick's Boston: 1846–1866.* Boston: Northeastern University Press, 1984.

O'Day, Edward J. "Constructing the Western Railroad: The Irish Dimension." *Historical Journal of Massachusetts* 11 (1983): 7–21.

O'Donnell, Patrick. *The Irish Faction Fighters of the 19th Century.* Dublin: Anvil Books, 1975.

O'Dwyer, George. *Irish Catholic Genesis of Lowell.* Lowell: Sullivan Brothers Printers, 1920.

O'Faolain, Sean. *King of the Beggars: A Life of Daniel O'Connell, the Irish Liberator, in a Study in the Rise of Modern Irish Democracy.* New York: Viking Press, 1938.

O'Farrell, Patrick. *Ireland's England Question.* New York: Schocken Books, Inc., 1972.

———. "Emigrant Attitudes and Behavior as a Source for Irish History." *Historical Studies* 10 (1976): 109–31.

O'Grady, Joseph P. *How the Irish Became Americans.* New York: Twayne Publishers, 1973.

O'Leary, Robert. "Brahmins and Bullyboy: William Henry O'Connell and Massachusetts Politics." *Historical Journal of Massachusetts* 10 (1982): 3–19.

O'Shea, James. *Priests, Politics, and Society in Post-Famine Ireland: A Study of Country Tipperary, 1850–1891.* Dublin: Wolfhound Press, 1983.

O'Toole, James M. "'That Fabulous Churchman': Toward a Biography of Cardinal O'Connell." *Catholic Historical Review* 70 (1984): 28–44.

Parkerson, Donald H. "How Mobile Were Nineteenth-Century Americans?" *Historical Methods Newsletter* 15 (1982): 99–109.

Patterson, Jon A. "The Impact of Sanitary Reform upon American Urban Planning, 1840–1890." *Journal of Social History* 13 (1979): 83–109.

Pawa, Jay. "Workingmen and Free Schools in the 19th Century: A Comment on the Labor-Education Thesis." *History of Education Quarterly* 11 (1971): 287–302.

Pease, Jane H., and Pease, William H. "Social Structure and the Potential for Urban Change: Boston and Charleston in the 1830s." *Journal of Urban History* 8 (1982): 171–95.

Pedulla, Marianne. "Labor in a City of Immigrants: Holyoke, 1882–1888." *Historical Journal of Massachusetts* 13 (1985): 147–61.

Pessen, Edward. "The Social Configuration of the Antebellum City: An Historical and Theoretical Inquiry." *Journal of Urban History* 2 (1976): 267–306.

Post, J. D. "Famine, Mortality and Epidemic Disease in the Process of Modernization." *Economic History Review* 29 (1976): 14–27.

Potter, George. *To the Golden Door: The Study of the Irish in Ireland and America.* Westport, Conn.: Greenwood Press, 1960.

Pred, Allen. *Urban Growth and City Systems in the United States, 1840–1860.* Cambridge: Harvard University Press, 1980.

Preston, Jo Anne. "'To Learn Me the Whole of the Trade': Conflict between a Female Apprentice and a Merchant Tailor in Antebellum New England." *Labor History* 24 (1983): 259–73.

Prince, Carl E. "The Great 'Riot Year': Jacksonian Democracy and Patterns of Violence in 1834." *Journal of the Early Republic* 5 (1985): 1–19.

Prince, Carl E., and Taylor, Seth. "Daniel Webster, the Boston Associates, and the U. S. Government's Role in the Industrializing Process, 1815–1830." *Journal of the Early Republic* 2 (1982): 283–99.

Prude, Jonathan. *The Coming of the Industrial Order: Town and Factory Life in*

Rural Massachusetts, 1810–1860. New York: Cambridge University Press, 1983.

Ralph, John H., and Rubinson, Richard. "Immigration and the Expansion of Schooling in the United States, 1890–1970." *American Sociological Review* 89 (1980): 943–54.

Rapp, Rayna. "Family and Class in Contemporary America: Notes toward an Understanding of Ideology." *Science and Society* 42 (1978): 278–300.

Ravitch, Diane. "The Revisionists Revisited: Studies in the Historiography of American Education." *Proceedings of the National Academy of Education,* 1977, (4).

Richardson, James F. *Urban Police in the United States.* Port Washington, N.Y.: Kennikat Press, 1974.

Rorabaugh, William J. *The Alcoholic Republic: An American Tradition.* New York: Oxford University Press, 1981.

Rosenberg, Charles E. "Social Class and Medical Care in 19th Century America: The Rise and Fall of the Dispensary." In *Sickness and Health in America,* pp. 157–72. Edited by Judith Walzer and Ronald L. Numbers. Madison: University of Wisconsin Press, 1978.

Rothman, David J. *Discovery of the Asylum: Social Order and Disorder in the New Republic.* Boston: Little, Brown & Co., 1971.

Rourke, Constance. *American Humor: A Study of the National Character.* New York: Harcourt, Brace & Co., 1931; reprint, New York: Anchor Books, 1953.

Rousey, Dennis C. "'Hibernian Leatherheads': Irish Cops in New Orleans, 1830–1880." *Journal of Urban History* 10 (1983): 61–84.

Rozenzweig, Roy. *Eight Hours for What We Will: Workers and Leisure in an Industrial City, 1870–1920.* New York: Cambridge University Press, 1983.

Rury, John. "Urban Structure and School Participation: Immigrant Women in 1900." *Social Science History* 8 (1984): 219–41.

Ruskowski, Leo F. *French Emigre Priests in the United States (1791–1815).* Studies in American Church History, no. 32. Washington, D.C.: Catholic University Press, 1940.

Ryan, Dennis P. *Beyond the Ballot Box: A Social History of the Boston Irish, 1845–1917.* Rutherford, N.J.: Farleigh Dickinson University Press, 1983.

Ryan, Mary P. *Cradle of the Middle Class: The Family in Oneida County, New York, 1790–1865.* New York: Cambridge University Press, 1984.

Scally, Robert. "Liverpool Ships and Irish Emigrants in the Age of Sail." *Journal of Social History* 17 (1983): 5–30.

Schrier, Arnold. *Ireland and the American Emigration, 1850–1900.* Minneapolis: University of Minnesota Press, 1958.

Schultz, Stanley K., and McShane, Clay. "To Engineer the Metropolis: Sewers, Sanitation, and City Planning in Late 19th Century America." *Journal of American History* 65 (1978): 389–411.

Scranton, Philip. "Varieties of Paternalism: Industrial Structures and the Social Relations of Production in American Textiles." *American Quarterly* 36 (1984): 235–57.

———. "Milling About: Family Firms and Urban Manufacturing in Textile Philadelphia, 1840–1865." *Journal of Urban History* 10 (1984): 259–84.

Shannon, James P. *Catholic Colonization of the Western Frontier*. New Haven: Yale University Press, 1957.

Shannon, William. *The American Irish*. New York: Macmillan, 1974.

Sheehan, P. A. "The Effect of Emigration on the Irish Churches." *Irish Ecclesiastical Record* 3 (1882): 602–15.

Shlakman, Vera. *Economic History of a Factory Town: A Study of Chicopee, Massachusetts*. New York: Octagon Books, 1969.

Shorter, Edward. *The Making of the Modern Family*. New York: Basic, 1975.

Silvera, Philip T. "The Position of Workers in a Textile Community: Fall River in the Early 1880s." *Labor History* 16 (1975): 230–48.

Simon, Roger D. "Housing and Services in an Immigrant Neighborhood: Milwaukee's Ward 14." *Journal of Urban History* 2 (1976): 435–58.

Siracusa, Carl. *A Mechanical People: Perceptions of the Industrial Order in Massachusetts, 1815–1860*. Middletown, Conn.: Wesleyan University Press, 1979.

Smith, Timothy L. "Protestant Schooling and American Nationality, 1800–1850." *Journal of American History* 53 (1967): 679–95.

Smyth, William J. "Social Geography of Rural Ireland: Inventory and Prospect." *Irish Geography Golden Jubilee* (1984): 204–36.

———. "Landholding Changes, Kinship Networks and Class Transformation in Rural Ireland: A Case-Study from Country Tipperary." *Irish Geography* 16 (1983): 16–35.

———. "Continuity and Change in the Territorial Organization of Irish Rural Communities." *Maynooth Review* (1975): 1:51–78; 2:52–101.

Solomon, Barbara. *Ancestors and Immigrants: A Changing New England Tradition*. Chicago: University of Chicago Press, 1956.

Stott, Richard. "British Immigrants and the American 'Work Ethic' in the Mid-Nineteenth Century." *Labor History* 26 (1985): 86–102.

Tansill, C. C. *America and the Fight for Irish Freedom, 1886–1922*. New York: Devin-Adair Company, 1957.

Taylor, George Rogers. *The Transportation Revolution, 1815–1860*. New York: Holt, Rinehart, 1951.

Taylor, Philip. *The Distant Magnet*. New York: Harper & Row, 1971.

Tharp, Louise H. *The Appletons of Beacon Hill*. Boston: Little, Brown & Co., 1973.

———. *Until Victory: Horace Mann and Mary Peabody*. Boston: Little, Brown & Co., 1953.

Thernstrom, Stephan. *The Other Bostonians*. Cambridge: Harvard University Press, 1974.

———. *Poverty and Progress: Social Mobility in a Nineteenth Century City*. Cambridge: Harvard University Press, 1964.

Thernstrom, Stephan, and Knights, Peter. "Men in Motion: Some Data and Speculations about Urban Population Mobility in Nineteenth Century America." *Journal of Interdisciplinary History* 7 (1976): 7–36.

Thernstrom, Stephan, and Sennett, Richard, eds. *Nineteenth Century Cities: Es-

says in the New Urban History. New Haven: Yale University Press, 1974.

Thompson, E. P. *The Making of the English Working Class*. New York: Vintage Books, 1963.

Thompson, Margaret S. "Ben Butler versus the Brahmins: Patronage and Politics in Early Gilded Age Massachusetts." *New England Quarterly* 55 (1982) 163–86.

Tilly, Louise A., and Scott, Joan W. *Women, Work and Family*. New York: Holt, Rinehart & Winston, 1978.

Tilly, Louise A.; Scott, Joan W.; and Cohen, Miriam. "Women's Work and European Fertility Patterns." *Journal of Interdisciplinary History* 6 (1976): 447–76.

Tobias, S. J. *Nineteenth Century Crime: Prevention and Punishment*. Newton Abbot, Eng.: David & Charles, 1972.

Towey, Martin G., and Lopicculo, Margaret Sullivan. "The Knights of Father Mathew: Parallel Ethnic Reform." *Missouri Historical Review* 75 (1981): 168–83.

Treacy, G. C. "The Evils of Trusteeism." *Historical Records and Studies* 8 (1915): 136–56.

Trefousse, Hans Louis. *Ben Butler: The South Called Him Beast*. New York: Twayne Publishers, 1957.

Tuathaigh, Geariod O. *Ireland before the Famine, 1798–1848*. London: Gill & Macmillan, 1972.

Tyack, David. "The Kingdom of God and the Common School." *Harvard Education Review* 36 (1966): 447–69.

Tyrell, Ian. *Sobering Up: From Temperance to Prohibition in Antebellum America, 1800–1860*. Westport, Conn.: Greenwood Press, 1979.

Ueda, Reed. "The High School and Social Mobility in a Streetcar Suburb: Somerville, Massachusetts, 1870–1910." *Journal of Interdisciplinary History* 14 (1984): 751–74.

Vinovskis, Maris A. "Quantification and the Analysis of American Antebellum Education." *Journal of Interdisciplinary History* 13 (1983): 761–86.

Walkowitz, Daniel J. *Worker City, Company Town: Iron and Cotton Worker Protest in Troy and Cohoes, New York, 1855–1884*. Urbana: University of Illinois Press, 1978.

Walsh, Francis R. "Who Spoke for Boston's Irish?: The Boston *Pilot* in the Nineteenth Century." *Journal of Ethnic Studies* 10 (1982): 21–36.

Walsh, James P. *The San Francisco Irish, 1850–1976*. San Francisco: Irish Literary and Historical Society, 1978.

Walsh, Louis S. *The Early Irish Catholic Schools of Lowell, Massachusetts*. Boston: Thomas A. Whalen Co., 1901.

Ware, Caroline. *The Early New England Cotton Manufacture: A Study in Industrial Beginnings*. Boston: Houghton Mifflin Co., 1931; reprint, New York: Johnson Reprint Corporation, 1966.

Ware, Norman. *The Industrial Worker, 1840–1860: The Reaction of American Industrial Society to the Advance of the Industrial Revolution*. Chicago: Quadrangle Books, 1960.

Weber, Michael P. "East Europeans in Steel Towns: A Comparative Analysis." *Journal of Urban History* 11 (1985): 280–313.

Weber, Michael P., and Boardman, Anthony E. "Economic Growth and Occupational Mobility in Nineteenth Century America: A Reappraisal." *Journal of Social History* 11 (1977): 52–74.

Weiss, Bernard J., ed. *American Education and the European Immigrant*. Urbana: University of Illinois Press, 1982.

Welter, Rush. *Popular Education and Democratic Thought in America*. New York: Columbia University Press, 1962.

West, E. G. *Education and the Industrial Revolution*. New York: Harper & Row, 1975.

West, Robert S. *Lincoln's Scapegoat General: A Life of Benjamin F. Butler, 1818–1893*. Boston: Houghton Mifflin Co., 1965.

Wheeler, Robert. "The Fifth Ward Irish: Mobility at Mid-Century." Seminar paper, Boston University, 1967.

Whelan, Kevin. "County Wexford Priests in Newfoundland." *Journal of the Wexford Historical Society* 10 (1985): 55–68.

———. "The Catholic Parish, the Catholic Chapel, and Village Development in Ireland." *Irish Geography* 16 (1983): 1–15.

Wieble, Robert; Ford, Oliver; and Marion, Paul, eds. *Essays from the Lowell Conference on Industrial History*. 2 vols. Lowell: U.S. Department of the Interior, 1981, 1983.

Wilcox, Jerry, and Golden, Hilda H. "Prolific Immigrants and Dwindling Natives: Fertility Patterns in Western Massachusetts, 1850 and 1880." *Journal of Family History* 7 (1982): 265–88.

Wittke, Carl. *The Irish in America*. Baton Rouge: Louisiana State University Press, 1956; reprint, New York: Russell & Russell. 1970.

———. *We Who Built America: The Saga of the Immigrant*. New York: Prentice-Hall, 1939; reprint, Cleveland: Press of Case Western Reserve, 1964.

Wolkovich, William. "Cardinal and Cleric: O'Connell and Mullen in Conflict." *Historical Journal of Massachusetts* 13 (1985): 129–39.

Woodham-Smith, Cecil. *The Great Hunger*. New York: Harper & Row, 1962.

Wyman, Mark. *Immigrants in the Valley: Irish, Germans, and Americans in the Upper Mississippi Valley, 1830–1860*. Chicago: Nelson-Hall, 1984.

Young, James H. *The Toadstool Millionaires: A Social History of Patent Medicine in America before Federal Regulation*. Princeton: Princeton University Press, 1961.

Zaroulis, Nancy. "Daughters of Freemen: The Female Operatives and the Beginning of the Labor Movement." In *Cotton Was King: A History of Lowell, Massachusetts*, pp. 105–26. Edited by Arthur Eno, Jr. Lowell: Lowell Historical Society, 1976.

Zimiles, Martha, and Zimiles, Murray. *Early American Mills*. New York: Bramhall House, 1978.

Zunz, Oliver. *The Changing Face of Inequality: Urbanization, Industrial Development, and Immigrants in Detroit, 1880–1920*. Chicago: University of Chicago Press, 1982.

There has been considerable research on Lowell in the twentieth century. *Surviving Hard Times: The Working People of Lowell* (Lowell: Lowell Museum, 1982), edited by Mary H. Blewett, is interesting particularly for its material on immigrant groups who followed the Irish and for their experiences in Lowell's mills. Frederick W. Coburn's *History of Lowell and Its People*, 3 vols. (New York: Lewis Historical Publishing, 1920), is an exhaustive informational catalogue of Lowell's history, while *Cotton Was King* (Lowell: Lowell Historical Society, 1976), edited by Arthur L. Eno. Jr., is an ambitious commemorative effort. John Coolidge's *Mill and Mansion* (New York: Columbia University Press, 1942) blends social and architectural history; Sara Swan Griffin, *Quaint Bits of Lowell History: A Few Interesting Stories about Earlier Days* (Lowell: Butterfield Printing Co., 1928) and George F. Kenngott, *The Record of a City: A Social Survey of Lowell, Massachusetts* (New York: Macmillan, 1912) amplify stories discussed in more traditional narrative histories, with Kenngott most important for his biased ethnocultural perceptions on Lowell's immigrants. Undoubtedly, Lowell's Yankee mill women have received the most serious scholarly treatment. Hannah Josephson's *The Golden Threads: New England's Mill Girls and Magnates* (New York: Duell, 1949; reprint, New York: Russell & Russell, 1967) and Caroline Ware's *The Early New England Cotton Manufacture: A Study in Industrial Beginnings* (Boston: Houghton Mifflin Co., 1931; reprint, New York: Johnson Reprint Corporation, 1966) are good examples of older scholarship, while Benita Eisler's edited collection, *The Lowell Offering: Writings by New England Mill Women* (New York: Harper & Row, 1977), Thomas Dublin's *Women at Work: The Transformation of Work and Community in Lowell, Massachusetts, 1826–1860* (New York: Columbia University Press, 1979), and his *Farm to Factory: The Mill Experience and Women's Lives in New England, 1830–1860* (New York: Columbia University Press, 1981) are among the best in the recent explosion of women's history literature to deal extensively with Lowell. While Lowell's immigrants have received little treatment beyond that of Kenngott, the few efforts to deal with them include George O'Dwyer, *Irish Catholic Genesis of Lowell* (Lowell: Sullivan Bros. Printers, 1920); Stella M. Mazur, *Roots and Heritage of Polish People in Lowell* (Lowell: Sullivan Bros. Printers, 1976); and Louis S. Walsh, *The Early Irish Catholic Schools of Lowell, Massachusetts* (Boston: Thomas A. Whalen, 1901). Beyond women's history, recent scholarship on Lowell includes Patrick M. Malone, *The Lowell Canal System* (Lowell: Lowell Museum, 1976); Albert Gibbs Mitchell, Jr., "Irish Family Patterns in Nineteenth Century Ireland and Lowell, Massachusetts" (Ph.D. dissertation, Boston University, 1976); Francis H. Early, "The French-Canadian Family Economy and Standard-of-Living in Lowell, Massachusetts, 1870," *Journal of Family History* 7 (1982): 180–99; Brian C. Mitchell, "Immigrants in Utopia: The Early Irish Community of Lowell, Massachusetts, 1821–1861" (Ph.D. dissertation, University of Rochester, 1981); and Robert Wieble, Oliver Ford, and Paul Marion, eds., *Essays from the Lowell Conference on Industrial History*, vols. 1 and 2 (Lowell: U.S. Department of the Interior, 1981 and 1983).

There are a number of good histories of Ireland which help one to understand the Irish heritage of American immigrants. The best include J. C. Beckett, *A Short History of Ireland*, 3d. ed. (New York: Hutchinson's University Library, 1966); Edmund Curtis, *A History of Ireland*, pap. ed. (New York: Barnes & Noble Books, 1968); T. W. Freeman, *Ireland: A General and Regional Geography* (London: Methuen & Co., 1969); and T. W. Moody and F. X. Martin, *The Course of Irish History* (New York: Weybright & Talley, Inc., 1967). Among Irish historians, there has been an ambitious tendency to relate Irish experiences to those occurring elsewhere in Europe. Two recent efforts are: L. M. Cullen and T. C. Smout, eds., *Comparative Aspects of Scottish and Irish Economic and Social History, 1600–1900* (Edinburgh: John Donald Publishers, 1977) and L. M. Cullen and F. Furet, *Ireland and France—17th–20th Centuries: Towards A Comparative Study of Rural History*, Proceedings of the First Franco-Irish Symposium on Social and Economic History (Ann Arbor, Mich.: UMI Press, 1980). For more specific periods of Irish history, see Gearoid O. Tuathaigh, *Ireland before the Famine, 1798–1848*, and Joseph Lee, *The Modernization of Irish Society, 1848–1918*, two works in a multivolume series from Gill and Macmillan; as well as Lawrence McCaffrey, *The Irish Question, 1800–1922* (Lexington: University Press of Kentucky, 1968); Giovanni Costigan, *A History of Modern Ireland* (New York: Pegasus, 1969); Patrick O'Farrell, *Ireland's English Question*, pap. (New York: Schocken Books, Inc., 1972); and J. C. Beckett, *The Making of Modern Ireland, 1603–1923* (New York: Alfred A. Knopf, 1966). Some of the best work in social geography includes Samuel Clark's outstanding *Social Origins of the Irish Land War* (Princeton: Princeton University Press, 1979), especially the first two chapters; William J. Smyth's "Continuity and Change in the Territorial Organization of Irish Rural Communities," Part I (1975): 51–78 and Part II (1975): 52–101 in *Maynooth Review;* his "Landholding Changes, Kinship Networks and Class Transformation in Rural Ireland: A Case-Study from County Tipperary," *Irish Geography* 16 (1983): 16–35; and his "Social Geography of Rural Ireland: Inventory and Prospect," *Irish Geography Golden Jubilee* (1984): 204–36; as well as James S. Donnelly, Jr., *The Land and People of Nineteenth Century Cork: The Rural Economy and the Land Question* (London: Routledge & Kegan Paul, 1975); Liam Kennedy and Philip Ollerenshaw, *Economic History of Ulster* (Manchester: University of Manchester Press, 1985); and William H. Crawford, "Economy and Society in South Ulster in the Eighteenth Century," *Clogher Record* 8 (1975): 241–58. On specific moments in Irish history, see R. B. McDowell, *Public Opinion and Government Policy in Ireland, 1801–1846* (London: Faber & Faber, 1932); G. C. Bolton, *The Passing of the Irish Act of Union: A Study in Parliamentary Politics*, Oxford Historical Series, 2d series (Oxford: Oxford University Press, 1966); and Kevin B. Nowlan, *The Politics of Repeal: A Study in the Relations between Great Britain and Ireland, 1841–1850* (London: Routledge & Kegan Paul, 1965) on the Act of Union and the Repeal movement; Angus McIntyre, *The Liberator: Daniel O'Connell and the Irish Party, 1830–1847* (London: Hamish Hamilton, 1965) and Sean O'Faolain, *King of the Beggars: A Life of Daniel O'Connell, The Irish Liberator, in a Study in the Rise of Modern Irish Democracy* (New York: Viking Press, 1938) on Daniel O'Connell; and Denis Gwyn, *Young Ireland and 1848* (Oxford: B. H. Blackwell, 1949) on the Irish revolutionary movement. Patrick O'Donnell's *The Irish Faction Fighters of the 19th Century* (Dublin: Anvil Books, 1975) is an informative although nonscholarly piece. Much of the Famine and pre-Famine study has evolved from Kenneth H. Connell's impressive *The Population of Ireland, 1750–1845* (Oxford: Clarendon Press, 1950) and two subsequent reappraisals—Joseph Lee's "Marriage and Population in Pre-Famine Ireland," *Economic History Review* 21 (1968): 283–95; and Michael Drake's "Marriage and Population Growth in Ireland, 1750–1845," *Economic History Review* 16 (1963): 301–13. Three of the strongest studies on the Famine are R. B. McDowell's "Ireland on the Eve of the Famine," in *The Great Famine: Studies in Irish History*: 402–56, edited by R. Dudley Edwards and T. Desmond Williams (New York: New York University Press, 1957); Cecil Woodham-Smith's *The Great Hunger* (New York: Harper & Row, 1962); and Joel Mokyr's provocative *Why Ireland Starved: A Quantitative and Analytical History of the Irish Economy, 1800–1850* (London: George Allen & Unwin, 1983).

Immigration: Historical Aspects of the Immigration Problem (Chicago: University of Chicago Press, 1926), edited by Edith Abbott, describes some of the historical emigration problems which have also been examined by Terry Coleman in *Going to America*, pap. (New York: Anchor Books, 1973); Philip Taylor in *The Distant Magnet*, pap. (New York: Harper & Row, 1971); and, most recently, by David Eltis in "Free and Coerced Transatlantic Migrations: Some Comparisons," *American Historical Review* 88 (1983): 251–80. There have been a number of specific studies on Irish emigrants including David Fitzpatrick's excellent *Irish Emigration, 1801–1921* (Dublin: Dundalgan Press, 1984) as well as William Forbes Adams's *Ireland and Irish Emigration from 1815 to the Famine* (New Haven: Yale University Press, 1932; reprint, New York: Russell & Russell, 1967); S. H. Cousens's "Regional Variations in Emigration between 1821 and 1841," in the *Transactions and Papers of the Institute of British Geographers* 37 (1965): 22–29; Patrick O'Farrell's "Emigrant Attitudes and Behavior as a Source for Irish History," *Historical Studies* 10 (1976): 109–31; Barbara Kerr's "Irish Seasonal Migration to Great Britain, 1800–1838," *Irish Historical Studies* 3 (1943): 38–62; R. Lawton's "Irish Emigration to England and Wales in the Mid-Nineteenth Century," *Irish Geography* 4 (1959): 35–54; Oliver McDonough's "Irish Overseas Emigration during the Famine," in *The Great Famine: Studies in Irish History*: 319–88, edited by R. Dudley Edwards and T. Desmond Williams (New York: New York University Press, 1957); Arnold Schrier's *Ireland and the American Emigration, 1850–1900* (Minneapolis: University of Minnesota Press, 1958); Robert Kennedy, Jr.'s *The Irish: Emigration, Marriage and Fertility* (Berkeley: University of California Press, 1973); Kerby A. Miller, Bruce Boling, and David N. Doyle's, "Emigrants and Exiles: Irish Cultures and Irish Emigration to North America, 1790–1922," *Irish Historical Studies* 40 (1980): 116–34; Lynn Lees and John Modell's "The Irish Countryman Urbanized: A Comparative Perspective on the Famine Migration," *Journal of Urban History* 3 (1977): 391–408; and Raymond L. Cohn's "Mortality on Immigrant Voyages to New York, 1836–1853," *Journal of Economic History* 44 (1984): 289–300.

The difficulties faced by Irish emigrants after their arrival are discussed in a number of studies on Great Britain and the United States. In addition to Michael Anderson on Preston, John Archer Jackson discusses *The Irish in Britain* (London: Routledge & Kegan Paul, 1963) while, more recently, Lynn Hollen Lees examines patterns of development, including family and household structure, among London's Irish in *Exiles of Erin: Irish Migrants in Victorian London* (Ithaca: Cornell University Press,

1979). There are a number of general studies of the American Irish including Lawrence J. McCaffrey, *The Irish Diaspora in America*, pap. (Bloomington: Indiana University Press, 1976); William V. Shannon, *The American Irish*, pap. (New York: Macmillan, 1974); Kerby Miller, *Emigrants and Exiles: Ireland and the Irish Exodus to North America* (New York: Oxford University Press, 1985); George Potter, *To the Golden Door: The Study of the Irish in Ireland and America* (Westport, Conn.: Greenwood Press, 1960); John B. Duff, *The Irish in America*, pap. (Belmont, Calif.: Wadsworth Publishing Co., 1971); David N. Doyle, *Ireland, Irishmen and Revolutionary America, 1760–1820* (Dublin: Mercier, 1981); Timothy J. Meagher, ed., *From Paddy to Studs: Irish-American Communities in the Turn of the Century Era* (Westport, Conn.: Greenwood Press, 1986); Andrew M. Greeley, *That Most Distressful Nation: The Taming of the American Irish* (Chicago: Quadrangle Books, 1972); and James G. Leyburn, *The Scotch-Irish: A Social History* (Chapel Hill: University of North Carolina Press, 1962). The question of assimilation has been treated in a general discussion by Marcus Lee Hansen in *The Immigrant in American History* (Cambridge: Harvard University Press, 1942); by Carl Wittke in *The Irish in America* (reprint, New York: Russsell & Russell, 1970) and in *We Who Built America: The Saga of the Immigrant* (reprint, Cleveland: Press of Case Western Reserve, 1964); by John Higham in a recent article, "Integrating America: The Problem of Assimilation in the 19th Century," *Journal of American Ethnic History* 1 (1981): 7–25 as well as in his "Current Trends in the Study of Ethnicity in the United States," *Journal of American Ethnic History* 2 (1982): 5–15; and, of course, by Oscar Handlin in *The Uprooted*, pap., 2d ed. (Boston: Little, Brown & Co., 1973). Building upon the work of Hansen and Wittke, many historians have dealt with questions of assimilation and acculturation through case studies. Robert Ernst's *Immigrant Life in New York City, 1825–1863* (Port Washington, N.Y.: Ira J. Freeman, 1965) and Oscar Handlin's *Boston's Immigrants: A Study in Acculturation*, rev. pap. (New York: Atheneum, 1977) became the standards by which other scholarship was measured. Twenty years ago, Nathan Glazer and Daniel Patrick Moynihan looked at the history of assimilation in America and its effect upon American culture in *Beyond the Melting Pot* (Cambridge: MIT Press, 1963). Since then, there have been a number of local studies of varying quality, including Dennis Clark's solid *The Irish in Philadelphia: Ten Generations of Urban Experience* (Philadelphia: Temple University Press, 1973), as well as Earl F. Niehaus, *The Irish in New Orleans, 1800–1860* (Baton Rouge: Louisiana State University Press, 1965); James P. Shannon, *Catholic Colonization of the Western Frontier* (New Haven: Yale University Press, 1957); Justile McDonald, *History of the Irish in Wisconsin in the 19th Century* (Washington, D.C.:

Catholic University Press, 1954); Dennis P. Ryan, *Beyond the Ballot Box: A Social History of the Boston Irish, 1845–1917* (Rutherford, N.J.: Farleigh Dickinson University Press, 1983); Mark Wyman, *Immigrants in the Valley: Irish, Germans, and Americans in the Upper Mississippi Valley, 1830–1860* (Chicago: Nelson-Hall, 1984); R. A. Burchill, *The San Francisco Irish, 1848–1880* (Manchester: Manchester University Press, 1979); Michael J. O'Brien's older *Pioneer Irish in New England* (New York: P. J. Kennedy & Sons, 1937); and James P. Walsh's lively account of the much-neglected San Francisco Irish community in *The San Francisco Irish, 1850–1976* (San Francisco: Irish Literary and Historical Society, 1978).

On American Catholicism, John Gilmary Shea led the way in 1890 with his *History of the Catholic Church*. Since then, much of the recent research has been influenced by John Tracy Ellis, *American Catholicism* (Chicago: University of Chicago Press, 1956) or by Thomas T. McAvoy, *A History of the Catholic Church in the United States* (Notre Dame, Ind.: University of Notre Dame Press, 1969). Bernard J. Weiss edited a collection on *American Education and the European Immigrant* (Urbana: University of Illinois Press, 1982). James Hennessey's *American Catholics: A History of the Roman Catholic Community in the United States* (New York: Oxford University Press, 1981) focuses less on institutional development and more on social history. An excellent new study on the social dimension within American Catholicism is Jay P. Dolan's *The American Catholic Experience: A History from Colonial Times to the Present* (New York: Doubleday & Co., 1985). John Cogley's *Catholic America* (New York: Dial Press, 1973) is less satisfying than Hennessey, Ellis, Dolan, or McAvoy, while Dolan's earlier *The Immigrant Church: New York's Irish and German Catholics, 1815–1865* (Baltimore: Johns Hopkins University Press, 1975) stands out for his brilliant and successful effort to depict the immigrant "in the pew." On the notion of a Catholic ghetto, see Martin E. Marty, "The Catholic Ghetto and All Other Ghettos," *Catholic Historical Review* 60 (1982): 182–205. For Boston, the three-volume *History of the Archdiocese of Boston* (New York: Sheed and Ward, 1944) by Robert H. Lord, John E. Sexton, and Edward P. Harrington, which was commissioned by William Cardinal O'Connell, is a scholarly treatment with an unfortunate tendency to exaggerate O'Connell's successes as recounted in O'Connell's *Recollections of Seventy Years* (Boston: Houghton Mifflin Co., 1934), while Donna Merwick's *Boston's Priests, 1848–1910: A Study of Social and Intellectual Change* (Cambridge: Harvard University Press, 1973) dealt effectively with the transition from the "Generation of '45" to the imperial rule of O'Connell. For the post-Fenwick era, refer to Thomas H. O'Connor, *Fitzpatrick's Boston: 1846–1866* (Boston: Northeastern University Press, 1984); James M. O'Toole, "'That Fabulous Churchman':

Toward a Biography of Cardinal O'Connell," *Catholic Historical Review* 70 (1984): 28–44; William Wolkovich, "Cardinal and Cleric: O'Connell and Mullen in Conflict," *Historical Journal of Massachusetts* 13 (1985): 129–39; and Robert O'Leary, "Brahmins and Bullyboy: William Henry O'Connell and Massachusetts Politics," *Historical Journal of Massachusetts* 10 (1982): 3–19. On trusteeism, see Peter Guilday, "Trusteeism," *Historical Records and Studies* 18 (1928) 14–73; G. C. Treacy, "The Evils of Trusteeism," *Historical Records and Studies* 8 (1915); 136–56; Patrick S. Dignan, *A History of the Legal Incorporation of Catholic Church Property in the United States (1784–1932)*, Studies in American Church History (Washington, D.C.: Catholic University Press, 1933); Patrick Carey, "The Laity's Understanding of the Trustee System, 1785–1855." *Catholic Historical Review* 44 (1978): 357–76; his "Republicanism within American Catholicism, 1785–1860," *Journal of the Early Republic* 3 (1983): 413–37; and finally, David A. Gerber, "Modernity in the Service of Tradition: Catholic Lay Trustees at Buffalo's St. Louis Church and the Transformation of European Communal Traditions, 1829–1865," *Journal of Social History* 15 (1982): 655–84, in which, unlike Lowell where the struggle with Bishop Fenwick masked serious internal divisions among parishioners, Gerber found that assertions of lay control of church affairs stemmed more from old-world traditions. On Irish Catholicism, see Desmond J. Keenan, *The Catholic Church in Nineteenth Century Ireland: A Sociological Study* (Dublin: Gill & Macmillan, 1983); S. J. Connolly, *Priests and People in Pre-Famine Ireland, 1780–1845* (Dublin: Gill & Macmillan, 1982) and "Catholicism in Ulster, 1800–50," in *Plantation to Partition: Essays in Ulster History in Honour of J. L. McCracken*, ed. Peter Roebuck (Belfast: Blackstaff Press, 1981); pp. 157–71; James O'Shea, *Priests, Politics, and Society in Post-Famine Ireland: A Study of Country Tipperary, 1850–1891* (Dublin: Wolfhound Press, 1983); Kevin Whelan, "The Catholic Parish, the Catholic Chapel, and Village Development in Ireland," *Irish Geography* 16 (1983): 1–15 and "County Wexford Priests in Newfoundland," *Journal of the Wexford Historical Society* 10 (1985): 55–68; Emmet Larkin, "The Devotional Revolution in Ireland, 1850–1875," *American Historical Review* 77 (1972): 625–52; David W. Miller, "Irish Catholicism and the Great Famine," *Journal of Social History* 9 (1975): 81–98; Oliver McDonough, "The Irish Catholic Clergy and Emigration during the Great Famine," *Irish Historical Studies* 5 (1947): 287–302, as well as P. A. Sheehan, "The Effect of Emigration on the Irish Churches," *Irish Ecclesiastical Record* 3 (1882): 602–15, which captures some of the pain involved in emigration. On the role of French-speaking priests in early immigrant communities, Leo F. Ruskowski's *French Emigre Priests in the United States (1791–1815)*, Studies in American Church History,

no. 32 (Washington, D.C.: Catholic University Press, 1940) offers a traditional view. There are several histories of the Sisters of Notre Dame available. They include: *American Foundations of the Sisters of Notre Dame,
Compiled from the Annals of Their Convents by a Member of the Congregation* (Philadelphia: Dolphin Press, 1928); *A Century in Lowell,
1852–1952: Courtesy of the Sisters of Notre Dame de Namur, May 30,
1952* (Lowell, 1952); Sister Miriam of the Infant Jesus, S.N.D., *The Finger of God: History of the Massachusetts Province of Notre Dame de
Namur, 1849–1963* (Boston: Mission Church Press, 1963); and Sister Julie
de la Sainte Famille, *History of the Rules and Constitutions of the Sisters
of Notre Dame de Namur*, n.d.

There are a number of New England community histories which reflect
conditions also occurring at Lowell. The earliest was Constance Mc-
Laughlin Green's *Holyoke, Massachusetts: A Case History of the Indus-
trial Revolution in America* (New Haven: Yale University Press, 1939), fol-
lowed by Vera Shlakman's *Economic History of a Factory Town: A Study of
Chicopee, Massachusetts* (New York: Octagon Books, 1969), originally
published as part of the Smith College Studies in History; Donald B.
Cole's *Immigrant City, Lawrence, Massachusetts, 1845–1921* (Chapel
Hill: University of North Carolina Press, 1963); John Borden Armstrong's
*Factory under the Elms: A History of Harrisville, New Hampshire, 1774–
1969* (Cambridge: MIT Press, 1969); Jonathan Prude's *The Coming of the
Industrial Order: Town and Factory Life in Rural Massachusetts, 1810–
1860* (New York: Cambridge University Press, 1983), as well as the work of
Handlin on Boston and Thernstrom on Newburyport. The major impetus
to additional community research has come from the Harvard University
Press series, especially Michael Frisch's *Town into City: Springfield, Massachusetts and the Meaning of Community, 1840–1880* (1972); and Kathleen Neils Conzen's *Immigrant Milwaukee, 1836–1860: Accommodation
and Community in a Frontier City* (1976). Regarding the development of
community, especially the whole concept of regional identity, see Allen
Pred, *Urban Growth and City Systems in the United States, 1840–1860*
(Cambridge: Harvard University Press, 1980); Francis X. Blouin, Jr., *The
Boston Region, 1810–1850: A Study of Urbanization* (Ann Arbor, Mich.:
UMI Research Press, 1978); and Burton W. Folsom, Jr., *Urban Capitalists: Entrepreneurs and City Growth in Pennsylvania's Lackawanna
and Lehigh Regions, 1800–1920* (Baltimore: Johns Hopkins University
Press, 1981), as well as David R. Goldfield, "The New Regionalism," *Jour-
nal of Urban History* 10 (1984): 171–86, among others. Michael J. Doucet
warns of the need to see land development as a unified process in "Urban
Land Development in Nineteenth Century North America: Themes in
the Literature," *Journal of Urban History* 8 (1982): 299–342. John Mc-

Clymer places community history squarely within American social history in "The Study of Community and the 'New' Social History," *Journal of Urban History* 7 (1980): 103–18, while Kathleen Neils Conzen emphasizes the role of process in "Quantification and the New Urban History," *Journal of Interdisciplinary History* 13 (1983): 653–77. On immigrants and their communities, refer to John J. Bukowczyk's "Immigrants and Their Communities," *International Labor and Working Class History* 25 (1984): 47–57 and Michael P. Weber's "East Europeans in Steel Towns: A Comparative Analysis," *Journal of Urban History* 11 (1985): 280–313.

The relationiship among technology, republican values, and urbanization has received serious consideration in three works: Thomas Bender, *Toward an Urban Vision: Ideas and Institutions in Nineteenth Century America* (Lexington: University Press of Kentucky, 1975); John F. Kasson, *Civilizing the Machine: Technology and Republican Values in America, 1778–1900* (New York: Grossman, 1976); and Leo Marx, *The Machine in the Garden: Technology and the Pastoral Ideal in America* (London: Oxford University Press, 1964). Several of the Boston Associates are treated in biographies. The best among them include Russell B. Adams, Jr., *The Boston Money Tree* (New York: Thomas Y. Crowell Co., 1977); Ferris Greenslet, *The Lowells and Their Seven Worlds* (Boston: Houghton Mifflin Co., 1946); Francis W. Gregory, *Nathan Appleton, Merchant and Entrepreneur, 1779–1861* (Charlottesville: University of Virginia Press, 1976); and Louise H. Tharp, *The Appletons of Beacon Hill* (Boston: Little, Brown & Co., 1973). *A Chronicle of Textile Machinery, 1824–1924, Issued to Commemorate the One Hundredth Anniversary of the Saco-Lowell Shops* (Boston: By the Company, 1924) and *The Saco-Lowell Shops: Textile Machinery Building in New England, 1813–1949* (Cambridge: Harvard University Press, 1950) by George S. Gibb are real treasures. Regarding the role of an urban elite on the environment, see the argument by Stuart Blumin in "The Hypothesis of Middle Class Formation in Nineteenth-Century America: A Critique and Some Proposals," *American Historical Review* 90 (1985): 299–338 and that by Michael B. Katz, Michael J. Doucet, and Mark J. Stern on the two-class social structure in nineteenth-century America in *The Social Organization of Early Industrial Capitalism* (Cambridge: Harvard University Press, 1982), as well as the article by Jane H. Pease and William H. Pease, "Social Structure and the Potential for Urban Change: Boston and Charleston in the 1830s," *Journal of Urban History* 8 (1982): 171–95; Geoffrey Blodgett, "Yankee Leadership in a Divided City: Boston, 1860–1910," *Journal of Urban History* 8 (1982): 371–96; Philip Scranton, "Varieties of Paternalism: Industrial Structures and the Social Relations of Production in American Textiles," *American Quarterly* 36 (1984): 235–57; his "Milling

About: Family Firms and Urban Manufacturing in Textile Philadelphia, 1840–1865," *Journal of Urban History* 10 (1984): 259–94, and the continuing discussion on "elites" encouraged by historians like Edward Pessen. On the tariff, recent research includes Carl E. Prince and Seth Taylor, "Daniel Webster, the Boston Associates, and the U.S. Government's Role in the Industrializing Process, 1815–1830," *Journal of the Early Republic* 2 (1982): 283–99 and Mark Bils, "Tariff Protection and Production in the Early U.S. Cotton Textile Industry," *Journal of Economic History* 44 (1984): 1033–45. On wages and productivity, see Robert G. Layer, *Earnings of Cotton Mill Operatives, 1825–1914* (Cambridge: Harvard University Press, 1968); Paul D. McGouldrick, *New England Textiles in the Nineteenth Century* (Cambridge: Harvard University Press, 1968); Pamela J. Nickless, "A New Look at Productivity in the New England Cotton Textile Industry, 1830–1860," *Journal of Economic History* 34 (1979): 889–910. On land and water transportation, two classics, George Rogers Taylor's *The Transportation Revolution, 1815–1860* (New York: Holt, Rinehart, 1951) and Edward C. Kirkland's *Men, Cities, and Transportation: A Case Study in New England History, 1820–1900* (Cambridge: Harvard University Press, 1948; reprint, New York: Russell & Russell, 1968), are a must. On Lowell's canal age, Patrick Malone's *Canals and Industry: Engineering in Lowell, 1821–1880* (Lowell: Lowell Museum, 1983) and Mary Stetson Clarke's *The Old Middlesex Canal* (Melrose, Mass.: Hilltop Press, 1974) are the best available local sources. In addition to Ware's work on early textile development, there are a few major studies which are national in scope. They include Douglas T. Miller, *The Birth of Modern America, 1820–1850* (Indianapolis: Bobbs-Merrill Co., 1970) and Douglas C. North, *The Economic Growth of the United States, 1790–1860* (Englewood Cliffs, N.J.: Prentice-Hall, 1961); as well as less inclusive studies, especially Carl Siracusa, *A Mechanical People: Perceptions of the Industrial Order in Massachusetts, 1815–1860* (Middletown, Conn.: Wesleyan University Press, 1979); Martha Zimiles and Murray Zimiles, *Early American Mills* (New York: Bramhall House, 1978); and Robert F. Dalzell, "The Rise of the Waltham-Lowell System and Some Thoughts on the Political Economy of Modernization in Antebellum Massachusetts," *Perspectives in American History* 9 (1975): 229–68.

On education, historians have revised substantially Elwood P. Cubberly's argument of the "public school triumphant" in *Public Education in the United States: A Study and Interpretation of American Educational History* (Boston: Houghton Mifflin, 1934). Bernard Bailyn opened the attack on Cubberly's position by suggesting that schools played only a secondary role to family, community, and church as educators in *Education in the Forming of American Society: Needs and Opportunities for Study*

(Chapel Hill: University of North Carolina Press, 1960). Lawrence Cremin echoed Bailyn's perspective by stressing a broader range of educational institutions in *The American Common School: An Historical Conception* (New York: Columbia University Press, 1961), while placing the school in a national perspective in his more recent *American Education: The National Experience, 1783–1896* (New York: Harper and Row, 1980). Rush Welter made an important connection in *Popular Education and Democratic Thought in America* (New York: Columbia University Press, 1962). There have been a number of studies examining the formative years of the American public school. They include Sidney L. Jackson, *America's Struggle for Free Schools: Social Tension and Education in New England and New York, 1827–1842* (New York: Russell & Russell, 1965); Carl F. Kaestle, "Social Change, Discipline, and the Common School in Early 19th Century America," *Journal of Interdisciplinary History* 9 (1978): 1–17; Frederick M. Binder, *The Age of the Common School, 1830–1865*, Studies in the History of American Education (New York: John Wiley & Sons, 1974); Emit Duncan Grizzell, *Origins and Development of the High School in New England before 1865* (Philadelphia: J. B. Lippincott, 1923); Reed Ueda, "The High School and Social Mobility in a Streetcar Suburb: Somerville, Massachusetts, 1870–1910," *Journal of Interdisciplinary History* 14 (1984): 751–74. Malcolm S. Knowles, *The Adult Education Movement in the United States* (New York: Holt, Rinehart, and Winston, 1962) and E. G. West, *Education and the Industrial Revolution* (New York: Harper & Row, 1975). David J. Bruck's unpublished undergraduate thesis on Lowell's schools is interesting for his concept of Lowell as a case study in "The Schools of Lowell, 1824–1861: A Case Study in the Origins of Modern Public Education in America" (undergraduate thesis, Harvard, 1971), while Louise H. Tharp's *Until Victory: Horace Mann and Mary Peabody* (Boston: Little, Brown & Co., 1953) is a suitable work on Horace Mann.

The more recent revisionists of Cubberly include Cremin; Michael B. Katz, *The Irony of Early School Reform: Educational Innovation in Mid-Nineteenth Century Massachusetts* (Cambridge: Harvard University Press, 1968) and *Class, Bureaucracy, and Schools: The Illusion of Educational Change in American Public Education* (New York: Basic Books, 1972); Samuel Bowles and Herbert Gintis, *Schooling in Capitalist America* (New York: Basic Books, 1976); Diane Ravitch, "The Revisionists Revisited: Studies in the Historiography of American Education," *Proceedings of the National Academy of Education* (1977); R. Freeman Butts, *Public Education in the United States: From Revolution to Reform* (New York: Holt, Rinehart, and Winston, 1978); John W. Meyer, David Tyack, Joane Nagel, and Audri Gordon, "Public Education as Nation-Building in

America," *American Journal of Sociology* 85 (1979): 591–613; Maris A. Vinovskis, "Quantification and the Analysis of American Antebellum Education," *Journal of Interdisciplinary History* 13 (1983): 761–86; Alexander James Field, "Educational Expansion in Mid-Nineteenth Century Massachusetts: Human- Capital Formation or Structural Reinforcement?" *Harvard Education Review* 46 (1976): 521–52; David Nasaw, *Schooled to Order: A Social History of Public Schooling in the United States* (New York: Oxford University Press, 1979); Myra C. Glenn, "School Discipline and Punishment in Antebellum America," *Journal of the Early Republic* 1 (1981): 395–408; Charles E. Bidwell, "The Moral Significance of the Common School," *History of Education Quarterly* 6 (1966): 50–91; William J. Gilmore, "Elementary Literacy on the Eve of the Industrial Revolution: Trends in Rural New England, 1760–1830," *Proceedings of the American Antiquarian Society* 92, pt. 1 (1982): 87–171; and Selma C. Berrol, "Urban Schools: The Historian as Critic," *Journal of Urban History* 8 (1982): 206–16.

The development of public schools and their relationship to nineteenth-century immigrants has received considerable attention, particularly in the work of Vincent P. Lannie, with its focus upon Catholicism and education. See Lannie's *Public Money and Parochial Education: Bishop Hughes, Governor Seward, and the New York School Controversy* (Cleveland: Press of Case Western Reserve, 1968) and his "Alienation in America: The Immigrant Catholic and Public Education in Pre-Civil War America," *Review of Politics* 32 (1970): 503–21; David Tyack's "The Kingdom of God and the Common School," *Harvard Education Review* 36 (1966): 447–69; Timothy L. Smith's "Protestant Schooling and American Nationality, 1800–1850," *Journal of American History* 53 (1967): 679–95; Brian C. Mitchell's "Educating Irish Immigrants in Antebellum Lowell," *Historical Journal of Massachusetts* 11 (1983): 97–103; Miriam Cohen's "Changing Education Strategies among Immigrant Generations: New York Italians in Comparative Perspective," *Journal of Social History* 15 (1982): 443–66; Timothy J. Meagher's "The Delayed Development of Parochial Education among Irish Catholics in Worcester," *Historical Journal of Massachusetts* 12 (1984): 44–59; John Rury's "Urban Structure and School Participation: Immigrant Women in 1900," *Social Science History* 8 (1984): 219–41; John H. Ralph and Richard Rubinson's "Immigration and the Expansion of Schooling in the United States, 1890–1970," *American Sociological Review* 89 (1980): 943–54.

Health and crime have come under increasing scrutiny lately. On health, see Gerald Grob, "The Social History of Medicine and Disease in America: Problems and Possibilities," *Journal of Social History* 10 (1977): 391–409; J. D. Post, "Famine, Mortality and Epidemic Disease in the

Process of Modernization," *Economic History Review* 29 (1976): 14–27; Charles E. Rosenberg, "Social Class and Medical Care in 19th Century America: The Rise and Fall of the Dispensary," in *Sickness and Health in America*, edited by Judith Walzer and Ronald L. Numbers (Madison: University of Wisconsin Press, 1978): 157–72; and Mark Aldrich, "Determinants of Mortality among New England Cotton Mill Workers during the Progessive Era," *Journal of Economic History* 42 (1982): 845–62. Jon A. Patterson, "The Impact of Sanitary Reform upon American Urban Planning, 1840–1890," *Journal of Social History* 13 (1979): 83–109; Stanley K. Schultz and Clay McShane," To Engineer the Metropolis: Sewers, Sanitation, and City Planning in Late Nineteenth Century America," *Journal of American History* 65 (1978): 389–411; Roger D. Simon, "Housing and Services in an Immigrant Neighborhood: Milwaukee's Ward 14," *Journal of Urban History* 2 (1976): 435–58; Richard A. Meckel, "Immigration, Mortality and Population Growth in Boston, 1840–1880," *Journal of Interdisciplinary History* 15 (1985): 393–417; Joan Underhill Hannon, "Poverty in the Northeast: The View trom New York State's Poor Relief Rolls," *Journal of Economic History* 44 (1984): 1001–32; Clayton R. Koppes and William P. Norris, "Ethnicity, Class and Mortality in the Industrial City: A Case Study of Typhoid Fever in Pittsburg, 1890–1910," *Journal of Urban History* 11 (1985): 259–79; and Amy Gilman, "From Widowhood to Wickedness: The Politics of Class and Gender in New York City Private Charity, 1799–1860," *History of Education Quarterly* 24 (1984): 59–74. "Social control" as applied to institutional development has received considerable thought not only in the writings of Bowles, Gintis, and Katz, for example, on education but also in David J. Rothman's *Discovery of the Asylum: Social Order and Disorder in the New Republic* (Boston: Little, Brown & Co., 1971); John T. Cumbler's "The Politics of Charity: Gender and Class in Late 19th Century Charity Policy," *Journal of Social History* 14 (1980): 99–111; and Lawrence Frederick Kohl's "The Concept of Social Control and the History of Jacksonian America," *Journal of the Early Republic* 5 (1985): 21–34. On crime, the strongest research includes David R. Johnson's *Policing the Urban Underworld: The Impact of Crime on the Development of the American Police, 1800–1887* (Philadelphia: Temple, 1979); Roger Lane's *Policing the City, Boston, 1822–1885* (Cambridge: Harvard University Press, 1967); James F. Richardson's *Urban Police in the United States* (Port Washington, N.Y.: Kennikat Press, 1974); S. J. Tobias's *Nineteenth Century Crime: Prevention and Punishment* (Newton Abbot, Eng.: David and Charles, 1972); Eric H. Monkkoner's "From Cop History to Social History: The Significance of the Police in American History," *Journal of Social History* 15 (1982): 575–91; Dennis C. Rousey's "'Hibernian Leatherheads': Irish Cops in New Orleans, 1830–1880," *Journal of*

Urban History 10 (1983): 61–84; and Carl E. Prince's "Great 'Riot Year': Jacksonian Democracy and Patterns of Violence in 1834," *Journal of the Early Republic* 5 (1985): 1–19.

There are a variety of studies which deal with issues affecting nineteenth-century Irish immigrants. Brian Harrison, *Drink and the Victorians: The Temperance Question in England, 1825–1872* (London: Faber & Faber, 1971); Ian Tyrell, *Sobering Up: From Temperance to Prohibition in Antebellum America, 1800–1860* (Westport, Conn.: Greenwood Press, 1979); William J. Rorabaugh, *The Alcoholic Republic: An American Tradition* (New York: Oxford University Press, 1981); and Jed Dannenbaum, "The Origins of Temperance Activism and Militancy among American Women," *Journal of Social History* 15 (1981): 235–52, as well as his *Drink and Disorder: Temperance Reform in Cincinnati from the Washingtonian Revival to the Women's Christian Temperance Union* (Urbana: University of Illinois Press, 1984), deal generally with temperance, while William Breitenbach, "Sons of the Fathers: Temperance Reformers and the Legacy of the American Revolution," *Journal of the Early Republic* 3 (1983): 69–82, and Martin G. Towey and Margaret Sullivan Lopicculo, "The Knights of Father Mathew: Parallel Ethnic Reform," *Missouri Historical Review* 75 (1981): 168–83, see the temperance movement among the Irish of St. Louis as mutually exclusive of the general temperance drive, unlike my findings on Lowell where its Yankees participated in the planning for Mathew's visit and where the Irish saw their movement as complementary to, not separate from, the general temperance drive. An interesting recent study of the Mathew crusade which has obvious significance for Lowell is H. F. Kearney's "Fr. Mathew: Apostle of Modernization," in Art Cosgrove and Donal McCartney, *Studies in Irish History: Presented to R. Dudley Edwards* (Dublin: University College, 1979): 164–75. On mid-nineteenth-century ethnic stereotypes, see Constance Rourke's masterful *American Humor: A Study of the National Character* (New York: Harcourt, Brace & Co., 1931; reprint, New York: Anchor Books, 1953); Dale T. Knobel's "Vocabulary of Ethnic Perception: Content Analysis of the American Stage Irishman, 1820–1860," *Journal of American Studies* 15 (1981): 45–71; and Joseph Boskin and Joseph Dorinson's "Ethnic Humor: Subversion and Survival," *American Quarterly* 37 (1985): 81–97. On Catholic Emancipation, see Thomas F. Moriarty's "The Irish American Response to Catholic Emancipation," *Catholic Historical Review* 66 (1980): 353–73; on the validity of the Boston *Pilot* as a spokesperson for Boston and Massachusetts Irish generally, see Francis R. Walsh, "Who Spoke for Boston's Irish?: The Boston *Pilot* in the Nineteenth Century," *Journal of Ethnic Studies* 10 (1982): 21–36; and on patent medicines, see James H. Young's *The Toadstool Millionaires: A Social*

History of Patent Medicine in America before Federal Regulation (Princeton: Princeton University Press, 1961). On the use of leisure time among the American Irish, two late nineteenth-century studies on Worcester are useful. See Roy Rozenzweig's *Eight Hours for What We Will: Workers and Leisure in an Industrial City, 1870–1920* (New York: Cambridge University Press, 1983) and Timothy J. Meagher's "Why Should We Care for a Little Trouble or a Walk through the Mud: St. Patrick's and Columbus Day Parades in Worcester, Massachusetts, 1845–1915," *New England Quarterly* 58 (1985): 5–26.

American labor history has fairly exploded in terms of the quantity of research as well as the quality of the effort to integrate work experience into family, women's, ethnic, religious, and urban history, among other fields. The call to redefine work experience was launched by E. P. Thompson in his seminal *The Making of the English Working Class*, pap. (New York: Vintage Books, 1963) in England and, shortly after, by Herbert Gutman in a provocative series of articles grouped into his *Work, Culture, and Society in Industrializing America: Essays in American Working Class History*, pap. (New York: Alfred A. Knopf, 1976). Their challenge to write "new" (left, urban, social) history has been taken up by many historians. Among the group are Daniel J. Walkowitz, *Worker City, Company Town: Iron and Cotton Worker Protest in Troy and Cohoes, New York, 1855–1884* (Urbana: University of Illlinois Press, 1978); Paul Fahler and Alan Dawley, "Working Class Culture and Politics in the Industrial Revolution: Sources of Loyalism and Rebellion," *Journal of Social History* 9 (1975): 466–80, as well as Dawley's separate discussion of Lynn's shoe workers; David Montgomery, "The Shuttle and the Cross: Weavers and Artisans in the Kensington Riots of 1844," *Journal of Social History* 4 (1972): 411–46; Susan E. Hirsch, *Roots of the American Working Class: The Industrialization of Crafts in Newark, 1800–1860* (Philadelphia: University of Pennsylvania Press, 1978); Michael H. Frisch and Daniel J. Walkowitz, *Working-Class America: Essays on Labor, Community, and American Society* (Urbana: University of Illinois Press, 1983); Philip T. Silvera, "The Position of Workers in a Textile Community: Fall River in the Early 1880s," *Labor History* 16 (1975): 230–48; and Maurice Neufeld's articles, "The Size of the Jacksonian Labor Movement: A Cautionary Account," *Labor History* 23 (1982): 599–607 and "The Persistence of Ideas in the American Labor Movement," *Industrial and Labor Relations Review* 35 (1982): 207–20. Other efforts include Bruce Laurie, *The Working People of Philadelphia, 1800–1850* (Philadelphia: Temple, 1980) and with Theodore Hershberg and George Alter, "Immigrants and Industry: The Philadelphia Experience, 1850–1880," *Journal of Social History* 9 (1975): 219–48; Norman Ware's classic *The Industrial Worker, 1840–1860: The*

Reaction of American Industrial Society to the Advance of the Industrial Revolution, pap. (Chicago: Quadrangle Books, 1960); Pamela J. Nickless, "Changing Labor Productivity and the Utilizing of Native American Workers in the American Cotton Textile Industry, 1825–1860" (Ph.D. dissertation, Purdue, 1976); William Mulligan, Jr., "Mechanization and Work in the American Shoe Industry: Lynn, Massachusetts, 1852–1855," *Journal of Economic History* 41 (1981): 131–56; and Stephen Dubnoff, "Gender, the Family, and the Problem of Work Motivation in a Transition to Industrial Capitalism," *Journal of Family History* 4 (1979): 121–36.

On Manchester, New Hampshire, Tamara Hareven has done much to explore the work experiences at the Amoskeag Mill. See, for example, "The Laborers of Manchester, New Hampshire, 1912–1922: The Role of Family and Ethnicity in Adjustment to Industrial Life," *Labor History* 16 (1975): 249–65, and with Randolph Langenbach, *Amoskeag: Life and Work in an American Factory City* (New York: Pantheon Books, 1978); as well as James P. Hanlan's recent *The Working Population of Manchester, New Hampshire, 1840–1886* (Ann Arbor, Mich.: UMI Research Press, 1981). John T. Cumbler looks at the relationship between urbanization and labor in "The City and the Community: The Impact of Urban Forces on Working Class Behavior," *Journal of Urban History* 3 (1977): 427–42, while Jay Pawa examines the labor-education argument in "Workingmen and Free Schools in the 19th Century: A Comment on the Labor-Education Thesis," *History of Education Quarterly* 11 (1971): 287–302. The role of the Irish in New England's work force has received attention in Howard P. Gitelman's *Workingmen of Waltham* (Baltimore: Johns Hopkins University Press, 1974); Stephen Dubnoff's "The Family and Absence from Work: Irish Workers in a Lowell, Massachusetts Cotton Mill, 1860" (Ph.D. dissertation, Brandeis University, 1976); Edward J. O'Day's "Constructing the Western Railroad: The Irish Dimension," *Historical Journal of Massachusetts* 11 (1983): 7–21; Marianne Pedulla's "Labor in a City of Immigrants: Holyoke, 1882–1888," *Historical Journal of Massachusetts* 13 (1985): 147–61; Isaac Cohen's "Worker's Control in the Cotton Industry: A Comparative Study of British and American Mule Spinning," *Labor History* 26 (1985): 53–85; Richard Stott's "British Immigrants and the 'Work Ethic' in the Mid-Nineteenth Century," *Labor History* 26 (1985): 86–102; Ira Berlin and Herbert G. Gutman's "Natives and Immigrants, Free Men and Slaves: Urban Workingmen in the Antebellum South," *American Historical Review* 88 (1983): 1175–1200; John J. Bukowczyk's "The Tranformation of Working Class Ethnicity: Corporate Control, Americanization, and the Polish Immigrant Middle Class in Bayonne, New Jersey, 1915–1925," *Labor History* 25 (1984): 53–82; and Jeffrey E. Mirel and David L. Angus,

"From Spellers to Spindles: Work Force Entry by the Children of Textile Workers, 1888–1890," *Social Science History* 9 (1985): 123–43.

The role of women in the labor movement is discussed in Josephson, Ware, and Dublin as well as in Louise Tilly and Joan W. Scott, *Women, Work and Family* (New York: Holt, Rinehart, & Winston, 1978); Virginia Yans McLaughlin, *Family and Community: Italian Immigrants in Buffalo, 1880–1930*, pap. (Urbana: University of Illinois Press, 1981); Philip S. Foner, *The Factory Girls: A Collection of Writings on Life and Struggles in the New England Factories of the 1840s* (Urbana: University of Illinois Press, 1977); Carol Groneman, "Working Class Immigrant Women in Mid-Nineteenth Century New York: The Irishwoman's Experience," *Journal of Urban History* 4 (1978): 255–74; Louise A. Tilly, Joan W. Scott, and Miriam Cohen, "Women's Work and European Fertility Patterns," *Journal of Interdisciplinary History* 6 (1976): 447–76; Carol Lasser, "A 'Pleasingly Oppressive' Burden: The Transformation of Domestic Service and Female Charity in Salem, 1800–1840," *Essex Institute Historical Collections* 116 (1980): 156–75; David M. Katzman, *Seven Days a Week: Women and Domestic Service in Industrializing America*, pap. (Urbana: University of Illinois Press, 1981); Faye E. Dudden, *Serving Women: Household Services in Nineteenth Century America* (Middletown, Conn.: Wesleyan University Press, 1983); Jo Anne Preston, " 'To Learn Me the Whole of the Trade': Conflict between a Female Apprentice and a Merchant Tailor in Antebellum New England," *Labor History* 24 (1983): 259–73; Laurie Nisonoff, "Bread and Roses: The Proletarianization of Women Workers in New England Textile Mills, 1827–1848," *Historical Journal of Massachusetts* 9 (1981): 3–14; and Donna S. Kenny, "Women at Work: Views and Visions from the Pioneer Valley, 1870–1945," *Historical Journal of Massachusetts* 13 (1985): 30–41, as well as the writings of Mary Blewett on women shoe workers in New England.

Conrad Arensburg and Solon T. Kimball discussed Irish family structure in their *Family and Community in Ireland*, 2d. ed. (Cambridge: Harvard University Press, 1968), as do many of the historians of Irish emigration such as Robert Scally in "Liverpool Ships and Irish Emigrants in the Age of Sail," *Journal of Social History* 17 (1983): 5–30. Irish-American families have received considerable treatment, most notably in the Danny O'Neill series from James T. Farrell and in Pete Hamill's *The Gift*, pap. (New York: Ballantine, 1974). Other work includes William Gibson's *A Mass for the Dead* (New York: Atheneum, 1968) and Edward McSorley's *Our Own Kind* (New York: Harper & Row, 1946). The impact of emigration upon Irish families is described by Lynn H. Lees; Michael Anderson's *Family Structure in Nineteenth Century Lancashire* (Cambridge: Cambridge University Press, 1971); John Modell and Tamara Hareven's "Urbanization and the Malleable Household: An Examination of Boarding and Lodging in American Families," *Journal of Marriage and the Family* 35 (1973): 467–79; and Richard L. Bushman's "Family Security in the Transition from Farm to City, 1750–1850," *Journal of Family History* 6 (1981): 238–56. The development of households is discussed in Peter Laslett's *The World We Have Lost* (New York: Charles Scribner's Sons, 1965) and in *Household and Family in Past Time* (Cambridge: Cambridge University Press, 1972); in Lutz Berkner's "The Stem Family and the Developmental Cycle of the Peasant Household: An 18th Century Austrian Example," *American Historical Review* 77 (1972): 398–418; in Lawrernce Glasco's "The Life Cycles and Household Structure of American Ethnic Groups: Irish, Germans, and Native-Born Whites in Buffalo, New York, 1855," *Journal of Urban History* 1 (1975): 338–64; and in the work of Tamara Hareven, including "The Family Process: The Historical Study of the Family Cycle," *Journal of Social History* 7 (1974): 322–27; "Cycles, Courses and Cohorts: Reflections on the Theoretical and Methodological Approaches to the History of Family Development," *Journal of Social History* 12 (1978): 97–109; and with Howard Chudacoff, "From Empty Nest to Family Dissolution: Life Course Transitions into Old Age," *Journal of Family History* 4 (1979): 69–83. See also A. Gordon Darroch and Michael Ornstein, "Family and Household in Nineteenth Century Canada: Regional Patterns and Regional Economies," *Journal of Family History* 9 (1984): 158–77; and Jerry Wilcox and Hilda H. Golden, "Prolific Immigrants and Dwindling Natives: Fertility Patterns in Western Massachusetts, 1850 and 1880," *Journal of Family History* 7 (1982): 265–88. Mary P. Ryan's *Cradle of the Middle Class: The Family in Oneida County, New York, 1790–1865* (New York: Cambridge University Press, 1984) is a fascinating analysis of the role of the family in society, while Edward Shorter's *The Making of the Modern Family* (New York: Basic, 1975) is less convincing. Josef Barton's *Peasants and Strangers: Italians, Rumanians, and Slovaks in an American City, 1890–1950* (Cambridge: Harvard University Press, 1975) compares various ethnic groups. Francis Early's work on Lowell's French-Canadians and Myfanwy Morgan and Hilda Golden's "Immigrant Families in an Industrial City: A Study of Households in Holyoke, 1880," *Journal of Family History* 4 (1979): 59–68, add considerably to the study of New England immigrant households. There have been a number of reviews of the progress made in understanding the history of the family. Christopher Lasch wrote a number of controversial pieces for the *New York Review of Books*, such as "The Family and History," 13 Nov. 1975, pp. 30–33; "The Emotions of Family Life," 27 Nov. 1975, pp. 37–42; and "What the Doctor Ordered," 11 Dec. 1975, pp. 50–

54. Barbara J. Harris wrote an impressive response in "Recent Work on the History of the Family: A Review Article," *Feminist Studies* 3 (1976): 159–72; and, finally, Rayna Rapp's "Family and Class in Contemporary America: Notes toward an Understanding of Ideology," *Science and Society* 42 (1978): 278–300, is a must. The best work recently on Irish immigrant women is Hasia R. Diner's *Erin's Daughters in America: Irish Immigrant Women in the Nineteenth Century* (Baltimore: Johns Hopkins University Press, 1983).

Much of the recent scholarship has centered around the issue of social mobility. Stephan Thernstrom opened the debate with his *Poverty and Progress: Social Mobility in a Nineteenth Century City* (Cambridge: Harvard University Press, 1964). Thernstrom followed his work on Newburyport with *The Other Bostonians* (Cambridge: Harvard University Press, 1974), which, like Peter Knights's *Plain People of Boston, 1830–1860* (New York: Oxford University Press, 1971), focuses upon the level of opportunity and the rates of persistence among Boston's residents. The techniques employed by such historians have prompted a wide debate reflective in the work of John Bodnar, Michael Weber, and Roger Simon in "Migration, Kinship, and Urban Adjustment: Blacks and Poles in Pittsburg, 1910–1930," *Journal of American History* 66 (1979): 548–65; of Stanley L. Engerman in "Up or Out: Social and Geographical Mobility in the United States," *Journal of Interdisciplinary History* 5 (1975): 469–90; Michael B. Katz, Michael Doucet, and Mark Stern in "Migration and the Social Order in Erie County, New York, 1865," *Journal of Interdisciplinary History* 8 (1978): 669–702; of Stephan Thernstrom and Peter Knights in "Men in Motion: Some Data and Speculations about Urban Population Mobility in Nineteenth Century America," *Journal of Interdisciplinary History* 7 (1976): 7–36; of Gary P. Kocolowski in "Alternative to Record Linkage in the Study of Urban Migration: The Uses of Naturalization Records," *Historical Methods Newsletter* 14 (1981): 139–42; and of Donald H. Parkerson in "How Mobile Were Nineteenth-Century Americans?" *Historical Methods Newsletter* 15 (1982): 99–109, in which Parkerson suggests that the persistence rates may be much higher than previously suspected.

Other studies on mobility include Clyde Griffen and Sally Griffen, *Natives and Newcomers: The Ordering of Opportunity in Mid-Nineteenth Century Poughkeepsie* (Cambridge: Harvard University Press, 1978); John N. Ingham, "Rags to Riches Revisited: The Effect of City Size and Related Factors in the Recruitment of Business Leaders," *Journal of American History* 63 (1976): 615–37; Michael Katz, *The People of Hamilton, Canada West: Family and Class in a Mid-Nineteenth Century City* (Cambridge: Harvard University Press, 1975); Glenna Matthews, "The

Community Study: Ethnicity and Success in San Jose," *Journal of Interdisciplinary History* 7 (1976): 305–18; Franklin F. Mendels, "Social Mobility and Phases of Industrialization," *Journal of Interdisciplinary History* 7 (1976): 193–216; Edward Pessen, "The Social Configuration of the Antebellum City: An Historical and Theoretical Inquiry," *Journal of Urban History* 2 (1976): 267–306; Michael P. Weber and Anthony E. Boardman, "Economic Growth and Occupational Mobility in Nineteenth Century America: A Reappraisal," *Journal of Social History* 11 (1977): 52–74; and Robert Wheeler, "The Fifth Ward Irish: Mobility at Mid-Century" (seminar pap., Brown University, 1967). On neighborhoods, see Howard P. Chudacoff, "A New Look at Ethnic Neighborhoods," *Journal of American History* 60 (1973): 76–93; Kathleen Neils Conzen, "Immigrants, Ethnic Neighborhoods, and Ethnic Identity: Historical Issues," *Journal of American History* 66 (1979): 602–15; and Oliver Zunz, *The Changing Face of Inequality: Urbanization, Industrial Development, and Immigrants in Detroit, 1880–1920* (Chicago: University of Chicago Press, 1982).

The finest study of Irish-American political activity is undoubtedly Thomas N. Brown's *Irish-American Nationalism*, pap. (Philadelphia: J. B. Lippincott Co., 1966). Other efforts include William G. Bean's "Puritan *vs.* Celt, 1850- 1860," *New England Quarterly* 23 (1924): 319–34; Daniel Patrick Moynihan's analysis in *Beyond the Melting Pot*; Edward M. Levine's *The Irish and Irish Politicians* (Notre Dame, Ind.: University of Notre Dame Press, 1966); C. C. Tansill's *America and the Fight for Irish Freedom, 1886–1922* (New York: Devin-Adair Company, 1957), as well as some of the popular literature ranging from Edwin O'Connor to the political biographies of John F. Kennedy. William L. Burton recently examined the participation of the Irish in Massachusetts in the Union Army in "Irish Regiments in the Union Army: The Massachusetts Experience," *Historical Journal of Massachusetts* 11 (1983): 104– 19. On Ben Butler, see Robert J. Holzman, *Stormy Ben Butler* (New York: Macmillan, 1954); Howard P. Nash, Jr. *Stormy Petrel: The Life and Times of Con. Benjamin F. Butler, 1818–1893* (Rutherford, N.J.: Farleigh Dickinson University Press, 1969); Hans Louis Trefousse's *Ben Butler: The South Called Him Beast* (New York: Twayne Publishers, 1957); Robert S. West, *Lincoln's Scapegoat General: A Life of Benjamin F. Butler, 1818–1893* (Boston: Houghton Mifflin Co., 1965); and Margaret S. Thompson, "Ben Butler versus the Brahmins: Patronage and Politics in Early Gilded Age Massachusetts," *New England Quarterly* 55 (1982): 163–86.

The best of the studies on Jacksonian American include the work of Arthur M. Schlesinger, Marvin Meyers, Bray Hammond, Edward Pessen, Lee Benson, and Richard Hofstadter, among others. Ronald P. Formisano discusses *The Transformation of Political Culture: Massachusetts Parties, 1790s–1840s* (New York: Oxford University Press, 1983); while Eric Foner, *Free Soil, Free Labor, Free Men: The Ideology of the Republican Party before the Civil War* (New York: Oxford University Press, 1971) and Oscar Handlin, and Barry A. Crouch, "Amos A. Lawrence and the Formation of the Constitutional Union Party: The Conservative Failure in 1860," *Historical Journal of Massachusetts* 8 (1980): 46–58, offer interpretations as to the changing political fortunes of national and local political parties from 1840 to 1860. The rise of the Know-Nothing movement has received considerable interest lately. Ray Allen Billington's seminal *The Protestant Crusade, 1800–1860: A Study in the Origins of Nativism*, pap. (Chicago: Quadrangle Books, 1964) was followed by two solid studies, John Higham's *Strangers in the Land: Patterns of American Nativism, 1860–1925* (New York: Atheneum, 1963) and Barbara Solomon's *Ancestors and Immigrants: A Changing New England Tradition* (Chicago: University of Chicago Press, 1956). Other studies include Theodore M. Hammett's "Two Mobs of Jacksonian Boston: Ideology and Interest," *Journal of American History* 62 (1976): 845–68; Thomas W. Kremm's "Cleveland and the First Lincoln Election: The Ethnic Response to Nativism," *Journal of Interdisciplinary History* 8 (1977): 69–86; Dale Baum's "Know Nothingism and the Republican Majority in Massachusetts: The Political Realignment of the 1830s," *Journal of American History* 64 (1978): 959–86 and his more recent *The Civil War Party System: The Case of Massachusetts* (Chapel Hill: University of North Carolina Press, 1984); Stephen E. Maizlish and John J. Kushma's *Essays on American Antebellum Politics, 1840–1860* (College Station: Texas A and M University Press, 1982); Michael F. Holt's "The Politics of Impatience: The Origins of Know-Nothingism," *Journal of American History* 60 (1973): 309–31; and John R. Mulkern's "Scandal behind the Convent Walls: The Know-Nothing Nunnery Committee of 1855," *Historical Journal of Massachusetts* 11 (1983): 22–34, as well as Vincent P. Lannie's traditional view in "Alienation in America: The Immigrant Catholic in Pre–Civil War America," *Review of Politics* 32 (1970): 503–21.

In addition to the sources suggested above, readers will appreciate the growing body of literature on other ethnic groups, particularly Southern and Eastern European, Mexican, and Asian-American community studies, which enhance our understanding of the role of the immigrant in American history.

INDEX

Abbott, Josiah, 73

Acre, the, 6–7, 98, 101. *See also* Corkonians; Fardowners

Act of Union, 72–73

Adams, William Forbes, 4

American Citizen, 99, 119–20, 136, 138, 141

Anderson, Michael, 18

Appleton, Nathan, 10, 81, 89

Bagley, Sarah, 81

Ballyshannon, 6, 26, 27

Bancroft, Jefferson, 76

Barry, James, 41

Bartlett, Homer, 116

Baum, Dale, 134

Beard, Ithamar W., 65–66

Bender, Thomas, 1

Billerica, Mass., 40

Blumin, Stuart, 155

Boott, John W., 10

Boott, Kirk, 10, 11, 15–16, 27–28, 36, 45, 47–48, 50–51, 56, 77

Boston, 69, 81, 83, 85, 90, 92, 106, 107

Boston Associates, the: as capitalists, 8–9, 117–19; on community, 81; and construction of Western Canal, 34; and decision to turn to Irish labor, 2, 6, 7, 89; and development of other mill towns, 79; and effect upon Lowell, 105; and employment practices, 100; and holdings in New England, 1; and labor unrest in 1840s, 88–89; and value of public schools, 89; and vision of Lowell, 3, 10–11; and visit to East Chelmsford, 10. *See also* Employment

Boston *Bee*, 65

Boston and Lowell Railroad, 81, 102, 110

Boston *Pilot*, 8, 15, 20, 73, 99, 140

Boston Repeal Association, 20

Bowles, Samuel, 1

Bremer, Frederika, 14

Brown, Thomas N., 4

Business recession of 1848, 92

Butler, Benjamin F., 48–49, 124, 134, 140–42

Byrne, Fr. Patrick, 14, 35–36

Caledonia, 74

Castles, Stephen, 95, 101, 124

Catholicism: in Lowell, 59–61; in New England, 39–40; in U.S., 58–59, 66

Centralville, 95, 153

Certificate of attendance, 113, 116, 146

Chapel Hill, 63, 95

Charitable Fuel Society, 30

Charlestown, Mass., 14, 15

Chelmsford Glass Works, 15

Chevalier, Michel, 14

Cheverus, Jean (bishop of Boston), 35

Cholera, 107, 109. *See also* Health

Church of the Holy Cross, 16, 35, 56

Churchill, T. W., 42

City death records, 20

Civil War, 21, 92, 153

Clark, Dennis, 4, 129

Cobden, Richard, 14

Collins, Patrick, 53

Community: among Irish, 154–55; in Lowell, 3–4. *See also* Family structure; Yankee factory women

Concord, Mass., 61

Connaught men, 24, 109. *See also* Corkonians; Fardowners

Connolly, Michael, 27, 29, 39, 61

Conway, Fr. James, 53, 63, 121